Edwar
Execut

Bozell

Bozell Worldwide, Inc.
Direct Marketing
40 West 23rd Street
New York, New York 10010-5201
212-727-5322

Database
Marketing

Other McGraw-Hill Books by Edward L. Nash

DIRECT MARKETING: STRATEGY/ PLANNNG/ EXECUTION, Second Edition, 1986

THE DIRECT MARKETING HANDBOOK, Second Edition, 1992

Database Marketing

The Ultimate Marketing Tool

Edward L. Nash

McGraw-Hill, Inc.

New York San Francisco Washington, D.C. Auckland Bogotá
Caracas Lisbon London Madrid Mexico City Milan
Montreal New Delhi San Juan Singapore
Sydney Tokyo Toronto

Library of Congress Cataloging-in-Publication Data

Nash, Edward L.
    Database marketing : the ultimate selling tool / Edward Nash.
        p.   cm.
    Includes bibliographical references and index.
    ISBN 0-07-046063-9 (alk. paper)
    1. Marketing—Data bases.   2. Data base management.   I. Title.
HF5415.125.N37   1993
658.8′00285′574—dc20   93-10124
                                                                CIP

1 2 3 4 5 6 7 8 9 0   DOC/DOC   9 8 7 6 5 4 3

ISBN 0-07-046063-9

*The sponsoring editor for this book was James Bessent, the editing
supervisor was Fred Dahl, and the production supervisor was Donald
F. Schmidt. It was set in Baskerville by Inkwell Publishing Services.*

Printed and bound by R. R. Donnelley & Sons Company.

This book is printed on recycled, acid-free paper containing a
minimum of 50% recycled de-inked fiber.

This publication is designed to provide accurate and authoritative information in regard to the subject matter covered. It is sold with the understanding that the publisher is not engaged in rendering legal, accounting,
or other professional service. If legal advice or other expert assistance is
required, the services of a competent professional person should be sought.
    *—From a declaration of principles jointly adopted by a committee of the
        American Bar Association and a committee of publishers*

To my wife, Diana,
who makes it all worthwhile.

Contents

Foreword

This is *the* time to be involved in direct marketing! The foundation built by Montgomery Ward, Sears, L. L. Bean, and other pioneers has developed into the marketing "happening" of the decade. No longer relegated to the dream book merchants, direct marketing is now teeming with an army of merchants peering into every demographic and psychographic nook and cranny to find the hidden niche that will yield a sales bonanza.

Like the many new users being found for aspirin, direct marketing may be good for what ails your business. Do you need new customers or a way to hold onto loyal customers? Want to find the rare household that really needs your product? How about continuing the life cycle of a fading product that can no longer support national advertising? Or starting a business on a shoe string? Direct marketing and, more specifically, database marketing can do all these things and then some!

Somehow Ed Nash has found a way to stay in the mainstream of direct marketing's evolution. He was present when the great copywriters demonstrated the power of the right headline. He was there when direct marketers discovered computers, then TV, and now the infomercial. When someone discovered you could sell beef by mail, then cheese, and even live lobsters, Ed was there. He was in the middle of the electronics revolution that helped statisticians raise response rates. Recently he has been an early advocate of direct marketing as a tool for package goods companies, and now he is right in the middle of the database revolution!

In this work, Ed demystifies the concept of the database as a key to the next generation of direct marketing breakthroughs. He manages to make it simple, yet comprehensive. Most of all, he challenges the reader to find new uses for the most powerful direct-to-consumer tool yet.

By paying careful attention to the following pages, you will have the opportunity to unravel the complex task of creating and utilizing a customer database for virtually any direct marketing application. The important strategic planning phases, the data acquisition tasks, the analytical opportunities, and the innovative final uses for this marvelous tool are all ahead of you. The reader can view this work as a "how-to" manual or as a strategic planning primer. In either case, the value will come in the form of increased sales, improved loyalty, and ultimately more efficient direct marketing efforts.

Bob Wientzen
Manager of Direct Marketing,
Procter & Gamble
Direct Marketing Association Board Member

Preface

Desert Storm made every American familiar with the newest terms of military warfare, such as "smart bombs" and "laser guidance." We saw missiles travel across seas and deserts to hit a specific building a hundred miles away. We saw batlike "Stealth" planes swoop out of the night to guide bombs through the doors of a hangar or down the chimney of a telephone center.

If you compare these weapons with those of World War II—dozens of planes dropping hundreds of bombs with the hope that at least a few would hit a military target, and rockets aimed to land anywhere within a huge city—you have a fair comparison of the precision power of the "Database" marketing weapon as compared with the dated marketing weapons that preceded it.

As in the military example, it is often wasteful and ineffective to aim messages at vast magazine and television audiences when it is possible to concentrate budgetary "firepower" on exactly the prospects you want to reach. And it is just as wasteful to settle for a superficial "impression" when it is possible to reach a prospect with a message that not only creates a *positive* impression, but that involves, motivates, persuades, assures, proves, overcomes objections, asks for—and gets—a buying decision right there, right then.

In a way, database marketing completes the circle of marketing evolution. All selling started with one-on-one communication across the counter or doorway, where the relationship between vendor and customer provided the "brand equity"—the trust and assurance that the buyer needed to try a new product. With mass marketing, that relationship deteriorated in many fields. Yes, Cartier and Dunhill and even specialty grocers maintained such relationships. But for the most part the vendor was K-Mart or Alexander's or A&P—where sales clerks barely knew if something was in stock and could never be counted on to make a recommendation.

The brand name became the source of trust and authority. Sara Lee or P&G could be counted on to provide good grocery products, Time-Warner or Reader's Digest to provide good reading, GE or Sony to stand behind good appliances. But even these fine companies could not compensate for the loss of the one-on-one advisory relationship or continuing service of the old-time sales outlet.

This required knowing the customer as an individual—each with needs, preferences, interests, and a personality all his or her own. Mass television couldn't do that. Mass magazines couldn't. Cable TV and specialty magazines grew in importance because they could at least identify an interest as part of a group with common characteristics. But until the recognition of the potential of database marketing, we could not relate to our customers individually.

I see database marketing not as a supplementary niche marketing tool, but as part of the primary marketing effort, to be planned and budgeted before all the money is committed to "feel good," pure image advertising. This is especially so because database marketing can provide both image and response at no extra cost!

How did we get here? How is it being used? How can you, the reader, use this new "smart weapon" in your own business? These are the questions that I have been dealing with for six years and that my agency deals with every day. I have tried, in this book, to give you the basics not just to understand it, but to help you persuade those who control the purse strings in your corporation that database marketing is not an option, but a necessity. Those who fail to master this marketing weapon will be left standing in the trenches as the laser beams of this most high-tech of all marketing methods flash overhead. I suggest you start reading now.

Remember, I told you so.

Edward L. Nash

Database
Marketing

1

The Ultimate
Marketing Tool

Database marketing is not an end in itself. It is a tool—a marketing tool, an advertising tool, a sales promotion tool. Yet it is not a direct extension of any of these disciplines, nor will it ever replace them.

To master it, you must first understand its roots in the field of direct marketing. Indeed, this book is best used as an advanced text for those who have read my *Direct Marketing: Strategy/Planning/Execution,* 2nd ed. (McGraw-Hill, 1991).

But you need not master database marketing to use it in your own business. Instead, you can enlist the help of professionals who have a background in direct marketing, along with an appreciation (if not mastery) of advertising and sales promotion.

Direct marketing is somewhat like laser surgery: a powerful, precise, and very effective tool in the hands of professionals, but a potential disaster in the hands of amateurs. We must approach it as if we are surgeons, not butchers, as if we are cabinetmakers, not carpenters.

What It Is, and Isn't

Webster's Ninth New Collegiate Dictionary refers to a *data base* as "a collection of data organized esp. for rapid search and retrieval

(as by a computer)." *Data* is referred to as "factual information. . . ."
They list *data base* as two words, although in current practice and
in this book it is used as a single term. But the differences are
obviously even greater.

The databases we will be dealing with are marketing databases—
the compilation of names and addresses of individual customers
and prospects for the purpose of communicating information, by
mail or telephone, that directly or indirectly results in sales and
profits.

The *names* may be compiled from internal sources (orders,
promotions, inquiries) or from external sources (rented lists, barter
with other companies, database compilation companies). Or they
may be created on a custom basis (in conjunction with other
advertising or promotional efforts), or on a cooperative or solo
basis (through mailed questionnaires or "name-generation" promotions).

Once the list is identified, various segments of the list may be
used like other advertising medium—to communicate with prospective customers. Whether this use is feasible depends on the resulting cost per targeted prospect, as compared with other advertising
media options.

The cost efficiencies of database marketing as a medium, in turn,
make possible the planning of various promotions that would not
be possible, or at least that would not be as cost-effective, using
alternative communication channels. These include "conquest"
promotions, "customer loyalty" promotions, "line extensions," "frequency or trade-up promotions," "retail support" promotions, and
"product introductions."

If this list seems familiar to those who have worked with direct
marketing, general advertising, and sales promotion, that is the
point! Database marketing is applicable to and effective with virtually all of the different marketing opportunities and problems
formerly dealt with by these disciplines separately. It works with
every type of situation: industrial products, business services,
consumer packaged goods, utilities, appliances, fund raising. You
name it. It combines elements of all these disciplines in a truly
integrated science, yet it is different in that it requires an entirely

different way of planning, budgeting, analyzing, and creative execution.

The term *database*, in the business world, originally was applied to a collection of market research data: collective information about markets, demographics, sales trends, competitive information, and so on. This application is still a useful one, but it led to a common mistake that I have found in many companies. *Database marketing* today, to the extent a management structure is based on this original use, is often still under the control of the Market Research Department or the Computer Services Department.

When database marketing is used as other than a sales or marketing tool, it is sometimes incorrectly applied backwards. The creation of the database comes first, the applications later. Under such conditions, companies gather their customer lists, rebate offers, contest entrants, and any other name source, and combine them in one large computerized list. In some cases this is an adequate place to begin. In others, it results in a huge investment, which may or may not result in a marketing tool that is unique, usable, or cost-effective.

The truth is that building your own list is not necessarily the first step, at least not until you have tested applications and determined that this method is cost-effective compared to other advertising and communications options. This may seem like heresy from a database marketing practitioner, but, despite the widespread enthusiasm to try this methodology, the truth is that it is not a panacea. Also, it is sometimes more cost-effective to use existing outside database lists or to custom-compile names as needed for specific promotions.

There is also no one database marketing application that can be taken "off the shelf" and used for every product and service. There are wide differences in applications between business and consumer products, between retail-distributed products and companies with ongoing direct communications, between consumer items that are bought once or sporadically and items (like condiments or paper towels) that are kept in stock, between business supplies (such as Laserwriter paper) and business equipment (such as the Laserwriter.)

Some companies regard database marketing as a customer list for research purposes only, as in the original definition. Some have built huge lists of their own customers, usable only for customer loyalty and brand extension. I have seen database programs that target prospects less effectively than a magazine ad, and others that are so cost-advantageous that they merit the entire advertising budget.

Comparison with Mass Advertising

Mass market, or general advertising, has been in decline as a percentage of total marketing budgets. This is because more and more companies have placed greater emphasis on "accountable advertising." This trend has switched substantial portions of ad budgets into promotional and direct mail programs. Unlike some overly enthusiastic direct marketers, I do not believe that mass advertising is obsolete. There are still some roles for which newspaper, magazine, broadcast, and outdoor advertising will never be replaced.

One is the establishment of credibility for the company and its products. The reputation of a publication is an implied endorsement of its advertisers. Another is television's ability to dramatize product features or establish emotional imagery for the product and its users. No media conveys emotion and gives a product a personality of its own as well as television. And—most important from the database marketer's viewpoint—mass media are essential to attract the calls and coupons needed to build new and unique databases.

Also, the mass media are changing to meet the competitive advantages of direct marketing and database marketing. Cable TV stations now reach narrower, selective audiences that can be much more cost-effective, for certain products and services, than the lowest-common-denominator pap that seems to dominate many general television stations.

Magazines are offering selected editions, not only for geographic regions, but for demographic audience segments. *Lear's* is an excellent example of a magazine targeted to mature women, for example, as is the "Silver Edition" of *McCall's* aimed at the same audience. *Farm Journal* now has different editions depending on the type of crop or farm animal a farm specializes in. And some magazines are experimenting with inserting different advertisements to different subscribers based on database information. This is their attempt to compete with the growing use of direct mail as an advertising medium.

Advertising agency media buyers are accustomed to looking at *CPM,* or *cost per thousand,* circulation. If you are looking for people who drink decaf coffee, for instance, research tells us that they represent 20 percent of all households.

The *McCall's* rate for a black-and-white page is about $15 per thousand. Let's say research indicates a 10-percent efficiency (or a 90-percent "waste factor") for the product category you are concerned with. The cost per M target market is thus ten times $15/M or $150/M. Take a product with a 5-percent efficiency and the cost is $300/M.

But many of these people already use your brand. Others are not deemed "convertible" for one reason or another, perhaps those who are using a brand totally unlike your image or flavor; so we have reason to believe they are not our customers. Say that only half of the category users are those you wish to reach. In that case the ten-percent efficiency is really 5 percent for $300/M. And the 5 percent is really 2½ percent for $600/M.

At first glance, these costs seem low in comparison with direct mail costs, but first glances are deceiving. Let's say we have designed a mailing with a total cost of $450/M. This will vary, of course, depending on the lists, the format, the postage class, and mailing cost.

If you mailed this only to the known prospects who fit the preceding criteria, the relative cost per thousand would be advantageous in one case and not in the other. It is also easy to see that it is hard for direct mail to compete with magazine advertising on the basis of targeting alone.

In the 10-percent example, and with higher media efficiencies, the use of direct mail can only be justified if the mailing "works harder." That is, it has to be a more powerful and persuasive message than the magazine ad. If the mailing does no more than "bribe" a prospect with a cents-off store coupon, it has no added value.

However, direct mail can include much more:

A personalized and versioned letter explaining how this decaf process is better than others.

An attractive brochure showing people enjoying their coffee without the effects of caffeine.

A sample packet of the product.

A precoded offer to induce trial, conversion, repeated use.

Or all of the above!

Direct mail can almost always be justified in this case if you use its added selling space, its ability to be relevant to the reader, and its capability of making response or redemption easier.

Now consider the availability of a database that not only identifies our ideal prospects, but also gives us data about their interests, tastes, lifestyle, or personality. We may wind up selecting only 50 percent of the previous list, making it much more profitable even on the basis of targeting alone.

Comparison with Conventional Direct Marketing

Conventional direct marketing has always dealt with broader categories of prospects—not lists of individuals who are *known* to be prospects, but lists of buyers, members, and subscribers who are *likely* to be prospects, sometimes called *suspects*. In fact, one typical direct marketing application is called *two-step selling*. This method is usually used for higher-priced products or to generate leads for in-person or phone sales. The first ad or mailing simply offers information, perhaps along with a free booklet or catalog. In current usage, we would say they are building a database.

A mailing piece or telephone call to a database is no different in cost, content, or effectiveness than to a broader mailing list. So the element of relative selling power appears to be even, except for one factor: relevance, which is discussed later. The main advantage is in the media economics.

As with the magazine example, lists must also be looked at with the same media planning principles. Suppose a list of homeowners is worth $50/M to a manufacturer of refrigerators, washers, and dryers. Wouldn't then a narrower list of homeowners whose age and income are known to be within the target demographics be worth, say, $75/M? And if such homeowners have recently made other substantial purchases and thus revealed themselves to have buying power or to be in an acquisitive mood, wouldn't it be worth still more to the same appliance manufacturer? And perhaps we can select these names geographically, sending our mail only to areas where we have adequate retail distribution.

Lists such as these, or lists of donors, magazine subscribers, bookbuyers, and the like, are in the realm of direct marketing, whether the product is sold directly by mail or through salespersons or retailers. In this example, a list of buyers of a book on kitchen decorating would be as valuable as any database list. Such an obvious fit, however, cannot always be found, and, if it is available, there may not be a significant quantity.

Now, for a moment imagine still another dimension: a smaller list of people about whom you know not only that they are home-owners with the right geographic and demographic characteristics but something else as well. They have stated their interest in buying a new appliance within the next six months! Perhaps they have also told you what kind of appliance and whether they prefer modern or traditional design. Perhaps you even know whether they like to entertain, or whether they do gourmet cooking, the size of their kitchen, and the kind and age of appliances they currently have.

In some of our newer applications, you may even be able to deduce something about their personality: whether their tastes are generally conservative or if they enjoy being "ahead of the crowd"; the first in the neighborhood to own the new style or to have a stove with the newest gadgets. This is the ultimate database: a list of genuine prospects for whatever it is you have to sell, pinpointing the type of person most likely to buy it.

Such a prospect list, being more highly targeted, is worth more—easily two or three times the value of a list of less qualified suspects. Exactly how much depends on the value to your organization of the sales or leads it produces.

Note that the preceding example discusses only mailing list cost, which is likely to be only 5 or 10 percent of the cost of the mailing. In a $500-per-thousand-piece mailing (50¢ per prospect), doubling the cost of the list from $50/M to $100/M, making the mailing cost $550/M, increases the total cost only 10 percent, not 100 percent. The increase in effectiveness, measured by actual sales, is worth far more than the added list cost.

To be fair, let me point out that some databases may cost, and be worth, much more—even $10 per name ($10,000 per M). And in some cases, where the unit sale or expected cumulative sale is substantial, this may be a very good investment indeed. In fact, the same theory applies to the format of the mailing (or series of mailings). Increasing the cost of the printing by adding personalization, involvement devices, and elaborate four-color brochures may increase the selling power and response rate far out of proportion to the increase in cost.

But media efficiency is just the beginning of the advantages. The creative options that such behavioral information offers are infinite. Premiums can be offered that appeal to known interests. Product usage examples can be relevant and appropriate. Testimonials or endorsers can be included from people whose opinions are likely to be respected.

The message itself can be made more relevant, and thus more interesting, to the recipient. Your mail not only reaches just the right people, but reaches them with appropriate information that is not likely to be considered *junk*—a term that applies to any message in any media that is not relevant to the prospective customer. For example, television commercials for automobiles are junk to viewers who are not in the market for a car. But someone actively looking to buy a car not only doesn't mind them but may even scan the stations looking for more. Perhaps some day the mass media will be able to transmit their ads and commercials only to those who are known to be interested, giving all advertising the unique desirability and effectiveness that database marketing already enjoys.

Comparison with Sales Promotion

Database marketing has been the key to the successful application of direct marketing to the packaged goods field, including supermarket and drug store products. Some of its principles had already been used extensively in automotive direct mail, but limited mostly to knowledge of the type and age of car presently owned.

As these developments took place, the line between direct mail and sales promotion became increasingly blurry. Direct marketing agencies like mine hired sales promotion specialists and opened premium sourcing subsidiaries to handle the new variety of assignments from general consumer clients. And sales promotion agencies returned the compliment. A new breed of marketing resource emerged, the *integrated* advertising agency or the *integrated communications* division of a general agency. Such ventures offered similar database marketing services, but were generally effective only to the extent that the executives in charge had genuine hands-on experience in both related fields, and had adequate independence from or equal influence with the entrenched practitioners of indirect advertising. My present position as Executive Vice President of Bozell, Jacobs, Kenyon & Eckhardt is an example of the latter approach.

One reason for this meshing of the two disciplines is that database marketing has assumed some objectives previously considered jobs for sales promotion specialists. For instance, one tool of many consumer products companies has been the distribution of "cents-off" coupons redeemable at supermarkets and other chain stores. While the emphasis on this sort of promotion has been under review, such coupons still provide productive means for tracking the effectiveness of promotions, even if the savings are an incidental rather than primary benefit.

The change has been the recognition that the cost of such coupons is more influenced by the pattern of the redemption than by the cost of distribution. For instance, a 50¢-off store coupon might cost just $25 per thousand (2½¢ each) to distribute in free standing inserts (FSIs). But if 90 percent of the coupons are redeemed by present users, the cost for each coupon redeemed by a new tryer is 10 times as much, or $5 each. On this basis database marketing is clearly more cost-effective than traditional sales promotion.

On the other hand traditional sales promotion media, such as FSIs as well as in-packs, on-packs, contests, and "shelf-talkers," often figured advantageously in planning to build databases in the first place. It was obvious that each field of experience had something to bring to the party, and that both working together could do more than either one alone.

The Underlying Basics

It is important to consider database marketing as a tool that is the product of an evolutionary process, in fact one that is still evolving. It did not spring into being as the sudden inspiration of a brilliant marketer.

Database marketing is rooted in direct marketing, which in turn is rooted in direct mail and mail order. Yes, all these fields have been influenced by the psychological subtleties of general advertising and the practical lessons of sales promotion. But database marketing must always respect the basics of direct mail even when the mails are not involved!

What are some of these basics? Here are some of the "commandments" of this original discipline that have a bearing on database marketing:

- *Targeting*: The more qualified the list is the more efficient the effort. But don't presume that new customers are necessarily identical to previous ones, or to so-called "heavy users." (See Clancy and Shulman, *The Marketing Revolution* (New York: Harper, 1992.)

- *Selectivity*: Weigh all the possible goals—conquest, loyalty, extension, product introduction, list building.

- *Personalization*: Tailor the message; make it relevant.

- *Involvement*: Involve the reader in story, picture, and proposition.

- *Salesmanship*: Use both reason and emotion to complete the sale. Don't rely on "bribes."

- *Testing*: Try several lists, media, messages, offers before committing to a roll-out.

- *Measurability*: Always include some method of determining the response to the initial message and to subsequent efforts.

- *Response-ability*: Have a clear idea of what you want the reader to do, and give him or her all the information and imagery to do it. The cheapest format is not necessarily the wisest.

- *Relationship building*: The relationship doesn't end when the sale is made. That's when it starts!

The Database as an Asset

One agency creative director was asked, "What's the difference between a database and a mailing list?" His answer: $50 per thousand!

That's a cute answer, but an amazingly common misconception. It's true that buying or building a custom database will cost at least twice the cost of a conventional mailing list of buyers, subscribers, and so on. And, in the short run, the results may be the same.

Understanding the difference requires an entirely different way of thinking about marketing. It requires that the database itself be looked at as an asset. In fact, just as mail order companies are often valued, when bought or merged, according to the size and effectiveness of their mailing list, I predict that we will see general marketers valued not just for the value of their brand names, but for the value of their database!

Once the database is established and its effectiveness demonstrated, it is not put away and forgotten. It is an asset like a brand name, or a good patent, or an efficient factory, and, as it should do with all assets, good management dictates that it be put to good use.

Modern companies today have been evolving from being product-based to being market-based. The database asset is the ultimate market-based tool. The consumers on the list should be looked at as an extended family of consumers whose needs can and must be served. This family should be "tracked" in terms of attitude and researched in terms of product improvements and product extensions. In return for the loyalty of this identified, growing, changing market, the corporation must establish a two-way communication that asks and listens to consumer needs, and then provides product features, service policies, and new products that fill those needs.

James Rosenfeld, the prominent San Diego consultant, summed up some of the basic premises of database marketing very nicely in an article in *Direct*:

1. Customers are more important than noncustomers.

2. Past behavior is the best indicator of future behavior.

3. Some customers are more important than other customers.

4. Customers are likely to share certain characteristics.

5. Prospective customers are likely to look like current customers. The exception is heavily advertised brands, where database marketing's greatest potential may be in positioning the product or service to new groups of users.

A database is not static, but a changing, growing, dynamic list. And—most important to remember—it is not just names and addresses and other data. It is made up of real people who have placed their trust in your company. They are not just your market; they are your future.

2

The In-House Database

The most valuable and usually easiest to obtain database is the master list of your own customers. In the mail order business, such a customer list, or *house list*, is the single most valuable asset the company has, responsible for between 50 percent and 80 percent of the total sales volume and usually 100 percent of current profits.

Why promote to customers you already have? One reason is that it costs less to hold on to a present customer than to win a new one. Another is that it is often more fruitful to increase consumption or to trade up present customers than it is to win new ones. And still another is that present, presumably satisfied customers are most likely to respond to line extensions or entirely new products using the brand name they have learned to trust.

One quick hypothetical example: You have 100 customers, each spending $100 a year, for a volume of $10,000. To increase sales by 10 percent it is often easier to get the present customers each to spend $10 more, than it is to win ten new customers. You already have a customer list of 100 users. To find ten brand new customers, you may have to first identify 100 category users and then win over 10 of them. The economics are clearly on the side of promoting to present customers.

Making Gold Out of Lead

If your company history includes the day someone found that boxes and boxes of potential names were discarded, don't despair. You are not alone. The exceptions are the rarity. Most non-mail order companies have failed to value their own incipient mailing lists.

One very famous jewelry company had been throwing away retail sales slips that carried customer names and addresses, as well as the items purchased and their value. The company's fear was that to use the list would risk embarrassing some of its customers (such as those who buy two Valentine's Day gifts).

Another client of mine, a major hotel chain, had a similar concern. It has always been the policy of innkeepers not to send letters referring to recent stays. But this was the best—in fact, the only way—a frequent guest program could be started for this chain.

In both cases the client was finally prevailed upon to make the list available. With extraordinary security precautions, the lists were finally compiled, and they turned out to be the basis for very successful promotions.

A famous cosmetic sales organization had a similar problem. Their representatives were well trained and very effective at getting new customers and making substantial initial sales. But little was done to get reorders from these customers. Most sales representatives simply sent customers envelopes stuffed with miscellaneous brochures once or twice a year, paying first class postage.

We helped set up a centralized program where, for the same overall cost to the salesperson, the representative's customer would receive a professional catalog, with immediacy incentives and personal letters, computer-signed by the salesperson and personalized in other ways as well. Sales were increased dramatically. Yet the original objective was simply to persuade representatives to give the company their mailing lists, so that, if a salesperson quit, the customer list could be contacted by a new representative.

But just owning names doesn't mean they will be valuable. For instance, Schenley conducted a very original promotion for their Pinch scotch. Advertisements in newspapers and *The Wall Street Journal* invited readers to select $100,000 in their choice of "fantasy" stock; the responder whose selection of stocks increased most in value would win valuable prizes including a trip to Scotland.

This Pinch stock promotion undoubtedly attracted a great many entrants, including myself. The telephone scripts exposed me to Pinch messages, and built an implicit association of Pinch as the scotch for successful investors. It was an interesting and well-executed sales promotion but it never crossed the line to become a database marketing program.

What was missing? It did produce a list, but it was a list of contest entrants interested in the stock market. The promotion would have been perfect for Merrill Lynch or Dreyfus, as the respondents displayed their interest in stocks. And, it also told something about the respondents' stock interest and knowledge (from the choice of stocks selected). The missing ingredient could have been supplied with a few additional questions: "Do you drink scotch? If not scotch, what other liquor? What brand? How often?" That would be a database for a liquor company, one of value in producing future promotions that could to help offset some of the costs of the original promotion. Such a list, with the unique information needed for future loyalty or conquest promotions, could then be enhanced with data from other lists, neighborhood characteristics, or other information.

Identifying Your Own
Customers Through Pomotions

Many of the lists discarded over the years were of people responding to classic sales promotion offers, many much less imaginative that the Pinch offer previously discussed.

Save three proofs of purchase and we'll give you a rebate.

This clever tote bag or T-shirt sent in return for proofs of purchase.

Enter our contest and win a trip to Hawaii.

Send for a free sample of this new product.

Such promotions are effective, if used judiciously and not as a substitute for building strong product images and strong customer relationships. But one of the most effective objectives was not discovered until recently—using such promotions *primarily* to build a database.

The person who sends in a proof of purchase or who requests a sample has at least tried the product. The person who sends in multiple proofs (such as from a six-pack of cola or a carton of cigarettes) can be presumed to be a customer. You have the publication or list that buyers responded to, which tells you something about them, as each different medium produces names of different quality. And you have the addresses, which can be very revealing if compared with known characteristics for the geographic area or even for the household, using the data available from other lists.

Even if this is all you have, the names are worth saving and using. But the more information a list includes, the more valuable it can be—both for profitable selection or segmentation, and for making relevant the message or offer.

The cigarette companies were the first to discover that you can ask additional questions at the same time you make the T-shirt or other offer without a significant decrease in response rates. In fact, some companies have reported increases in response rates; others have research showing that people like to make their preferences and needs known.

It costs no more, except for nominal data entry costs, to ask some additional questions, providing they are relevant and seem to indicate a genuine desire to know the customer. Ask which flavor of the product they buy, or what kind of store they buy it in, or what size or packaging they prefer. Ask about favorite music, or spectator sports, or summer activities, to enable you to tailor future promotions to their interests. In one promotion I developed, we asked for the prospects' astrological signs, and in another we asked for a vote on their favorite singing groups, because we could build promotions on this unusual data.

The questions asked must be relevant to the product, the theme of the advertisement, and the imagery of the product. Asking about football can suggest a macho brand image, while asking about favorite flowers can be appealing in connection with a fashion or fragrance offer.

The choice of such questions must be marketing-driven, not research driven. If the research department gets in on the act they'll want to ask about age, income, and education. These are not only the most risky questions, in terms of possibly turning off the prospect and reducing response rates, but they are also usually the least usable. How old someone is, or claims to be, is not nearly as valuable in designing database promotions as how old they act in terms of their activities and interests.

The In-Pack Media:
A Billion-Dollar Unused Asset

All types of marketing ideas are ultimately judged by economics. Database marketing is no different. Every name that does not have to be bought from commercial compilers or generated through advertising media increases the chances of the promotion surviving the economic modeling test. Therefore, names that are a by-product of general advertising or sales promotion are a free bonus. So are names and data generated by *free ride* inserts in or on packages, or included with bills, statements, or shipments.

In-pack describes a promotional offer inserted into a package, such as a cereal package. Black & Decker built a major list and the beginning of their direct marketing business by offering vacuum cleaner bags in an in-pack insert packed with their Dust Buster shipments. Lea & Perrins built a substantial list of their sauce buyers by offering recipe books. Mattel Toys established their award-winning Barbie Pink Stamp Club with millions of in-pack inserts—each only $1\frac{1}{4} \times 4$-inch when folded—in millions of packages of Barbie doll fashions and accessories. This was one of my proudest accomplishments, developed for Mattel's brilliant marketing executive, Rick deHerder.

On-pack refers to offers that are either printed on the package or attached to the package. The same Mattel promotion eventually was printed on the back of the store display cards on which the merchandise was packaged, once the long packaging schedules could catch up with faster moving promotional needs.

One extension of the on-pack concept is the use of in-store promotions, such as *shelf talkers*—pads of rebate or other offers attached to the shelf where the merchandise is displayed. Contests or promotions mounted on counter cards, wall posters, or other displays can also present database-building offers to the public.

Warranty Cards

For many kinds of products, warranty cards have been one of the key sources of names and information about customers. While originally intended to limit a company's obligations to repair or replace a defective item, they gradually developed a secondary use—as a research tool. "Where did you buy this?" and "Where did you hear about it?" later led to demographic questions—age, income, occupation.

One of the most significant innovations in the development of database marketing was Jock Bickert's creation of National Demographic Lists, now part of the Polk organization. Jock had the idea of offering manufacturers an analysis of their customers in return for using NDL questions on their warranty cards and letting NDL use the names commercially. NDL was the first to ask respondents to check off interests such as those in Fig. 2.1.

My first reaction to this type of questionnaire was skepticism. I was concerned that more people would check off, say, "tennis" than could possibly play the game. This would be a negative factor for a classic mail order marketer selling tennis balls, for example. But later experience provided indications that for many advertisers the self-image of the respondent was useful regardless of whether the activity was a reality or an aspiration. How people think of themselves is often as useful to know as their actual behavior.

Ownership names derived from warranty cards are more important to some companies than to others. Take the example of Polaroid, a client I worked with when I headed BBDO Direct. The rate of film usage after buying a camera is a critical element in

To help us understand our customers' lifestyles, please indicate the interests and activities in which *you* and/or *your spouse* enjoy participating on a regular basis.

01. ☐ Bicycling Frequently	16. ☐ Flower Gardening	31. ☐ Fashion Clothing	46. ☐ Wildlife/Animal Protection
02. ☐ Golf	17. ☐ Sewing	32. ☐ Fine Art/Antiques	47. ☐ Environmental Issues
03. ☐ Physical Fitness/Exercise	18. ☐ Crafts	33. ☐ Foreign Travel	48. ☐ Dieting/Weight Control
04. ☐ Running/Jogging	19. ☐ Automotive Work	34. ☐ Travel in the USA	49. ☐ Science/New Technology
05. ☐ Snow Skiing Frequently	20. ☐ Electronics	35. ☐ Travel for Pleasure/Vacation	50. ☐ Self Improvement
06. ☐ Tennis Frequently	21. ☐ Home Workshop/Do It Yourself	36. ☐ Gourmet Cooking	51. ☐ Walking for Health
07. ☐ Camping/Hiking	22. ☐ Recreational Vehicles	37. ☐ Wines	52. ☐ Watching Sports on TV
08. ☐ Fishing Frequently	23. ☐ Listen to Records/Tapes/CDs	38. ☐ Coin/Stamp Collecting	53. ☐ Community/Civic Activities
09. ☐ Hunting/Shooting	24. ☐ Buy Pre-Recorded Videos	39. ☐ Collectibles/Collections	54. ☐ Home Video Games
10. ☐ Power Boating	25. ☐ Avid Book Reading	40. ☐ Our Nation's Heritage	55. ☐ Motorcycles
11. ☐ Sailing	26. ☐ Bible/Devotional Reading	41. ☐ Real Estate Investments	56. ☐ Improving Your Health
12. ☐ House Plants	27. ☐ Health/Natural Foods	42. ☐ Stock/Bond Investments	57. ☐ Home Video Recording
13. ☐ Grandchildren	28. ☐ Photography	43. ☐ Entering Sweepstakes	58. ☐ Career-Oriented Activities
14. ☐ Needlework/Knitting	29. ☐ Home Decorating/Furnishing	44. ☐ Casino Gambling	59. ☐ Moneymaking Opportunities
15. ☐ Vegetable Gardening	30. ☐ Attending Cultural/Arts Events	45. ☐ Science Fiction	60. ☐ Current Affairs/Politics

Figure 2.1. National Demographic Lists. Interests and activities. *(Reprinted by permission. © 1993 R.L. Polk Inc.)*

Polaroid sales. When they introduced their high-tech Spectra camera, they wanted to produce the maximum registration from their warranty cards. We were able to double the usual rate of response by adding several response requests instead of just the warranty registration. We included a free enlargement offer, a research form, and a contribution to one of several charities, to be designated by the new camera owner. The four cards were premarked so that a response to any of the offers would be recorded as a new owner.

Alternatives

I have had several occasions to work with clients who had valuable uses for lists of their own customers but had failed to acquire them in the past. For one product we had to purchase lists of buyers of our client's own packaged goods product from compilers. Packaged goods advertisers, faced with this type of catch-up situation, can create some type of name-generation offer for on-pack or in-pack use. But this is only applicable if it is an expendable item that is purchased on a regular basis. Usually, if you don't identify the new refrigerator or computer owner at the time of purchase, it is likely that you never will. For this reason every effort must be made to identify the maximum number of customers when the purchase is first made.

This is, of course, not a problem for services such as banks, phone companies, cable television operators, and others with ongoing relationships. Here a more common problem is failing to record the information in a usable manner. Many insurance companies, for instance, fail to transfer to tape the priceless information about age, income, and family configuration that is available in their hard file of application forms. Others, such as Allstate or Citibank, look at information the way a butcher looks at a hog. Everything but the squeal is put to good use.

3
Names for Sale

In the conventional advertising world, the science of media is based on reaching groups of people more likely to become customers than the average population. To serve the changing needs of advertisers, specialty magazines are created that will be attractive to interest groups that advertisers want to reach.

Consequently there are senior magazines such as *Golden Years* and teen magazines such as *Sassy*. *Lear's* uniquely reaches the active woman over 40. And a variety of "buff" magazines reach computer users, amateur photographers, sailors, baseball card collectors—you name it.

Mailing lists were originally created not out of need but availability. Lists are collected, offered through list managers and brokers, and rented to those who can use them. Some are used often, others not at all.

The database compilation industry has arisen in both ways. The original pioneer was a company called JFY, Inc. With the quiet backing of R. J. Reynolds, this company began the first effort to build a different kind of advertising medium: a product and brand usage database providing names and addresses based not on probable usage but on individual, consumer-provided claims of actual usage.

JFY's primary "bread and butter" assignment was to begin the task of assembling names of smokers—a priority for RJR in the face of impending legislation restricting advertising. But while they were at it, the millions of questionnaires sent through the mail, inserted in co-op mail and in free standing newspaper inserts, asked about other interests as well. Much of this effort was speculative, and JFY undertook the job, difficult at the time, of selling advertisers on the value of obtaining such name lists. The questionnaires requested information on demographics, category, brand, and personal preferences.

Prior to JFY the best tool available was called *geodemographics*, or *the cluster system*. Suppliers such as Claritas developed the PRIZM system which matched neighborhoods by similarities based on 73 different items of information available from the U.S. Census. From this they compiled 40 different types of clusters representing not just demographics but apparent lifestyle. With clever names like Station Wagon Country and Blue Blood Estates, they enabled mailers to target those parts of the country more likely to make a particular purchase, subscribe to a particular magazine, watch a particular television show, and so on, than others—often by factors of three or four times the population average. Later they added behavioral data compiled by market research firms such as MRI, Simmons, and Stanford Research.

Stanford Research Institute has a similar segmentation tool called *VALS*, which stands for Values and Life Style. This is based on SRI's own questionnaires sent to neighborhoods, and offers areas in eight lifestyle groupings ranging from Strugglers to Achievers.

Other principal cluster lists, available through advertising agencies and list brokers with database units, are ClusterPlus, ACORN, and Vision.

All of these are based on the reasonably accurate assumption that "birds of a feather flock together." It appears that people in similar neighborhoods are likely to spend like their neighbors, on cars, lawn care, appliances, etc., even though there may be radical differences in their true financial capabilities.

But all of this represents only areas, not individuals. If neighborhood clusters could provide three times the marketing efficiency, then individual lists could often have 10 or 12 times the power. Even with this relative efficiency, the usefulness of cluster lists is far from over. Where large-scale coverage is needed and budgets permit, they can often provide the market penetration needed in situations where coverage is more important than marketing efficiency. At least for now.

Today there are half a dozen commercial suppliers of database names, and by the time this book is out there will probably be a dozen more. I have been working with two companies myself on plans to develop new databases in areas not adequately covered by those databases currently available.

No one database is perfect. None has every category or brand usage detail you might want. None has all the names up to date and *cleaned* (corrected for address changes, duplications, and other errors) And none offers 100-percent penetration of a given category. But taken all together, combining perfect information from one source and imperfect information from another, they still represent a powerful marketing tool.

How and Where to Buy Database Lists

An entire industry has developed in recent years, dedicated to building lists, refining them, and making them available to marketers. At the time of this writing, several principal suppliers are in the field, each with its own strengths and its own reputation for helpfulness or lack of it.

R.L. Polk & Co. This company offers about 80 million unduplicated households addressable by name, compiled by cross-indexing a score of information sources containing over a billion names. These include:

- 120 million auto and truck registrations
- 66 million telephone book listings
- 50 million birth records and school registrations
- 50 million homeowners
- 60 million direct mail respondents
- 150 million credit card holders

- 50 million names from questionnaires or canvassers

Thirteen million names from the NDL lists are available individually or included in this database. This list is updated six times a year, and matched with the post office's NCOA (National Change of Address) service. A wide variety of selection data can be selected from this database.

Donnelly Marketing.   Another enormous mass list containing over 80 million households, Donnelly's uses telephone directory names as its base source. These have been enriched with data from auto registrations, voter lists, and other sources.

This supplier also includes brand/category usage surveys in over 25 million Carol Wright co-op packages each year. The respondents to these surveys, plus other brand usage lists, are available to Donnelly customers under names such as DQ2 and ShareForce. These questions can be customized—often on an exclusive arrangement—to the needs of individual advertisers.

Metromail.   This company offers the database business 80 million households and twice that number of individual names within those households. Having purchased Market Development Corporation, they have particular strength in identifying new parents, families with children of specific ages, and households with high school and college students.

With select use of Metromail's database and R.R. Donnelly's Selectronic binding technology, the firms work together to produce a variety of versions of magazines and catalogs that can be sent to those people for whom they will have relevance and from whom a response is most likely to be elicited.

Behavior Bank.   A questionnaire-generated list offered by CMT Data Corporation, this is the ultimate category/brand list. It is one of the prime suppliers for sophisticated "conquest" promotions in the packaged goods industry, including several of those described later in Chap. 7, "Conquest Direct Mail."

Their questionnaires include a wide variety of other questions, including political and philanthropic preferences, ailments, intentions to move or make major purchases, and other unique data.

Lifestyle Selector.   The pioneering concept created by database pioneer Jock Bickert, was the first company that made it possible to either rent an existing list or overlay to a company's house list. While the list is best-known for its questionnaire-based information on 50 different interests and avocations by individual, it also records actual purchases of products sold by the eighty or so manufacturers whose warranty cards bear NDL's survey. The result is almost 30 million names which combine demographic data, actual purchase category, and individually stated preferences. The company is one of the most cooperative in the field, assisting new users of database technology in determining the best combination of characteristics to make a program successful. As these often turn out to be other than the obvious, their modeling and analytical services are often crucial for new database marketers.

TRW.   One of the major credit bureaus serving retailers and the financial community, TRW has become a major supplier of names or data to the mailing industry. If you ever receive a mailing that says, "Your credit has already been approved ...," it is likely that the list was either supplied by TRW or another list has been overlaid with TRW selection factors. Called Performance Data System, TRW's database includes the consumer credit history of over 140 million individuals. Note, though, that the company is very sensitive to the privacy issue, and does not rent the specific data on its list or any individual information other than to banks, retailers or others evaluating a credit application. Instead TRW works by providing a list of names and addresses of people who fit agreed-upon specifications, omitting individual detail and names of those who don't fit the specifications.

Datalinx, Inc.   This is a unique database of 100-percent mail order buyers, in a 12-dynamic-month file of 30 million names known as National Mail Order Buyer Registry. The most interesting part, however, is its 30-day Netbase hotline mail order buyer service, which just one month earlier consisted of actual buyers for 83 mailers who supply names to Datalinx. For the first time, mailers can select 30-day or 90-day hotline mail order buyers, gaining the invaluable "Recency," so important to response with net mailed pricing.

Netbase has definite database characteristics with one of the largest data sets in the industry (256 characters per record) for analysis and modeling. Where specific category of purchases is needed, 9 categories provide prior mail order purchase data. Demographics have been developed to the point that family size, adults by name, gender, and age are available, as well as children. This one file that response modelers love. They receive millions of records from Netbase, model a select group of a few hundred thousand; yet they pay only for the names mailed. this Net Net Billing is an industry first, but a direction in which modeling is leading most mailers.

Netbase also provides conventional selections, independent of modeling. Another departure is that Netbase can be matched to current and customer files, or mailed solo on a net basis, for which the mailers pay only for the names actually mailed.

Finally, under contract, Netbase can be received each month at the mailer's site in its approximately 3-million, 30-day hotline release. Netbase was introduced to major suppliers in 1992 and is one of the ideas to watch in this decade.

For more details on all of these suppliers I recommend that readers review the excellent section on database marketing written by Jock Bickert, a distinguished industry leader, for my second edition of *The Direct Marketing Handbook* (McGraw-Hill, 1992).

All of these database suppliers invest in media, printing, and advertising or mailing costs to develop category and brand information on behalf of clients or on a speculative basis. In almost every case they will cooperate with their "competitors" to obtain additional data in order to meet a client's needs.

For example, one company may have a list of car owners by brand and age. A particular strategy—perhaps for a sportier model—might be aimed at people who think of themselves as youthful. (As opposed to people who really are.) A conventional direct mail list supplier has lists of people whose youthful self-image is indicated by the magazines they subscribe to, the interests they claim to have, or even the books they read. Such lists can be combined to select those names that represent the needed combination of car owner-ship and behavior by a process called a *list overlay*, where the characteristics from one list are added to another.

These suppliers often work with each other, and cross-license their data, so that a customer only has to deal with a principal supplier to get access to all the data they need. That supplier probably also licenses or has access to other enhancement services. These might include NCOA, the Postal Services address correction service, and the DMA Mail Preference Service list of people who would prefer not to receive advertising mail.

Business List Sources and Selection Methods

While most attention has been on consumer applications of data-base marketing, the business-to-business sector should not be over-looked. This is an area where there are fewer commercially available lists, but where there is even greater opportunity.

The U.S. Census estimates there are thirty million people with jobs that can be classified as executive, management, professional or technical. Yet even the largest multititle magazine publishers do not have names of more than one and a half million of them. As a result, much business mail is wasted on shotgun approaches, ad-dressed to the president, addressed by title, or mailed to names that may be available but belong to individuals who are neither influ-encers, deciders, nor approvers.

Mail addressed to the president of a company can be effective, providing the president's secretary takes the time (and has the knowledge) to forward it to the person who would be interested in your product or service. How much more effective it is, however, to send it specifically to the right person and to be able to follow it up.

I have been involved in an effort (thus far fruitless) to help develop the ultimate business database, with over 10 million names indicating not only areas of interest but also areas where the individual can influence, approve, or decide. Imagine how valuable this would be for those who seek to sell phone services, air freight, car leases, office equipment, machinery, training services, consulting and similar services. Development plans are in place. All that's missing is the sponsor with the foresight to move it forward.

In the meantime, the lists that are available—by company name and SIC code, can be effective. Many, however, are incomplete. Surprisingly, one of the major suppliers of business names has never conformed them to DMA list maintenance standards, causing incredible waste and irritation. A proper list should have separate fields for prefix, first name, last name, city, state, and zip. And they should follow standard industry practice on abbreviations.

Business lists are particularly difficult, and require superior merge-purge and print conversion programs. Otherwise you are likely to be sending your mail to companies like IBM and BBDO. And some of your letters can end up being addressed to "Dear No First Name."

The long-term value of each sale or appointment in business marketing is usually too great to risk offending anyone, so it is often better to compile your own list. This also applies to some high-ticket consumer products and services. I have often recommended sending out questionnaires or making offers of information or related premiums that would only be of interest to the person you want to reach. Either of these methods can be used to compile a successful list.

For a manufacturer of office storage cartons, we offered a chart with information on tax and legal record retention requirements. This chart in itself was a motivator to organize and expand record storage, and the person requesting it would be the right person to buy the cartons. We sent mail to "President" and to "Office Manager," hoping that the offer would be forwarded, and ran advertisements in certain business magazines.

When we obtained these names, the information was entered in the database and appropriate offers were sent. When we didn't, yet had reason to believe from the SIC code and size of company that the company was a prospect, it was worthwhile for this manufacturer to make a phone call to identify by name the person concerned with record storage. In fact they eventually organized their phone bank into two separate groups—one to solicit orders, and the other devoted only to identifying decision makers within the company. By the way, this type of telephoning is sometimes referred to as *bird-dogging*, a phrase borrowed from the encyclopedia sales and stock brokerage businesses which, oddly, often use similar sales methods.

Using Mail Order Names

In the frenzy to apply the new science of database marketing, it is too easy to overlook the original source of direct mail targeting: so-called "mail order lists." While lacking the individual category and brand information that distinguishes database lists, conventional mail order lists can often be equally effective at reaching prospects for a product or service.

It is helpful to remember a basic axiom of the direct mail business. "Response lists" are, by definition, more responsive than "compiled lists." All database lists, other than mailed-in questionnaires, are basically compiled. The person sending in a questionnaire or selecting fields of interest is not necessarily someone who is inclined to respond to mailed or telephoned offers.

Mail order lists may consist of subscribers to a specialty publication, or buyers of a certain kind of book from a book club, or buyers from a certain kind of catalog. They are people who like to respond by mail. Even though they may not be as selective as those on a database, they may turn out to be just as profitable, if not more so.

For example, you might send a line extension offer to buyers of your basic product. You know they are in the category and they respect your brand name. And such a mailing may produce a 10-percent redemption rate. But perhaps you have only 100,000 of such names.

In the meantime, there is usually at least one magazine that deals with the basic field, and whose subscriber names are available for rent. These are all people who have bought and paid for a magazine subscription. It is entirely possible that half of the readers may not be appropriate at all, but the other half are because they have already proven themselves to respond to mail offers.

Even more important, there are likely to be five or ten times the number of names on commercially available mail order buyer lists than are available at the initial stages of database building, on the company's own list. Using these conventional lists as part of the program not only increases the total penetration of the market but serves to build the company database at the same time.

Combination programs designed to produce product trial from such lists—at the same time as building the database—often turn out to be the most profitable approach for a company first using database marketing.

Bartering and Co-op Efforts

The database business in the United States is somewhat like the basic mailing list business in developing countries. For example, we do a lot of consulting in South America, where the mailing list industry is in its infancy. Time and again our local associates come up with ideas for clients that seem to have an insurmountable obstacle—the lack of an appropriate mailing list. Yet, with only one exception, we have eventually been able to locate just the list we need by dealing directly with companies who are not primarily in the list business.

Often we have been able to rent or exchange lists with publishers of specialty magazines. In other cases, certain businesses have assembled lists for their own purposes. By exchanging lists, or offering to add information to a list, we have been able to work out deals. In one case, we were able to develop a co-op mailing program combining offers from several companies dealing with the same age group.

What do you do if there are no existing lists available, on any basis? No problem! That's the subject of the next chapter, and represents one way in which the database industry is growing in all countries.

4

How to Build
Your Own
Custom Lists

For most companies, the best lists are custom lists designed expressly for the unique needs of the company and its brands, not only for the present but into the future. But this database nirvana is not available to most firms, particularly those first learning to use this powerful but elusive tool. Accordingly, recogizing the inherent imperfection of the process, we most often have to start with "accidental" lists, derived as by-products of other efforts.

The trick is to make do, and find ways to turn this unrefined ore into precious metal. To quote Victor Schwab, one of my first direct marketing teachers, we must "turn the lemon into lemonade."

One trade article addressed this subject as "Surprise! You already have a database," referring to collections of booklet requests and contest entries. Based on my experience, I don't share this definition. Too often such lists lack the selectivity and refinement of a modern database, and even fail to do as well as conventional mailing lists, available for routine rental.

List Building as a Bonus of Sales Promotion Efforts

One of the gray areas of database marketing is its relationship with sales promotion. There are two reasons for this. One is the fact that many company databases began with a collection of names derived as an incidental result of a sales promotion effort. The other is that some companies use their databases as just another way to distribute sales promotion offers, such as store coupons. In this chapter the first is most relevant. Some of the largest companies derive their initial lists of customers this way. But the result is not necessarily a database, any more than you can drop a truckload of bricks in a pile and call it a house.

Some lists are derived from contests where, depending on the entry qualification, you have nothing more than a list of people who would like to go to Hawaii or win a million dollars. Some sales promotions produce people who would like a clever T-shirt or tote bag and who are willing to make a nominal purchase to get it. And others are simply of frugal homemakers whose redemption of a $2 mail-in rebate is more of an indication of their lack of any brand loyalty than their usage of a particular brand.

A name and address are not the defining characteristics of a marketing database. Usable segmentation information is. Stated category usage is, and so is stated brand preference. However, this is not to say that there is no usefulness to names from other sources. They may simply not be as useful as names that have been collected primarily with database building in mind.

To make such lists part of a database, we must find ways to get more information. The obvious way is to mail out a questionnaire. Such efforts usually produce as little as 5 percent or as much as 30-percent response, depending on the wording of the offer and the nature of the product.

One important qualifier is responsiveness. Who among the list are most likely to respond to offers sent by the list owner? Such offers can, in themselves, be selling efforts. These might be for an information booklet for appliances, a savings coupon for a food product or a retail store, a contest, or any of the other tools used to create the list in the first place. Incidentally, people are most likely to respond to the kind of offer that first added their names to the list. Contest entrants, for instance, are more likely to respond to contests than other offers.

The difference between such "enhancement" or "follow-up" mailings and the initial list generation effort is that this mailing can ask the additional questions needed to make the list more useful in the long run.

Of course, the cost of this follow-up mailing has to be carefully evaluated. Sometimes it is better to keep the imperfect list until the new product introduction or other promotion is scheduled, asking for enhancement information as part of the "live" promotion. In other cases, particularly where the follow-up use of the database involves costly multiple mailings, catalogs or phone calls, the enhancement effort will always be worthwhile.

Promotions That Acquire
Usable Names

So far we have talked about taking lists that were created as by-products of other promotions and making them useful. I have faced this situation frequently, and have begun database programs with boxes of sales slips, handwritten lists of names compiled by salespersons, requestors of recipe booklets, and—yes—respondents to T-shirt offers.

Obviously the most cost-effective approach is to design the original promotion to generate usable names in the first place. Enlightened agencies and marketing executives consider list building an objective at the very start of the strategic planning process. However, this requires the close cooperation of general and direct marketing specialists, a factor that as of this writing is still the rarity and not the rule.

Offers in Newspapers
and Magazines

A simple but effective way to gather a list of your own customers is to make an uncomplicated offer in the media. One example is Shell Oil's schedule of 2-column-by-ten-inch advertisements in newspapers: "$1 off on a tankful of gas," redeemable at any Shell station. The resulting list is one of actual buyers, though not necessarily of loyal customers. An interesting by-product is the ability to determine which newspapers are most effective at producing sales in a given area.

Johnson & Johnson offered free samples of an incontinent aid in women's magazines, helping them compile their reported 6-million-name database in this category. A cigarette company offered, in magazine spreads with bind-in cards, a free package of cigarettes to anyone filling out a brief questionnaire. And still another ran ads and distributed co-op mail flyers with a "National Survey" promising only the possibility of samples and special offers "from time to time."

Budweiser, one of the beverage companies now using database marketing, offered $1 million in gold in their "Bud Summer Games" contest. A questionnaire (not required to enter the contest) appeared on the entry blank. It asked for age, phone number, birthdate, gender, "Brands you drink regularly," and "In a typical week, how many beers do you drink?"

I generally prefer to identify prospects by offering information rather than discounts or samples. For one client I planned a series of booklets on related home improvement subjects, to be offered free "in return for answering a few questions." The choice of booklets, on issues such as designing your kitchen or fixing your roof, was a reliable indicator of a contemplated purchase.

For an airline I set up a contest in which respondents could win a trip to Europe. Twelve "tour packages" were offered, carefully selected to indicate not just destination choices but also vacation styles. The entrants had to rank the three they preferred, and also answer a few more questions. The choices and the rankings provided a clear-cut guide to help us select which destinations and tour packages to promote to whom.

Television and Radio Uses

Theoretically, broadcast advertising should be as effective in building a mailing list as newspapers and magazines. And it is increasingly used for this purpose.

Automobile companies list a phone number for a dealer name, or an offer of road test results, as the final tag on some commercials. Manufacturers of health aids, such as Attends incontinent garments, offer a free sample at the end of theirs. And such efforts have been known to produce substantial numbers of new names of people interested in the various products.

There is no harm in this kind of advertising, as the request for inquiries can be viewed as a free by-product. But the primary purpose is the general advertising message, and every element of creative and media planning has (and should have) that as its primary purpose.

But a tag line at the end of image advertising, in broadcast or any other media, is not a substitute for a true direct response advertisement. If getting names is the objective, every element of media and creative planning should aim to produce inquiries at the lowest possible cost per response.

For example, general advertising will target an audience segment and pay to get precisely the frequency and time or date deemed most desirable. Direct response advertising will negotiate for remnant advertising space or preemptible broadcast time, trading flexibility in timing for rate advantages.

And the offer, instead of being an afterthought to the primary message, *is* the primary message. All of the lessons of direct response broadcast apply to lead-generation (database building) just as they do to mail order propositions. This means that the phone number should stay visible for at least 20 seconds, the offer should be stated and demonstrated very clearly, objections or concerns should be addressed, guarantees offered, and credibility established—just as clearly and dramatically as you would if you were selling Ginsu knives. Most of all, the purpose of the message—its objective—should be to make the phone ring. Adding to product image and awareness is a secondary objective. There are no other valid criteria. Winning an award from one's creative peers doesn't enter the picture at all. In database marketing as in any aspect of direct response, the "judges" are all in the marketing analysis department.

One deterrent to the use of broadcast for database building is the cost of handling incoming phone calls. Costs vary between $1 and $2 depending on the length of the average call; the more questions you ask, the more the call costs. The handling costs of inquiries from space advertising, on the other hand, vary only slightly according to the number of questions and are always substantially less, even providing business reply postage.

The data handling costs, added to the media costs, usually tend to make broadcast less cost-effective than other media. However, there are exceptions to every rule.

Using Direct Mail to Build a Database

At first glance, the idea of using a list to build a list doesn't seem to make sense. And, in fact, it doesn't always.

It depends on the database applications that are planned, which is why I always recommend preparing a preliminary application plan before working out the database building plan. If promotions are planned only once or twice a year, it might be more profitable to include largely unqualified lists than to first refine them and then mail to them.

It depends on what you're mailing. If it is a low-value offer, it might cost less to mail to lists where only 20 or 25 percent of the names are genuine prospects. With a high-value product sample, or where multiple promotions or sales calls are required, it might pay to use mail to sift out the good names from the bad.

An example of the former strategy is National Liberty's Veteran's Insurance programs. They mailed to lists of people whose age indicated a probability of their being veterans, addressing them as "Dear Veteran," even though they knew that a large percentage were not. In this case, it did not pay for them to requalify their mailing list. On television they did not make the offer directly, but invited viewers who were veterans to send for information about their insurance and other benefits.

An example of the latter strategy is a promotion by Skil home tools, who offered a free copy of a homecraft magazine to identify prospects to whom it would be worth sending announcements of their new power tools.

Another example, is any airline or hotel, which finds it profitable to mail to the 2 percent of passengers who provide a third of their profits, according to some studies. In this case, however, the airline or hotel can identify its customers from its own booking information. The trick is to get names of frequent travelers who are using a different airline or hotel chain. The solution to this problem has often been to arrange joint promotions and information exchanges with collateral travel suppliers, including car rental and credit card companies.

If you do use mailing lists to solicit business directly or to build your database, all the experience and skill of the direct marketing business come into play. For instance, responder lists do better than compiled lists. Recent names do better than older ones. Letters always increase results. And self-mailers are seldom the best solution.

Because list costs and postage are such a large part of the direct mail investment, it doesn't pay to skimp on the creative and graphic part of the message. It amazes me how so many large companies use mailing lists to send out what amounts to postcards with a store coupon or mail-in coupon. And how many fail to use personalization or other basic tools of direct mail.

Even more amazing is how companies who wouldn't dream of running an advertisement in *Grocery News* without getting professional help from an ad agency, can send out a million samples without using a direct response agency or a list broker. I think the applicable phrase is "Penny wise . . . ."

Co-op Mail, and How to Start Your Own

One frequent solution to the economic realities of direct mail as a database builder is the use of co-op mailings. Co-op mail is an advertising medium in its own right. The best-known commercial co-op mailings are sponsored by two fine companies: Larry Tucker and Donnelly. Each of them send—to millions of selected consumers—assemblages of offers from over a dozen different advertisers at rates that amount to about 10 percent of what a solo direct mail piece might cost. Each has its own selection factors and offers coverage of important demographic groups. Tucker for instance has co-op mailing options of new parents, parents of toddlers, of teenagers, of older families, and of seniors 50 to 64 and 65 plus. Tucker and Donnelly can provide coverage of hispanic and black consumers as well.

The space and weight limitations make it difficult to use this medium for an elaborate sales message, though some limited sampling is possible. Arm & Hammer used it, for instance, to send out samples of their baking soda toothpaste in the Tucker mailing to ages 50 to 64.

I have had good results using this medium as a way of identifying prospects to add to client databases. While both companies offer a great deal of flexibility, I have found the Tucker organization to be particularly helpful in designing customized coverage to help solve special database problems.

For companies with substantial database operations, it is often possible to set up your own special purpose co-op mailing. If yours is a large multiproduct company, perhaps a publisher of business books, you probably have enough different magazines, newsletters, directories, books and other services to be able to combine them—along with a database-building offer—in your own co-op mailing. The same might apply for an office equipment manufacturer or any multiproduct food manufacturer.

Quaker Oats, for instance, planned a major program based on combining their products and noncompetitive outside brands in a combination promotion. The program was eventually discontinued because they were unable to attract enough outside participation to make the program cost-efficient.

I have had occasion to use this technique for Weight Watchers, as part of a two-million-piece reactivation mailing. To bring the costs in line, we sold participations to other weight-related products, covering half of the total costs. The Tucker organization offers a consulting and sales service for companies interested in using this approach.

Where to Start

Building a custom database is a major undertaking and requires a substantial investment, whether you start with your own collection of names or not. I generally recommend that you first develop and test applications, using commercially available lists or simulating your own database through mathematical modeling.

Once you have established the potential of database marketing, the database building or enhancing investment will be easier to justify. Think of the database as a tool. Like investing in other tools, you want first to establish that there is a market for what the tool will make.

5

List Segmentation

Once you have a list, whether it be of customers or prospects, it has to be put into a form that will enable successful and cost-effective direct mail and telemarketing programs. The physical aspects of list maintenance, a computer process, will be dealt with in a later chapter. For now I am referring to the need to segment or enhance the list with information that will facilitate its use.

Basic Information

The first consideration is to be sure to code each name with all available information. Often, important available data is lost because only the basic name and address is retained. And even that is not in its ideal form. Here's what should be included.

Name and address should not be taken for granted. It is important that these appear in full, and in upper and lower case format. Lists that are stored as all-capitals are not as easy to use as others when trying to simulate letters or other personalized formats.

Company names should be limited to 30 characters, and may omit legal terms such as Inc. or Company.

Standard formats should be used, so that the list can be merged with other lists as necessary. The U.S. Postal Service can provide a list of approved formats and abbreviations, as well as zip code tapes to verify accuracy. Professional database maintenance organizations are already familiar with formats and the latest variations.

Problems often occur when lists are maintained by in-house computer departments or by computer service companies who are not direct mail specialists.

One consideration is the need for separate fields for first name and last name, for instance, and for courtesy title (Mr., Ms., Professor, etc.) and any add-ons such as Jr., or III, or MD. Another is the need to standardize abbreviations for Road, Street, Avenue, East, West, etc. And states are now standardized into two letter codes, such as NY and ND. International lists are particularly complex, and it may be many years before lists from various countries can be accurately intermixed.

It is also necessary to provide for other information that is available in the raw, hard-copy format but that may be lost if not included in the tape preparation. These include:

- The *date* the name was obtained (as opposed to when it was finally put into computer format), as well as the date and type of the most recent transaction.
- The *source*—magazine, mailing list, TV spot—by key.
- The *offer or promotion*—contest, premium, inquiry.

Some databases even record names of people who sent in complaints. Obviously the potential responses will vary by all of these factors.

After the basic list is formulated, subsequent actions or purchases will be recorded. This list then might include:

- *Supplemental actions*—store coupons redeemed, direct purchases, referrals, and so on. If a purchase or premium catalog is used, the specific items should be supplemented with details as to categories and price range, which may be subject to further analysis, more so than the micro details.
- *Information provided by the subject*, such as answers to questionnaires about product usage and personal or business interests.
- *Outgoing actions*—promotions sent, rentals or exchanges, and the like.

This information can all be enhanced with information acquired from other sources, or obtained from questionnaires, surveys or as promotional by-products. These methods will all be discussed in the next chapter. Just how much is desirable to add will depend on (a) cost per name added and (b) name worth, in terms of the ability to add sales, before and after such enhancement.

It is not always cost-effective to enrich an entire list with a variety of additional data. Unless the list is used frequently, the added data can often be added as part of a particular promotion, on a less costly one-time basis. Some common exceptions are for business and consumer relationships that lend themselves to repeat purchases, or for which margins justify repeat promotions.

Categorization

While database marketing permits infinite selection of names according to single or multiple characteristics, promotion planning often requires some type of categories, each with a current count of names which fit that categorical description.

The obvious categories are those of customers. The classic RFP formula, borrowed from classic mail order, are usually the primary characteristics. R stands for recent or current customers. F stands for frequent or multiple buyers. P stands for the price category—not just high or low but, for some businesses, full price versus discounted. If some buyers respond only to sales and special offers, you may as well plan your mailings accordingly.

Of course, depending on the business, geographic, demographic or psychographic segments may be desirable.

- *Geographic*—Related to sales territories or to retail trading zones. Airlines often segment by location of nearest airport. Firms marketing cold remedies or garden supplies divide the country by weather patterns. And many companies maintain unique divisions relating to dealer support and traffic building.

- *Demographic*—Classic age, income, education patterns. These, of course, depend on specific company objectives. In a business market, new companies are more likely to buy their first copier or fax machine, while expanding firms are apt to be interested in more expensive models. With consumer products, names of younger prospects are generally worth more because they will be buyers for many more years than older ones, yet older buyers are more likely to afford premium products.

- *Psychographic*—The newest segmentation/relevance tool and most difficult to use so far. To the extent that a category or a brand has a personality, it can be matched to the personalities of prospects. I have worked with psychographic characteristics for scented soaps, automobiles, perfumes, musical preferences, and lingerie.

Cigarette marketers have been particularly adventurous in developing psychological profiles of smokers, asking questions obviously designed to establish social attitudes, degrees of adventure seeking or risk taking, and other questions. One interesting ad asked smokers to choose from four differently colored cigarette lighters, offered as gifts with purchase. The color choices probably indicate key personality traits, just like available data on car colors and models. For one cigarette company, this type of data was used to vary premium offers, selecting those most likely to appeal to different groups.

Other List Segmentation Methods

Now let's itemize several ways to divide your list or to enhance it. Which is right for your product or service depends first on application (what will work) and second on availability (what information you can get economically). There is no one answer for every product.

Horizontal Positioning

In my earlier book, *Direct Marketing: Strategy/Planning/Execution* (McGraw-Hill, 1992), I introduced a concept called *horizontal positioning*, namely, considering the stage of the customer's decision-making process in segmenting or versioning direct mail campaigns. I originally dealt with the five stages outlined in this section. To the extent you can determine which of these stages a consumer is likely to respond to, you can dramatically increase response rates.

1. *Creating a need,* or selling the category. In this stage the customer is considering a first purchase of something, for which he or she has not yet fully developed or realized an urgent need. This might apply to a computer, home fax, cellular telephone, or cable TV service. It might apply to selling a car owner on a van instead of another sedan, or an audiophile a digital stereo instead of an ordinary one. Taking automobiles as an example, antilock brakes, when first introduced, would be an example of a new need that first had to be created.

2. *Fulfilling a need,* announcing the answer to an existing problem. In this case the customer knows they have a need, often a problem, and need only be told that there is now a way to meet that need. This might apply to a kitchen soap that's gentle on your hands, or a shampoo that fights dandruff, or a diaper that can't leak. In the automobile field, this might relate to other needs, even such a simple one as a holder for a soft drink or a coffee cup—a simple but effective advantage when first introduced in the United States by foreign car makers. This is why the best marketing investment is often the research to discover what customers really want and the development fund to produce it.

3. *Competitive,* or why ours is better than theirs. In a mature product category, this is where the action generally takes place. In some cases there is a quality advantage, in other cases a styling or convenience feature.

Today most products are unable to maintain an advantage for more than a year without being copied by a competitor. So competitive marketing often involves user imagery—establishing an identification with the product for people who see themselves as smarter, more successful, more attractive, younger, or more sophisticated than buyers of other products.

In automobiles there are clear personalities for every car—sporty, stylish, practical, independent, high-tech, rugged, and sometimes sexy. It is only those cars that attempt to be all things to all people that end up lacking any brand personality and appealing to no one. Detroit learned this painful lesson in the 1980s.

Cigarettes, beer, colas, fragrances—these all compete on the basis of brand personality. Coca Cola, for example, has always been the drink for traditional, mature, active people. Pepsi Cola has been the nonconformist, independent drink, for people who want to associate with the "younger generation" and who use supposedly hip jargon like "Uh Huh." And Snapple is positioned as the smart, new choice for the "natural" generation.

4. *Value, or price.* The last resort, when all else fails, is to bribe the consumer with lower price, or extra features that others charge for. It is no accident that manufacturers with a long range share perspective usually use the first three horizontal positionings, while retailers, concerned with moving inventory and making each month's sales quota, usually use price advertising.

I believe the two approaches are contradictory, and confuse the consumer. Yet many manufacturers divert funds that should be spent on image building or product improvement to couponing and price cutting deals. Most co-op allowances given by manufacturers to retailers are used to subsidize ads featuring price, and to contradict the images the general advertising is attempting to build.

5. *Immediacy, or action.* As opposed to price cutting, which just cheapens the product, this category concentrates on action now—a necessary aspect of every direct mail program.

A mail order tradition says that "Later means never," and that it is imperative to give people a reason for making the phone call or sending in the coupon now. Database marketing programs must give people a reason for acting now—perhaps an expiration date for a store coupon, or a limited quantity for a sample or premium offer, or a gift if they respond now to a data-generation questionnaire.

For instance in one Kellogg promotion, we gave consumers 12 store coupons offering savings on milk and fruit instead of on cereal—a way to avoid the appearance of price cutting even when the effect is the same. Each coupon was good only for a one-month period.

The Relationship Ladder

A more common way to look at a database is called the relationship ladder. The idea is that you have some relationship with everyone on your list, and that the idea of each promotional effort is to move them up the ladder, rung by rung.

Suspect.   This term applies to a name that has a strong possibility of being a customer. For instance, if you are selling white wine, anyone who plays golf or tennis would be a suspect. And working women are more likely suspects for wine than, for example, older men in blue collar occupations. These are more likely, along with male college students, to be beer drinkers.

This information is about all that general advertising has to work with in media buying. It is applicable to database marketing in that the same techniques can be used to select the media or lists that will be most effective in running name-generation promotions.

Promotions aimed at suspects are useful in building databases, but such media or lists—whether purchased from the outside or generated in the company's own computers—should not be considered as databases until they reach the next stage.

Prospect.   A prospect is someone who in some way is reasonably certain to buy your product, or a competitor's, in the near future. Such genuine prospect lists can be worth $5 or $10 a name to some marketers, while ordinary (suspect) mailing lists may be worth only 50¢ or $1 a name. On the other hand, they are expected to produce five or ten times more business than a comparable mailing sent to suspects.

Who are prospects? They can be people who have actually bought a product in your category. For an airline client we were able to get people who have flown to a country served by our client.

They can be people who have said they buy your category of product, by filling out a questionnaire. Or they can be people who have sent for a booklet, subscribed to a specialty magazine, asked for a sample, or sent in a proof of purchase for a sales promotion offer in your category. Someone who has stated that they use a competitive brand or service, or that they use the category of brand or service, is an ideal prospect.

Depending on the penetration of the product and brand, whole categories of lists might be prospects. For instance, every boat owner is a prospect for a new item of safety gear, and every trout fisherman for bug repellent. Every new parent is a prospect for disposable diapers, even though a few still use less sanitary cloth diapers.

There are middle grounds of potential effectiveness, where the probabilities make a promotion to better-than-average suspects worthwhile even though the list is not totally comprised of prospects. For example, a new barbecue sauce can be introduced to premium steak buyers, to recent buyers of barbecues, or to buyers of other premium condiments. In each case they are somewhere between suspects and prospects. As a result, the promotion is not a sure thing and has to be tested—preferably to all three groups as well as to line extension lists of the company's other sauce buyers.

There is one important exception in all these cases. I have generally referred to new product introductions, where no one has been using the product. In cases where the product or service has previously been introduced, it is necessary to deduct the share already owned by the brand in calculating incremental sales increases. If you already own half or more of the market share, only one half of the list will be worth sending a conquest mailing. That's why conquest mailings are most effective in new product introductions or for brands with less than half of the share of their market.

User.   This term applies to someone who is known to have purchased your product at least once. This can be evidenced by use of a trackable store coupon or mailing in a proof of purchase for a sales promotion offer or contest entry. The term does not apply to someone who has simply asked for a sample or who has been sent one.

The idea of a user mailing is to generate repeat purchase. Often it is necessary for someone to use the product over a period of time before it becomes their regular choice. It is a matter of taste, or comfort, or habit, depending on the product.

Customer.   One way to look at the difference between a user and a customer is to consider a term used in computer programs: default. This is the option that a program reverts to unless an alternative is chosen. One example would be page margins, which are preset, but which can be adjusted. Resetting the default is an option in some programs, such as Microsoft Word, for example, but not in Microsoft Works.

To continue the analogy, our objective is to reset the customer's default position. Our brand or service should be the first that comes to mind (unaided awareness) or that is the "safe" choice when making a considered purchase.

A cigarette smoker or bourbon drinker can be very loyal to the brand they are used to, and so can the buyer of spaghetti, air freight, or car rentals.

If someone buys a Plymouth once, they are a product user. They would only become a customer, in this vocabulary, when they buy their second or third one. However, that is not completely correct. A product that is used frequently, such as a car or a refrigerator, will have more brand awareness impact (presuming that the experience is a satisfactory one) than a consumable product. A satisfied user of a Panasonic VCR will be more receptive to a Panasonic bicycle, for instance, than someone who has bought a Panasonic battery, which is out of sight once inserted.

It is a customer, not just a user, who has accepted a brand to such an extent that they are likely to try any new line-extension product that bears the same brand name. This is why multiproduct companies or companies with repeat purchase products are among the leaders in developing applications of database marketing.

Advocate.   Few general advertisers appreciate the enormous value of this "advocacy" category, but it is one of the most valuable tools of direct marketing. The basic idea is to take your best, most loyal customers and give them the information and motivation to help you build your business. They can be a small army of unofficial salespeople.

One common method is to request referrals. The terms *GAF* (get a friend) and *MGM* (member get a member) are basic direct marketing tenets easily applied to database marketing. Two basic methods are to either provide a flyer which can be given to a friend or to ask for one or more friend's names and addresses. Usually some kind of small gift or special offer is made to reward both the referror and the referree.

It is also possible to design programs to motivate customers to provide multiple referrals or even customers. The MCI Friends and Family promotion, by which customers can save on calls to friends who also sign up, is an excellent example of such a program.

A plan I prepared for an automobile company gave buyers a coupon book which they could give to friends, entitling them to a test drive and a free gift. The referror could also earn gifts, in this case car accessories, depending on how many friends turn in the test drive coupons or actually buy or lease a car.

While the advocacy step is still rarely used as of the time of this writing, I predict that it will become one of the most important uses of database marketing.

Identifying Present Customer Status

How do you know which category to put a name in? These categories are just ways of sorting available information, to the extent it is known. Each one permits a different type of promotion. They are simply ways of relabeling information gathered from other sources. For instance, someone who says they use your category of product or service, or has a high probability of doing so, is obviously a prospect. If they redeem one of your store coupons, they have tried it at least once. If they respond to a multipurchase premium offer, they are probably customers.

The horizontal positioning spectrum is often dictated by external marketing factors outside the database, usually the life cycle of the product category. For example, at the time of this writing, interactive computer services such as Prodigy and CompuServe are at different horizontal positioning stages with different market segments. To those without their first computer, these services must create the need, and sell their services as one of the reasons to buy a computer. For those who are already using computers, the services either have to sell competitively against each other or must go to the action stage, providing a reason for acting now rather than later. The latter stage would apply to anyone who has inquired about the service and not activated it. Seldom is this a case of fulfilling a need.

For many products the differences are not always this clear. But, thanks to this discipline's origin in direct marketing, the answers are easily obtainable by direct mail testing. Simply prepare promotions presuming different positions and see which one works best, and to whom. Often these tests can be compared by broad segments or original list sources. And often they require individual characterization by a variety of data, sometimes not the information you would suspect to be most meaningful.

To approach any of these segmentation or sorting questions, I suggest you begin with the premise that every name on your list belongs in one category or the other. Once that's established, it is a certainty that some type of data interpolation or test promotion will solve this question, with a high probability of accuracy.

6

Data Acquisition

There are three fundamental ways to add information to your list:

1. Updating files for new transactions.
2. Asking for information.
3. Buying the information.

The first method is a matter of updating files for any new transaction. If you are supplying business, banking, or investment services, for example, the presence of many new transactions increases the advisability of using the name for various types of promotions. Mail order companies, for instance, rely heavily on past purchasing experience to predict the likelihood of future purchases.

Credit companies, such as American Express, have enormous data-gathering capabilities, based not only on their own relationships but on observations of type of stores patronized, unit sales, travel patterns, and other information that they use to refine their many direct marketing programs.

Ito Yokado, parent company of 7-11, captures customer IDs with a unique system of customer charge cards. One of the most valuable items of information for this giant chain of retailers is the time of day a purchase is made. This information has enabled them to segment their database into distinct segments of lunchtime customers, workday customers, and home-bound customers.

One hotel chain I've met with is enhancing their database not only with hotel stays and financial data, but also with whether a smoking or nonsmoking room was requested, what pay-TV shows were watched, and exactly what drinks (and how many) were ordered in the hotel lounge. While this kind of detail may have some application to future promotions, I can't help wondering if they are not over the line in terms of the privacy issue. Certainly I can imagine a loss of business if guests realized that so much information was being recorded.

What about the other basic ways to enhance a list? One is to ask for information, by mail or phone, as a by-product of ongoing sales efforts, and the other is to buy or rent information from owners of other lists or similar sources. These two methods comprise the major part of this chapter.

Asking for Information

Certainly the more information you have, the more valuable a name is. Many types of information can be obtained from external sources, as discussed in the next section of this chapter. But few external sources will be able to give you the specific information you may need for your own marketing programs.

It would be ideal if the initial name acquisition came complete with the answers to every question you might want to ask. And I have designed several programs in which this is built in for most acquisition sources.

However, there are always some names that must be acquired in the simpler forms and enriched later. For example, there may not be enough room to ask many questions in small space ads. And it is both costly and annoying to the caller to ask too much during a phone call made in reply to a radio or television commercial. And, of course, there are often bundles of names produced as a by-product of sales promotion efforts or purchased from outside sources. All of these may require more data before they can be fully utilized.

Questionnaires

The obvious solution is to prepare questionnaires and mail them to the list to get information. But even the most professionally prepared database refinement mailings produce only a limited response. This can be increased by suggesting or promising that the respondents will receive money-saving offers or samples of new products.

The problem with this type of list enhancement is that it is very costly. If a questionnaire costs, say, $500/M and the response rate is 10 percent, the cost of enhancing each name is $5 each. There are few individual products whose long-range margins can afford this type of investment.

However, a multiproduct company can promote several products at once and amortize the investment. For example, if you have five different product categories that can benefit from the same list, the cost of adding the facts you need comes to only $1 a brand. It is easy to see why the huge multibrand companies, such as General Foods and Procter & Gamble, have made major commitments to database marketing. So too are companies where the lifetime value of a customer is sufficient to justify the expense. Some examples are airlines, cigarettes, liquor, automobiles, diapers, health remedies, and office services such as air freight and telephone services.

It is also possible for two or more companies to profitably work together on data enhancement projects, much as they do on sales promotion projects.

Telemarketing

Telemarketing is a highly effective tool to solicit information needed to make a list usable. It is obviously more expensive than using the mail, but this is often worth the added expense because of the higher response rate. Certainly it is the most effective way of refining a business-to-business prospect list—obtaining the vital identity of the initiators, influencers, and decision makers worth promoting to.

Large-scale outbound phone companies can handle the entire project, from researching the phone numbers to making the initial calls and follow-up calls to add this information to a high percentage of the list.

The difficulty is in getting a high percentage of the people being called to answer a long list of questions. Some people might, but usually these are fewer than those who would tolerate a briefer call. Also, those willing to sit still for 20 or so questions may not be typical of the entire list. Consider also that the phone services base their rates on the length of the calls, so that the more questions, the more expense. I generally recommend phone services when pure research is involved (such as reactions to a mailed questionnaire) or when data is too complex to handle in writing. However, there is no better way to find out whom to write to or call in the first place when you are selling to businesses.

One very successful telemarketer, Paige Storage Boxes, maintains two separate telephone groups. One works at finding out the name of executives in charge of maintaining accounting and other records; the other calls to solicit sales of the companies storage cartons. In other words, half of the marketing investment is devoted to identifying prospects and building a database, the balance to using it.

In some cases, the name of a particular decision maker can be solicited from the president's secretary. This can facilitate a particularly effective mailing featuring a statement such as "Mr. Big's office suggested that you are the executive who would be interested in . . . ." But don't translate this into a telephoned solicitation unless you want to generate long-lasting resentment.

Some data can be compiled by asking the respondent to punch keys in a touch-tone phone. Elsewhere in this book I describe a program I designed for an airline, asking about choice of destinations and travel plans as part of a contest promotion. Many phone promotions are designed to get very simple answers such as a birthdate for life insurance companies, a policy renewal date for car and boat owners, or a lease expiration date for residential and business tenants. It is relatively easy and inexpensive to get simple information like this, but much harder to get long lists of opinions and preferences.

Promotional Add-Ons

Even where the value of an enhanced name does not justify mail or phone efforts to add data to the list, it can often be added as a by-product of subsequent promotions. For instance, a mailing offering a product sample or a premium for purchase can ask for needed data as a condition of receiving the sample. Rather than discourage response, such offers actually improve the quality, if not the quantity, of response, and produce the information as a bonus.

In this type of promotion the questions become a justification for the offer. They answer the consumer attitude first identified by the world-famous copywriter Tom Collins, "Why are you being so good to me?" The questions become a consideration and therefore make the offer even more believable.

Bounce-backs are another approach to soliciting needed data. These are simple requests for information inserted with product shipments, bills, premium deliveries, and other communications. What is surprising is the very high response such requests for information produce, even when the respondents are asked to pay their own postage and no specific reward is promised.

Warranty cards are basically a form of bounce-back, and should be given much more attention than they are usually afforded. The reward is the warranty registration, but response is usually discouraged in several ways—making the type too small, the questions too wordy or complex, and the card itself graphically unimportant. And rather than have an incentive for fast response, they include a subtle encouragement to defer returning it until there is a problem. If the warranty runs for a fixed time period from the return of the card, there is no reason to turn it in right away. It would be better to have a weaker warranty that lasts an indefinite period, or that runs from the date on the sales slip rather than from the date the card is returned. If that can't be done, than the warranty card should not be the only means to identify the purchaser.

There are several other ways that warranty card response rates, or any other bounce back for that matter, can be improved. Black & Decker offered a free replacement dust bag with their Dust

Buster. Skil Saws offered a free magazine. Apple Computer, in common with the JK Lasser tax guides, offered an update service. Some food products offer a recipe book. Even the slightest incentive can substantially increase such response rates. It is much less expensive to use every means to get information about customers at the time of purchase than to have to mail or phone at a later time.

Creative Strategies

Database marketing is a form of direct marketing and subject to all of its science, strategies and superstitions. Rather than cover the whole field of direct marketing creativity in this specialized book, I will offer some examples of creative applications, mostly in offer construction. Each of these is a recommendation I have made to one client or another.

- An international airline needed to identify which European vacation destinations were of interest to their past travelers, in order to effectively promote off-peak fares. We devised a "Europe calling!" contest offering a free trip to any of the dozen destination choices. The entrant was asked to review the alternatives, select a first, second, and third choice, and enter by calling an electronic phone response service, punching in the numbers of the preferred trips. Supplemental questions were asked about seasonal preferences and if there was flexibility to take advantage of last-minute special offers.

- A major publisher of specialized business publications was considering building a database to enable them to reach middle management executives in the fields they covered. Existing lists, as in most industries were primarily of top officers. Sales managers, personnel managers, production managers, and others were addressable by title only, making any personalization impossible. One solution was to publish an industry directory, sort of a *Who's Who*, listing executives not only by company and name but also by areas of responsibility and authority. Combined with previously available information about each company this directory list, when complete, will be in demand not only by publications but by also by any marketer of business products or services. In addition, the directory itself will be sold as an incremental profit source, and there is a built-in incentive for those listed to keep the listing up to date when changing titles or employers.

- The Dialogo agency in Milan, Italy, developed a particularly effective program around an offer of a magazine, *Noi Con Te*, inserted in packages of Star Tea. Information about beverage and food interests were compiled, followed by offers in the magazines—primarily porcelain tea pots and cups in exchange for proofs of purchase and referrals. Fifteen percent of those receiving the magazine responded to multiple purchase incentives. And a similar promotion for pasta produced a 25 percent response.

- For another advertiser, we planned to offer a choice of booklets on various subjects of interest to homeowners, such as kitchen remodeling, floor covering, landscaping, roof and siding repairs, and home workshop projects. Any booklet was free, in return for answering the database questions. Additional booklets were available for $2 each, helping to establish the value of the booklet offered free. The choice of booklets, in itself, was as valuable as the questions in determining which offers could be sent to which segment of their list.

This free booklet approach is actually a throwback to the earliest days of direct marketing. Booklet offers can be on any subject: food preparation, pet nutrition, baby care, health problems. The difference is that the booklets are offered in connection with requests for information. There are many variations on the booklet approach: slide rules, wall charts, pocket guides, or sample issues of a newsletter or magazine. The idea is the same.

External Sources

So far this chapter has dealt with the generation of information through internal files or promotions. Often it is possible to obtain useful information by combining the company database with information from outside sources. While such information would never enhance 100 percent of a list, it could still provide enough information to most of the names to make promotions possible that might not otherwise be profitable.

Financial marketers have long been able to compare their prospect lists with the credit files at TRW and other credit bureaus, without which they would not be able to make offers of "preapproved" credit cards.

Family composition—ages of children in the household—is available for about half of the households in the United States. And about the same number have filled out questionnaires from various name compilers indicating if they drink, smoke, eat peanut butter, and other data. While these lists are often rented as primary lists, it is sometimes economical to use them to add certain data to an existing list. Sometimes an exchange can be arranged, where your company's names are offered to the compiler in return for data you need. A great variety of individual data is available from a dozen or so prime suppliers. Interests, occupations, hobbies, health—these are all available from list compilers, who often will also help arrange an analysis to see which of their data would be meaningful if added to your list.

Just examining the options suggests marketing promotions. For example, say you have a list of buyers of your steak sauce, and you are about to introduce a barbecue sauce. You match your steak sauce list against lists of barbecue owners and of charcoal buyers. You have just identified which of your names are most likely to be interested in your new product category, steak sauce.

Introducing a new after-shave lotion? Designed for people who think of themselves as outdoorsmen? Take your list of brand-loyal buyers and match it against readers of outdoor magazines, people who say they like hiking and sailing, owners of convertibles and sports cars. Or perhaps match it with buyers of entirely different kinds of products that happen to have the same brand personality. And, while you're structuring the test, use some of these names even if they are not already on your own list. You may find that the personality match is more relevant than the past brand usage.

Not all information is individual. Lists can be enriched just as well with information based on other factors, particularly geographic information. As people in neighborhoods tend to vote, pray, save, and buy like their neighbors, information based on zip codes, and census tracts is highly useful. Any information ever compiled by the U.S. Census or by publishers of telephone books and community directories is available.

The range of available data is amazing. Not just average income, age, education, family composition, home ownership, length of residence, but much more. Freezer ownership? Number of bathrooms? Ethnicity? Political party registration? You name it, and it's probably available.

While such information, compiled by neighborhood and ever smaller segments (the latest is postal carrier code) is less accurate than individual data, it has the advantage of applying to 100 percent of the names being matched.

The process just described is often referred to as *matching*, or *overlay*, meaning that one list is overlaid on the other. To do this, the names must be "merged," which is a computer process that compares files to determine that addresses match. The efficiency of this matching varies depending on the manner in which the file was prepared. Some lists are difficult to work with because they have first and last names in one field rather than in separate ones; others fail to provide gender codes or titles. The quality of the list compilation should be taken into account when first selecting lists to be matched.

A Name Is a Name
Is a Name—or Is It?

Is all this worth the trouble and, more to the point, the expense? The key is what you intend to do with the names, how often, and what kind of income it will generate. This factor is critical if the advertiser is going to make an informed decision about how much to spend on building and acquiring a database.

In a later chapter we will be reviewing the formulas for evaluating database investments. For now, let me just point out that it is necessary to add acquisition cost, enrichment cost, and maintenance cost to determine the total cost per thousand names in your usable database.

Total expenses must be compared with the expected sales margin resulting from the promotions. As discussed, if the unit sale is high enough (as with a car or a long-term continuing product), or if the list has secondary uses (such as rental or exchange), the investment can prove very profitable.

My premise is that it is no longer a great challenge to build the database or to enrich it. This task is predictable, except for the eventual quantity. The real question is how much is the extra enrichment worth in terms of added sales. Ultimately the decision to build or enrich a database depends, as with all marketing, on the results it will produce.

7

Conquest
Direct Mail

No objective of database marketing has captured the imagination of modern marketers as much as "conquest marketing." Instead of advertising to people who already buy your product, you concentrate your spending on people who buy someone else's. Instead of providing discounts to everyone, used mostly by those who are already your customers, you offer much more generous incentives only to those who presently patronize your competitor.

It is this aspect of database marketing that has justifiably been treated as the Manhattan Project of big league marketing, that has warranted planning reminiscent of D-Day, and has generated secrecy that the CIA would have difficulty penetrating. And it is this kind of marketing that has enabled me to maintain my own enthusiasm about a specialty that by logic should no longer be challenging to me.

Virtually none of the tests and experiments are reported in the trade press, until they reach a scale too enormous to be overlooked. Because of the nature of direct mail, little is reported, and when a project is unveiled, it is very difficult to discover to whom it was mailed and in what quantity. Only when the next share-of-market reports come out does the competition learn that they have become the victims of a devastating sneak attack.

Conquest marketing is not necessarily limited to database marketing. Any advertisement aimed specifically at users of another brand can fit this category. The "Pepsi Challenge" is one example. Another is the highly competitive analgesic category, where television commercials almost always provide comparisons with the leading brand. Conquest marketing is any offer that says, "Send us a wrapper from the other brand and we'll send you a sample of ours," or that says, "Turn in your old credit card." For that matter, so is most political advertising, often the most tasteless example of selling one "brand" by denigrating another.

Database conquest advertising is differentiated by making such offers specifically to users of the competing brand, or to people who have a strong probability of being such. The direct mail medium provides for efficient targeting in many situations. More important, it permits efficient sampling, requests for data, and the use of specific of images and copy points that might be relevant for special markets but not for mass advertising. In direct mail it is also possible to make generous offers of samples or store coupons that would not be economical if offered to current users.

Unfortunately some of the best illustrations of this technique, including some I have been involved with, are still concealed by confidentiality agreements. And for good reason. If it worked once, it can work again to a larger list or for another brand. And it may be adapted to work in reverse, to be used as a counterattack by the dazed competitor. (Except that in most cases the successful database marketer has quietly secured the best sources of names and perfected their lists in a way that would be hard to duplicate.)

Examples of Conquest Direct Mail

Soap

In this example one of my clients was on the receiving end of a database assault. Lever's Dove soap developed a mailing, probably after testing several creative approaches, targeted at users of Ivory soap. Using commercial database compilers, they assembled Ivory user names, and sent out a mailing which included a mini-sample and a litmus strip to demonstrate a "less-acidity" claim against Ivory. News of the test leaked because the agency entered the mailing in the Direct Marketing Association's Echo award competition and included the impressive results as part of the entry. I personally copied the entry portfolio to send the news to Ivory.

Within months the industry rumor mill carried news that the test had been a failure—"much ado about nothing." This too was passed along and the promotion passed by as an interesting but unimportant experiment. But, as it turned out, the rumors were deliberate misinformation worthy of the best foreign intrigue.

About half a year later the same test mailing was brought into the office by several members of our staff who had indicated on questionnaires that they were Ivory users. My estimate is that between two and five million pieces had hit the mailboxes of Ivory users all over the country! Here is sampling, demonstration, product claim—all concentrated in one dynamite mail package and placed in the hands of the consumers most likely to respond to the message—a marketing equivalent of a Tomahawk missile.

Soft Drinks

In this case no one I know spotted the testing that must have taken place. And the trade papers didn't pick it up until it had already been mailed and received. Yet it is probably one of the biggest and best examples of conquest marketing.

According to the press, Pepsi Cola sent one million 24-can cases of Pepsi to identified Coke drinkers. At first glance this might seem extravagant. "Why 24 cans?" is a logical question. My guess is that they had tested how many cans one must drink before the new taste seems natural, and the old Coke taste seems strange. Instead of relying on the logic of a taste test—"Try ours and compare"—they are actually trying to get the prospect accustomed to a different taste. And why not? Isn't that how we got attached to our "favorite" brands in the first place?

Some early testing by cigarette manufacturers indicated just that. Trying one cigarette or even one pack of cigarettes will not necessarily get someone to change brands. Up to a certain point, any brand taste other than the one they are accustomed to will seem to taste "strange." While some might adopt a new brand after two or three packs, many required as much as two cartons—40 packs of cigarettes. And others could not be changed at all. In this light, 24 cans of a soft drink seems quite sensible.

What about the cost? Let's presume UPS charged about $3 per shipment on a special basis. (If they didn't create a special rate, they should have.) Then let's presume list compilers provided and processed the name for less than $1 each. That's $4 a shipment, before figuring the manufacturer's cost of the product being shipped. I guessed about $6, which would make the program cost about $10 per prospect—admittedly a high price.

But it's not high at all when you consider what the response rate might be and the lifetime value of a converted soft-drink-consuming household. Five hundred cans a year is not an unreasonable estimate, for a typical family, with a manufacturer's margin on incremental sales of at least 10¢ a can, for a net of $50 per year. Figure on 10 years and you eventually have almost $500 in profit per converted customer.

At these figures, all of which are estimates, they would break even if only one out of 50 recipients converted; based on 10 years of use, that's $500 (50 × $10 cost). And that's only a 2-percent response. I would guess that the expected conversion rate could be ten times this figure, or 20 percent.

Look at it another way. At these figures, the promotion is a break-even in the first 12 months. If the conversion rate is higher than 20 percent (which this one probably is), this mailing will show a first-year profit and a long-range, very profitable change in market share.

One way to gain experience with database marketing is to work out the figures like this for any database program you receive or that you hear about. When you do, some of them will not add up no matter how you work out the costs, probable margins and response rates. How could these companies make such an offer or send out the samples? I have news for you: They probably didn't, and that database manager is probably getting his resume in shape.

In database marketing, as in all kinds of direct marketing, it doesn't pay to buck the odds.

Banking

One simple change in data storage made it possible for Chase, Citibank, and all major banks to become major users of database marketing. Only 10 years ago most banks kept each account separately, with no cross-index. A customer might have checking accounts, savings accounts, trusts, CDs, mortgages, business loans, credit cards. But each would be on a separate file. The bank knew how many accounts they had—so many IRAs, so many auto loans, and so on—but they had no idea how many customers they had. Combining all the account names into a single database opened up the whole world of database marketing options.

The conquest factor can be deduced from two simple assumptions:

1. Most customers in a given economic status have or will need a predictable combination of banking services.
2. If they aren't getting that service from us, they're getting it from someone else.

With these premises it was possible to develop programs designed to deepen the relationship the bank had with its customers. Instead of mailing a credit card invitation or loan rate announcement to everyone, they were able to concentrate on winning over those customers who already had at least one relationship with the bank.

Chase Manhattan approached the database marketing opportunity in a particularly sophisticated manner. They added data on income from mortgage applications or transaction records. When no individual data was available, they enriched the list by adding evaluations based on neighborhood. When such area-based information was not enough to grant a loan, it did make the prospect a reasonable bet to be receptive to certain marketing offers over others.

This data enabled Chase to segment lists not only by present account status but also in wealth categories. With response rates consistently exceeding 10 percent, they were able to target product offers to exactly those list segments most likely to be interested. Households with combined incomes over $250,000 were offered private banking services. Less affluent households were offered credit cards and CDs. Others were cross-sold savings or loan products.

Liquor

One of the earliest marketing executives to recognize the potential of database marketing was Richard Shaw of the House of Seagram. As early as 1986, Seagram began to participate in commercial surveys soliciting information about what people drink, how often, and what brands.

As a multibrand, multicategory company, they were able to ask buyers sending in a response to one brand's promotion what other brands they used. And, by performing mathematical analyses of these lists, they were able to develop very specific market profiles of the types of people who were attracted to different types of brand images.

Recognizing the testing process inherent in direct mail strategy, Seagram's approached database marketing very professionally. Direct marketing agencies were brought in for different brands, and each one encouraged to develop a range of creative promotions and offer options appropriate to the brand. This type of multiple testing approach, while routine in the world of direct marketing, is still foreign to most packaged goods companies that prefer to select one option and execute it without alternative testing.

A program I proposed for Seagram's Herradura Tequila offered contests and prizes which, in themselves, dramatized the ultra-macho image of this "shooter" brand, and was targeted to people with appropriate self-images.

Another we did for Seagram's Gin presented the summer refreshment approach, positioning this gin as an excellent mixer for cool, refreshing drinks. The main "selling" message was pictorial—closeups of iced, carbonated drinks. The support came from drink illustrations and recipes, plus an "invitation" to dramatize the party idea. The offer was a multiple purpose one: an individually coded store coupon (in those states where such offers are legal), plus a choice of mail-in offers— free preprinted party invitations, ice cube trays shaped like tennis rackets or golf balls, and battery-operated fans in the shape of oranges and lemons.

We were able to send these mailings not just to gin drinkers, but to buyers of those specific brands of gin most likely to be switchable to our client's brand. Additional mailings were sent to rented lists of individuals who have a high probability of being gin drinkers as well as being likely to entertain frequently. Based on Simmons data, we selected tennis and golf players, and adapted the premiums to interest each list.

Cigarettes

If necessity is the mother of invention, the tobacco industry should be the most inventive user of database marketing. And it is. Anticipating the curtailment of its right to advertise, both in media and content, it embarked on the development of database marketing in the 1980s, even before the term came into general use.

R. J. Reynolds entered into an arrangement with JFY, the first company to compile large scale brand and usage data. While the arrangement was not made public, JFY solicited information about smoking habits in millions of households—who in the family smoked, how often, what brands, and what variation and packaging of the brand.

I was running BBDO Direct when BBDO was handling Camels, and was fascinated at the sophistication of the research methods that were available for this type of product and the creative ways in which visual expressions of self-imagery could be used. We had the opportunity to apply some of the theories for this brand, and developed a variety of interesting ideas. The one that got furthest was a plan to offer, for proofs of purchase and a nominal shipping cost, a series of adventure booklets with "how-to" information on kayaking, mountain climbing, Amazon exploration, Sahara desert survival, and other subjects that reflected what was then the Camel image. This would have been sent by mail directly to smokers of the competing Marlboro brand.

Today most conquest promotions in this field are done with mailed samples, or with mailed coupons good for discounts or even free packs of cigarettes. To avoid problems with regulatory bodies, these are sent only where ages can be verified and where there is a signed consent to accept mailed tobacco samples. If this information is not available when the name is first obtained, it is solicited in subsequent promotions.

Where I have been involved with such promotions, for other cigarette companies, I have tried to match the product imagery with the offer, usually offering a contest or a merchandise premium that supports the brand image.

One interesting strategy I want to try for a tobacco client is deliberate image diversion, which can be done only through database direct mail. For instance, if you are selling Kools to Newport smokers, you can show social groups of three of more smoking Kools. Newport usually has this image while Kools shows one clean-cut smoker at a time. While you would not want to confuse your image in public advertising or with your own consumers, there is no risk and much opportunity in doing it to competitors.

This prior example reflects a positioning based on what is called the *sociability spectrum*. The same methods can apply to any positioning image: adventure versus relaxation, blue collar conformance versus self-satisfied elitism, nationalism versus prestige import. In my earlier book, *Direct Marketing*, I point out that you can be all things to all people, just not at the same time. Image diversion is the database tool to accomplish this.

In this field where taste and quality claims are increasingly difficult, photographic imagery is the competitive weapon. Like any weapon, it should be adapted to fit the target and the battlefield.

Automobiles

The grand-daddy of conquest advertising goes back to the 1970s, when Ford Motor Company hired the noted telemarketing pioneer Murray Roman to help introduce some new Ford models. With Ford executives, he developed a program that was, for the time, highly experimental.

R. L. Polk provided the names of car owners who fit three criteria:

1. They owned cars that were at least two years old and thus were ready for trade-in.

2. The brand and model of car was one that was inferior in some respect to comparable new Fords.

3. The prospect lived in a community which, according to census data, indicated the probability of adequate buying power.

At that time there were no automated ways to obtain telephone numbers, and hundreds of homeworkers were recruited to make the allowed three requests for information (which at that time was free). A huge telephone bank was established just to handle this program. Actors, students, and other part-timers were recruited and trained by the hundreds. And within a three-month period over one million car owners were called and invited to visit their local Ford dealer.

The Ford campaign was so successful that this type of conquest promotion became a standard part of automotive advertising and today is practiced to some degree by virtually every brand. Usually direct mail is the primary medium, not telephone, but telemarketing still plays a major role in many conquest programs.

Before joining Bozell, which handles Chrysler-Plymouth, I had met with Nissan, Toyota, and Volkswagen. All three of these foreign car manufacturers were first exploring database marketing, with various degrees of sophistication. The dramatic differences in their progress derived from the level at which this marketing tool was being considered.

In one, the company's U.S. President personally directed that database marketing be tested, and their first promotions were in the mail the same year. In another, a merchandising executive with no prior experience in direct marketing and less interest had been designated to study this field. We spent one hour with him answering superficial and irrelevant questions and never heard from him again. As far as I can tell, that company is still the exception, where the widespread use of database marketing in the automotive field is concerned. This marketing method, like any form of advertising, works best when top management takes an interest.

Targeting Promotions to Competitive Users

One should not presume that just because someone is buying your competitor's product or service that they merit being reached with a database conquest program. It's not that simple.

For one thing, the present brand use has to be what I call "conquestable." By this I mean that there has to be some reason why a consumer, if they try your product, will want to continue using it.

In the Seagram's example, we did not mail our gin promotion to buyers of Tanqueray, Bombay, or House of Lords gin. These are "real" gins, full-bodied, for people who drink their gin straight or in a martini. These people want to taste their gin. The larger mass of gin drinkers really like the taste of tonic water or orange juice. It was to these that Seagram's, a lighter, fresh-tasting gin, would appeal. And it is only to these that we mailed.

General Motors would not offer their new Chevrolet to owners of Lincoln Town Cars, but they are likely to send a Cadillac offer. And Nissan's hot sports cars would be promoted to other sports car owners, not to buyers of station wagons.

There are exceptions, of course. If you're promoting the popular Plymouth vans, you would obviously target station wagon owners. But you can also mail to families who don't have a wagon or van but should have. We are not limited to selection by car ownership. We can address such an offer to heads of Little League teams and Boy Scout troops, to families with three or more children, to owners of boats and second homes, to people who patronize lumber yards, go on camping trips, collect antiques, or any other interest or occupation which indicates a need for a more spacious form of transportation.

Another exception: real uses versus vicarious uses. Take the same automotive example. If you were assembling a lifestyle list for a Jeep Grand Cherokee or a Ford Explorer, you might select those drivers in rural areas who really need the four wheel drive option such cars feature. But you would be missing those people who are not buying it for a practical reason but for an emotional one—catering to their own self-image as a rugged, individualist, nonconformist (the real motivation). That's why such cars are as popular in Connecticut's affluent Fairfield County and Florida's Palm Beach as they are in Colorado's mountains. And, anyway, it might snow heavily some-day (the purchase justification)!

Offers: Sampling, Couponing, Premiums

What do you mail to prospects, to get them to try your product or service rather than the one they are using now? There is no limit to the offers and copy appeals that are usable. Here is where "integrated marketing" comes in. This choice can be made from the entire range of experience in advertising and sales promotion as well as in direct marketing. At Bozell, which is an integrated agency, executives from several specialties may participate in this type of planning.

Sampling. Many companies have found that sampling is their most effective marketing tool. Witness the Pepsi and cigarette examples, and note these important decisions.

How many samples to send?

All at once or over a period of time approximating usage patterns?

What kind?

Cigarette companies, for example, try to send the same packaging their customer prefers—hard pack or soft, the long, wide, or thin version or the standard one, the mild version or the regular. While writing this I am in the midst of a sampling test for a different product, between two samples or three, the regular or the extra-strength version, or a choice of three different formats of the product. Which will work best? If we knew that, we wouldn't be testing.

Where sampling is the preferred choice, it is often practical to time the program so that a database acquisition or enrichment program offering a sample—perhaps at that point a mystery sample—precedes the mailing of the new improved product. In that way the cost of the sample is nonincremental for the data building program, since it was to be sent anyway.

Of course, in sampling offers in general media, care must be taken to avoid fraud. Not only must all the appropriate legal warnings and prohibitions be included, but the fulfillment house should be cautioned to spot duplicated certificates or other mass requests. I sometimes have recommended advertising only a single sample even if several are to be sent, so as not to attract too many people who just see it as an opportunity to get something they can sell or swap. That mailing list we don't need. However someone should start compiling a list of offer and coupon abusers that can be shared to spot fraud, in the same way the original Hooper Holmes "deadbeat" list of mail order nonpayers proved valuable to the entire industry.

Discount or Free Coupons.   The most frequent use of database marketing is the least creative: mailing coupons for discounts. When database marketing is a responsibility of executives whose roots are in sales promotion, they often view this tool as merely an extension of other coupon distribution tools.

A major cereal company tried an individually coded multicoupon mailing to a specific target audience of generic cereal users, with database building as a secondary objective. The test was not repeated because the manager reported that the redemption was not as high as they get from co-op free standing inserts. True, but this leaves out the fact that between 80 and 90 percent of such coupons are redeemed by consumers who would have bought the product anyway, while the mailed coupons were used mostly by those who would not have done so.

That reasoning would be correct for a new product introduction, where virtually everybody is a prospect for cereal and nobody would have bought this product before. But it is totally unsound for an existing product, or for one that is of interest to less than 20 percent of the readers of an FSI or other mass publication.

When coupons are used in conquest direct mail, targeted only to claimed or probable competitive users, almost 100 percent of the redemption budget is going to win new customers. This efficiency not only pays for the cost of building, maintaining, and promoting to the database, but also allows the redemption funds to be concentrated where it will do the most good, to win new customers.

Thus, where an FSI offer extends 25¢ off to everyone, a mailed conquest promotion can offer $1 and still be more cost-effective. It can go beyond that, to offer the product completely free! Where a product is not easily mailed, perhaps because of weight, bulk, fragility, or the risk of breakage (soft drink? steak sauce?), this type of free offer becomes an efficient substitute for sampling.

However the entire concept of store coupons themselves should really be evaluated. Some very sophisticated packaged goods marketers now believe that this practice has been overused. It inflates the "regular" price of products for nonredeemers and for those who do redeem coupons. And it "trains" many consumers to buy only when they have coupons. Instead of rewarding brand loyalty and product improvement, it makes the consumer promotion-dependent. In other words, many customers become "hooked" on couponing, and won't buy without them.

Premiums.   As in sales promotion, premiums are often used instead of or in addition to discount coupons. One advantage is that premiums should have a higher perceived value than their cost. So, if a program can only afford a $2 premium, it is often possible to design and source items that are perceived to be worth $10—five times their wholesale cost. Sometimes such a premium can be offered for "only $2"—representing a saving to the consumer while making the promotion self-liquidating for the advertiser.

Another advantage is that the item can reinforce the brand imagery. If you want to add an English image to Kent or Chivas Regal, offer a Wedgewood ashtray. Or a compass for a product with an outdoor image. Or a recorded compact disc or tape to make your product seem hip, or jazzy, or classical, or Western, as the case may be.

Lately I have been using premiums as indicators of interest or personality. Which travelog video do you want? Which home improvement tape? Which recipe guide? The choice is used as an indicator to facilitate future segmentation.

Relationship Marketing

To me the ultimate database offer is one that doesn't rely on "bribery" with coupons or with premiums. It is the one that has as its main purpose the establishment of a relationship between company and consumer. True, gifts and savings can be one element in such a program. But in this case they are used not as ends in themselves but as tools to help involve the consumer in a "family" relationship with the manufacturer. This approach will be discussed at greater length in the section on customer loyalty programs. For now let me just point out that the same approaches can be used as "front-end" incentives as well as "back-end" ones.

Look at Pepsi Cola, which had been offering a "Gotta Have It" card in general advertising. They asked you to make a purchase and send in for the card, which made you a privileged person by association.

The Mattel Barbie promotion, designed originally as a customer loyalty promotion, was eventually promoted front end as well. Gifts and "pink stamps" were even given away at McDonald's, to get children to make any Barbie purchase, perhaps their first one. And banners appeared on packages, calling attention to the offer enclosed as another motivation for purchase.

One promotion I designed for a condiment manufacturer invited the recipient to join the Royal Order of the Barbecue and offered a diploma and wall poster in return for, you guessed it, the answers to a few questions. If they wished to send in their favorite barbecue tip they would receive a prize (a gold-plated barbecue set) if their idea was included in the poster. The promotion offered instant fame and unique conversation-piece gift items. Other special gifts would be available on a self-liquidating nominal cost just for buying the full range of the company's condiments.

For another product aimed at working women, we created a Woman's Executive Network featuring the product name. Membership included a unique appointment diary with women's issue inspirational messages, a list of special discounts for women who travel a lot, and a newsletter dealing with the issues facing businesswomen. There was one membership fee for the general public, and a substantially reduced one for customers who sent in the product proof of purchase. The client never proceeded with this program, but I was secretly pleased to see Virginia Slim's repeat, year after year, their very well done "You've come a long way, baby" appointment book, a broader execution of the same general approach. Nothing demonstrates better that the idea was a sound one.

It is not easy to develop a relationship promotion like this. They take more time and are more complex than simpler coupons and premium offers. But the reward is worth the effort.

Nondirect Response

The programs discussed so far in this chapter are the kind of incentive-related efforts that combine database marketing with the tools of sales promotion. Many of them also apply to traditional mail order. The difference is that the order is being asked for directly rather than through a later transaction with a retailer, agent, or salesperson.

But we should not forget database techniques can also be akin to general advertising as well. The week I wrote this chapter I completed a direct mail program for a soap product that involved no response mechanism at all: no sampling, no store coupons, no premiums. Yet it was an excellent and easily cost-justified example of database marketing.

This particular promotion used all the other tools of the trade. Targeted were buyers of other soap brands. It was highly personalized, addressed to the recipient by name, including lifestyle data as available. There was a printed brochure describing the product in more detail and dramatizing its imagery with beautiful full color photography. And it included a scent strip, inviting prospective buyers to smell the product's unique fragrance.

But that's where the similarity ended. The consumer was asked to buy the product at their store, but no incentive to do so was provided. Yet the selling message and the product appeal was so powerful that it will probably be highly successful.

Ordinarily I would prefer to include an individually coded store coupon to find out exactly how many people, and who, actually heeded our message and made the purchase. But this client preferred not to, and relied instead on a proven telephone research method they have perfected. They call recipients to see what they remembered and how many made a purchase.

Selling Message

Because so many users of database marketing came out of sales promotion or general advertising, they often fail to utilize one of the most valuable benefits of direct mail: sheer space! If they look at this specialty merely as a way of distributing store coupons, they end up sending out postcards with Cheshire labels and a store coupon. If they see it as an economical sampling vehicle, they slap a label on a carton and ship out the sample with a token printed message inserted in the package.

Such mailings miss the opportunity to use all the experience of direct marketing to help sell their product: involvement, story value, demonstration, evidence, explanation, testimonials, guarantees, applications, and photos of attractive people using the product and obviously enjoying their lives.

Does it cost more? Not really. The basic cost of the list, list processing, and postage are virtually the same whether you mail an empty envelope or a full one. Printing is usually less than a third of the cost. If you double the printing cost by adding more elements, you increase the total mailing cost by only one-third. Yet you are doubling the selling power of the message.

Is it harder to write and design? Yes, particularly for packaged goods marketers, accustomed to concentrating their efforts on television or in magazine ads. For such advertising, it is necessary to reduce the sales story to one simple, dramatic message that appeals to all potential buyers. The selling point and its support must be expressed in 30 seconds, or 30 words in an ad, or in even less on a billboard. Most packaged goods creative departments are geared for this.

No wonder that panic ensues when a direct marketer shows up and presents a 4-page sales letter and a 16-page brochure selling the same product. The direct marketer has the space to tell the whole story, and knows it is wasteful not to. To approve such copy requires more meetings with the legal department, more projects for the research department. Where database marketing is an executive's primary responsibility, he or she will do what has to be done. Where it is just one sporadic task of a product manager with a dozen other responsibilities, the temptation is to take the easy route. No wonder the best database marketing executions are produced by company and agency executives whose first priority is to apply these techniques.

But this will change. There was a time when television advertising was handled by people trained only in print ads. And when marketing data was handled by the accounting department because they had the computers. Database marketing will also come into its own, when it is the primary responsibility of marketers whose careers depend on using it effectively.

8

Customer Loyalty Promotions

With all the new marketing weapons designed to win business from competition, it is just good sense to presume that some of these weapons are in the hands of *your* competitors. While you sit and plan an exciting conquest campaign, they may be doing the same, with an eye on your customers.

Military history recalls many examples of armies that have set forth to conquer foreign lands, leaving their home cities undefended. It is the ultimate irony to triumph over an adversary only to return home to a pile of ashes. Modern marketers are not exempt from this lesson.

Why spend millions of dollars trying to win new customers while letting present ones slip out the back door? Let's say you have a 20 share, and are trying to get to 25. If this effort is worth $5 million, isn't it worthwhile to make some appropriation, usually much less, to avoid losing the same number of present customers?

This week my Bozell Direct team worked on a marketing plan for a packaged food product with just this kind of arithmetic. Because the category was an almost universal one, with a relatively low unit sale and lifetime value, database marketing was not included in the conquest stage of the plan. However it was assigned a $1 million effort to identify and retain present customers.

To some, this may seem like a large appropriation. To others, it may seem like too little. Such an effort is easily justified in terms of sales potential and leverage. Because it is easier to obtain names of your own customers than those of competitors (and because there is already brand awareness and presumably product satisfaction), the $1-million "defensive" appropriation can have as much of an impact on net sales volume as the "offensive" appropriation five times larger.

Remember, also, that your present customers are most likely to respond to line extensions and trade-ups. For some product or service categories it may also be easier to increase total sales by 10 percent, by encouraging present customers to increase usage, than it would be to find 10 percent more customers.

The Marketing "Death Wish"

"Many markets have settled into maturity," according to Professor Phil Kotler of Northwestern University.

> There are not many new customers entering the category and the costs of attracting new ones are rising as competition is increasing. In these markets it costs about five times as much to attract a new customer as to maintain the good will of an existing one.

In *The Marketing Revolution* (Sourcebooks, 1991), authors Kevin J. Clancy and Robert S. Shulman decry the "death wish" that finding and selling new customers (acquisition programs), is more important than holding onto current customers (retention programs) or increasing volume from current ones (expansion programs.) They chart what they call the Death-Wish Parodox, as shown in Table 8.1.

Table 8.1. The Death-Wish Paradox

Customer type	Marketing effort	Value to marketers	Cost of programs
New customers (acquisition)	High	Low	High
Current customers (retention)	Moderate	High	Moderate
Current customers (expansion)	Low	Moderate	Low

SOURCE: Courtesy of The Database Marketing Newsletter (Markham, Ontario).

"Converting" Triers into Customers

Enormous investments are made to induce trial, to get a buyer to take a chance with a product or service. Unfortunately, not everyone who tries will buy again, even when they are favorably impressed. Even when the switch is entirely logical. Even when it represents good value.

Once trial is induced, the hidden resistance still has to be overcome. These include habit, inertia, nostalgia, or just plain forgetfulness. Campaigns such as "I could have had a V-8" are an interesting general advertising approach recognizing that consumers do not always exercise their choice, in this case for V-8 juice.

I find it amazing that so few marketers follow through their trial-inducing efforts by concerning themselves with this issue. They send out samples with no incentive for a second purchase. They offer discounts on an initial purchase and none for repeat purchases.

Sales promotion specialists have long ago learned that it is necessary not only to sample but to "convert" into a purchase. Otherwise the good-looking young folks handing out cigarette or cereal samplers on street corners, or offering tasty samples in supermarkets, would not have, in every package, an incentive to also make a purchase. Experience shows that it is simply a waste of time to solicit trial without inducing at least one more purchase.

The practitioners of mail order, for so long ignored by general advertisers, faced these problems long ago and perfected methods for dealing with them. Respect for turning triers into customers is evident even in the terminology of mail order. We use the terms *respondents*, *triers* and *starters* to describe one-time buyers. Only later do they become *customers*, *members*, and *subscribers*.

When I ran Capitol Record Club, we had a million respondents "join" each year, seeking the free record offers that were common at that time. But we reserved the term *members* for those who were making the required purchases and paying for them on a timely basis.

Magazines routinely offer free issues or introductory rates, and accordingly begin to send magazines and bills to those who request them. But, in most cases, only half of those who start will become paid subscribers. And only half of those will renew after the initial subscription.

Fundraising organizations send out mass mailings or run newspaper ads seeking nominal donations for a specific cause. But contributors are not considered donors until they make a second contribution. Only then do donors justify ongoing communications, which encourage degrees of more substantial financial support.

Conversion

The process of turning a trier into a customer in the mail order business is called *conversion*. It is a basic part of the promotional process in every business that makes its living dealing directly with the customer. The real mystery is why it is not treated with more respect in every form of business—not only packaged goods but appliances, business services, and other products or services.

Welcome Kits.   The conversion process should begin with the very first purchase. Mail order companies send a "welcome kit" with special offers and resell materials to begin the process of relationship building. The concept can apply to any field.

MCI sends a friendly explanation to new Friends and Family enrollees. UPS sends a starter kit to new business accounts. Manufacturers of appliances often issue user-friendly instruction manuals, with ideas on how to get the most out of the new purchase. But these are still in the minority.

Why doesn't every food manufacturer offer recipe booklets and serving suggestions—the most obvious idea for this category? This simple promotion, featured right on or in the package, can identify the customer, get valuable database information, provide incentive for a repeat purchase, and maybe even increase the rate of consumption. True, it is not a clever idea, though there is room for creative variations. But the obvious effort is better than nothing at all.

Loyalty/Conversion Processes

Many more ambitious programs are possible, and all of them do double duty. For the first-time buyer, they aid the conversion process. For the repeat buyer, they serve to reinforce the relationship and discourage brand switching.

Many of them reflect the sales promotion influence in database marketing. The simplest is a discount coupon on the next purchase, but this fails to provide the name. It is far more effective, for long-range promotional planning and database marketing, to provide some type of mail-in offer. The mail order term is a *bounce-back offer*.

One obvious approach is the historical "nylon" offer, originally offered at the retail level by means of a punched membership card. The mail-in equivalent might be, "Mail in 10 proofs of purchase, and get a coupon good for another item free."

There are two problems with this kind of offer. First, it has the effect of reducing paid sales from those multipurchase customers who would have bought the eleventh anyway. Second, it does nothing at all for the first-time buyer who is not yet prepared to consider a 10-item offer, and who must first be motivated to make the second purchase.

It is far better to avoid what I call "bribery" and, instead, to offer premiums in such situations. Premiums, if selected with taste and imagination, can accomplish much that money cannot. They can represent a higher perceived value, dollar for dollar, than cash. They can be unique, and so appeal to people who would not respond only for savings. They can encourage product use. They can enhance the product image or the buyer's self-image. They can, in themselves, help position a product. They can even be self-liquidating. Let's look at some examples.

Gift Offers

Condiment jar, butter dish, special spaghetti bowl, wine glasses, steak knife, barbecue accessories, casserole dishes. Anything that adds prestige and convenience to the product adds brand equity. These are packaged goods examples, but there are applications to any field.

Black & Decker built an enormous database by offering replacement bags for its DustBuster vacuum. Appliance manufacturers offer a handy chart or a simple accessory. Information sources offer an update. Stockbrokers offer a record-keeping diary or portfolio. Tangible or intangible, the principle is still the same.

But these items cannot be selected just on design and value. They are, in themselves, part of the brand imagery. They must be selected to be attractive to the same demographic and psychographic markets as the product. They must project the personality of the brand, adding their own image of value to the brand's equity.

Information Formats

Understanding an ailment . . . a guide to investment techniques . . . planning for retirement . . . recipes . . . guidebooks . . . maps . . . newsletters . . . a magazine. Any kind of information, in any format, is not only welcome but has a relatively high perceived value. It is fairly simple to produce a unique booklet or newsletter that is not available anywhere else. I have produced such publications for everything from incontinence to barbecuing, from investing in gold to collecting miniature cars. And all have been successful.

A publication has both immediate and long-range use. A free copy can be the motivation to get the name at the outset. And subscriptions of various lengths can be offered for combinations of proofs of purchase or fees to build a longer term relationship.

Procter & Gamble, for example, produces a magazine for new parents. Kimberly-Clark produces one just for people with bladder control problems. Fidelity has a magazine on investments. Phillip Morris for cigarette smokers. These are just a few that this author has already seen in distribution; there are bound to be many more in existence.

Gift Catalogs. "Save these Betty Crocker Points and redeem them for big savings on hundreds of kitchen, home, gift and children's items! For catalog send 50¢ with your name and address to: General Mills. . . ." You'll find this message, along with a small Betty Crocker "point" certificate, on the top of every box of General Mills cereals. It is probably one of the longest-lasting premium catalogs in the world of marketing, offering substantial savings on hundreds of useful kitchen items, from silverware to linens, toys to housewares.

One of the newest is from Land o' Lakes Butter, which offers a free catalog of "top-quality, brand-name merchandise from Royal Doulton, Reed & Barton, Corning Ware and more." While these offers seem similar, the differences are significant. Land O' Lakes is free while General Mills charges 50¢. Both can be ordered by phone or mail, and both features prestige brand names rather than commodity products.

The Land o' Lakes catalog adds equity to the brand through its association with similarly upscale merchandise. General Mills only offers value. Perhaps that's why Land O' Lakes has an inch-wide banner with "New! 1992 Catalog Offer" on three of the four package display sides. What about the fourth, back panel? That one is devoted entirely to the catalog offer, as is the entire inside of the carton. "Reward Yourself" is the theme. Inside are lists that show the point values assigned on different Land O' Lake products. Also found is an offer for a Chip n' Dip Plate that can be purchased using a quantity of points and requiring just one additional purchase, ultimately for less than half the retail price. This last offer satisfies the need to provide a motivation to buy just one more pound of this brand of butter. The catalog offers reward for continued loyalty. Once they decided to make the offer, this company made the most of it. The free catalog is featured on-pack, and is presented as a reason for buying this brand in the first place.

This type of premium catalog offers little value to the company or to the consumer unless there is some point of difference other than price. Manufacturers are ill-equipped to compete with J. C. Penney only for a handful of proofs of purchase. Unless there is something unique, it is just another form of bribery.

If a manufacturer is to develop a premium catalog, it then should be a logical extension of the positioning of the brand it promotes. The selected merchandise should have greater perceived value because of the brand identity. In return, the merchandise should reinforce the brand imagery.

As in a mail order catalog itself, the selection in a premium catalog should offer a distinct consumer appeal. In the mail order business, a catalog must bring the consumer the best value, the best selection, or a unique boutique viewpoint. Only the latter is appropriate for a premium catalog.

An excellent example of a mutually supportive premium catalog was Camel Gear, offered by R. J. Reynolds for its Camel cigarettes. At that time Camel was positioned as the adventurer's or risk taker's brand. The merchandise in this promotion included safari jackets, back packs, rain ponchos, and a variety of camping gear. More recently Marlboro has announced a very similar program.

For a well-known fruit juice brand, positioned as a "natural" product, I planned a Mother Earth catalog featuring kitchen and dining items with an environmental or natural theme. For a cigarette aimed at a more feminine female than its competitor, Virginia Slims, I set up a catalog with a variety of bath and kitchen accessories, luggage and linens, all custom-designed with the same floral border used on the cigarette packages. For another cigarette with an English heritage, the catalog offered typically English products.

But don't make the mistake of depending on value alone. Too many such catalogs, backed by major investments, have produced disappointing results, because they did not reflect a clear and unique image. AT&T's Opportunity Calling and Citibank's Citidollars both come to mind.

If a product is convenient, offer convenient products. If it is upscale, make the items upscale. If it is imported, let the products be the same. This applies to any image. Outdoorsy? Fitness-oriented? American-made? Environmentally safe? Individualistic? College-y? For teen-agers? For parents? Sexy? Romantic? Any positioning can be reflected in the catalog, either by selecting appropriate items or by custom-designing them.

**Premium Catalogs—
Right and Wrong Ways**

Relationships can be built in two ways: with rewards and with recognition. The most successful loyalty programs offer a combination of both.

Let's say you develop a premium catalog for frequent buyers. If you give away the product you are asking them to buy, you cheapen your product image. If you offer a commodity catalog of reduced price items, you in effect bribe the customer to continue buying a brand that instead should merit repurchase on its own merits.

But take the same catalog, and fill it with a unique assortment of items that are not easily available elsewhere. Perhaps they have a unique decorating theme or a clever slogan. The choice should show that you understand the needs and interests of your customers. Let the items add prestige to your brand, and in turn appear to be more valuable because of the association with your brand.

Clubs and Societies

Now take the same premium catalog and make it one of the benefits of membership in a club. Now you are not just offering reward but "recognition" as well. A recognition token can be a membership card, a decal, a certificate, a listing in a directory. Let it be whatever is appropriate for the reciprocally reinforcing images of the brand and the customer.

Now change the catalog to a newsletter, or a magazine, or a set of cards, looseleaf pages, or files. Then add a special service phone number, and extra privileges—tangible or intangible—to make the buyer feel special. After all, this customer is probably among the 20 percent of all your customers who produce 80 percent of your sales, and probably an even higher percentage of your profits. (One airline study indicated that the top 2 percent of their customers produced one-fourth of the dollar volume and one-half of the airlines profits!)

Above all, stress the recognition element. In recent years I have created clubs, societies, and other organizations for every group from Barbie owners, Hot Wheels collectors, women executives who use a particular shampoo, teen-agers who want to be "in the know" about beauty and fashion, popcorn lovers who see it as "pop" culture, to restauranteurs who have demonstrated their excellent taste by serving my client's brand of champagne. The common element in all of these is the sense that the "member" is being treated by the manufacturer as someone special.

Seeing and Being Seen

A tenet of direct marketing copywriting is the idea that personalization does not just refer to knowing the customer's name, but to making the message relevant to the reader's interests. Another aid to making a letter seem personal is not just to show that you know something about the reader, that you "see" them, but to let them "see" the writer as well. For this reason clubs, communications, and publications are improved if the writer is a "real person," preferably just like the customer or like the customer would like to be. This latter idea is sometimes called *aspirational imagery*. This is the concept, identified by modern research methods, that people don't want to identify with people exactly like themselves, rather with people who are a little younger, thinner, richer, healthier, better looking, or in some way "better." Note that I say "little." The improvement has to be reasonably achievable, not unrealistic fantasy.

Recently I wrote a direct mail package over my daughter's name and personality, aimed at other high school girls, and another over my mother's name for seniors who share a particular health condition. In both cases, the letters sounded more personal and believable than a sales letter obviously written by a corporation or over a purely fictional name.

Line Extensions and Cross-Brand Promotion

One of the best uses of a database is to offer line extensions to present brand users or to get buyers of one of your brands to buy another. In both cases you are building on the presumed satisfaction with the original purchase.

A common mistake in cross-brand and line extension promotions, particularly in the investment and banking fields, is to use the database strictly as a way of selecting prospects, overlooking the opportunity to make the messages relevant. Of course, there are numerous cost efficiencies in selecting and scoring the likelihood of individual customers purchasing another type of financial product.

Various analytical methods can select the most likely prospects in the database, allowing the size of the mailing or phone canvass to be reduced. This type of approach, concentrating on cost efficiencies, would be expected from financial institutions. However they are missing a bet if they don't concentrate on the creative execution and test various personalization and relevance approaches. It is sad to see so many banks imitating each other with mailings of fake plastic insurance cards or of messages that "You are already qualified for our credit card . . . ," when there are so many other alternatives. This is especially so when there is such an abundance of data about financial services customers and their banking or investment preferences.

One obvious creative aspect is to remind the prospect of the existing relationship, and explain how the new product shares many of the same standards or objectives. Another is to discuss and reinforce the total relationship:

- A bank that can look after and coordinate all your financial needs.
- A soap for every purpose.
- A product for all your child care needs.
- A range of toys or books to help develop all your child's educational skills.
- Condiments for every type of food.

It is amazing how multiproduct or multiservice companies fail to build on the unique strength of their present relationship and the ability to personalize, based on data they alone have.

Frequency Programs

As mentioned earlier, it is sometimes easier, depending on share, to get present customers to buy 10 percent more than to get the same volume by winning new customers. This, of course, depends on current share, the size of the database, and many other factors.

If the economics work out right, there are many ways to motivate purchasing more of a product or service. Other promotional ideas in this chapter are designed to persuade consumers to buy your product or service rather than a competitor's. These comments are directed at getting present, loyal customers to buy more.

Stock-up promotions are one way. People who buy packaged goods in the "large economy size" or by the case will generally consume more.

Usage ideas are another. Recipe books and serving ideas are common and can be effective, by providing visual representation of the finished dishes as well as the recipes. For one liquor account we related the brand to party giving, an effective way to increase consumption whether for present customers or winning new ones. Phone services routinely remind people to keep in touch with loved ones, nearby and overseas. Airlines and hotel chains circulate information about destinations they serve, sometimes simply by making parts of their database available to tourist boards.

Building Relationships

Most companies use mass advertising to create awareness and desire. They use promotions to generate trial. But what do they do to turn triers into buyers? In most organizations, the answer is nothing.

In the mail order roots of database marketing, companies often devote their entire marketing budget to attract a first time buyer, confident in the knowledge that repeated mailings and offers will make up for the investment. The so-called "back-end" promotions are considered the most profitable aspects of the business.

I happen to be familiar with two different companies that make miniature automobile models, mostly bought by or for young boys. One encloses offers of clubs, newsletters, and display cases with every car, turning one-time buyers into collectors. The other does nothing at all to convert buyers into customers. You can guess which of the two companies has been growing faster.

Most department stores send their customers bills with a few manufacturer statement stuffers. Neiman Marcus billing statements add up the amount the customer spends with the store and totals it as InCircle Points—one for each dollar. After 3000, they get a newsletter, a cookbook, and free giftwrap, among other privileges. As the total increases, so do the rewards—wine, crystal, even vacation trips. This type of promotion is not aimed at every Neiman-Marcus customer, only the best ones.

Convenience

A whole new category of customer retention is the creation of an ongoing link that makes the relationship so convenient that it would be difficult to find a new supplier. They do, in effect, harness inertia for the marketer.

They also recognize the fact (long-known to direct marketers) that different people prefer different ways of shopping. A marketer who wants to serve all segments of the public should utilize every distribution channel. For some that means owned or franchised outlets, sales forces, and mail order, as well as conventional retail distribution.

My earliest recollections of this type of convenience include the milkman and the newspaper deliveryman, each providing home delivery on an ongoing basis. It wasn't easy to turn off these suppliers. At my first advertising agency job, I remember that the photostater, the engraver, and the messenger services had direct phone lines to our office. Again, it was too convenient to call the established suppliers and not bother to try new ones. You might say they were the earliest negative option plans. In recent times, such plans have been created for investment programs, burglary and emergency response protection, prepackaged diet foods, disposable diapers, pet foods, and—thanks to Amway—even cleaning products.

Many families welcome the convenience of home delivery, or at least of being able to attend to business at home, at their convenience. Often a company decides not to sell directly to avoid retailer complaints. Since retailers have no complaint about the company selling to other retailers, and since the family that prefers to buy direct is probably not buying at their store anyway, this is an empty and unfair complaint. All they have accomplished so far is to force consumers to buy brands that are sold direct or, to force manufacturers to bring out new brands in the same category.

Whether or not some type of alternative distribution channels are right for your particular product or service, it is still important to recognize that many consumers welcome the convenience of shopping from home. Even office managers and business executives often prefer to fill their office service and equipment needs by telephone.

Maintaining some type of telephone ordering service or information service is one aspect of relationship building. Announcing it as a service for customers is an effective promotion, perhaps enclosing a sticker or card with a special phone number. With all the tangible advantages of airline frequent flyer plans, the special phone number for reservations is one of the most appreciated features of the relationship.

New technology has widened the range of such relationships. Computer modem services such as Prodigy permit computer buffs to arrange their own airline schedules, order groceries, and a hundred other conveniences. Soon, in-house faxes and interactive television will widen the options even further.

But no matter what the distribution channel or the communications method, the principles are the same. Your marketing plans should include provision for selling to the customers you already have. And there are better ways to do this than to offer discounts.

In both consumer marketing and business marketing, a simple "thank you for your business" can go a long way. Your customers will think your company and its brands are special, providing that you recognize that so is your customer.

9
Tactical
Approaches

It is one thing to know the basic strategic approaches to database marketing. It is another thing to add value by making the most out of the many tactical and creative alternatives within every project.

Up to now, we have stressed communications channels, offers, and concepts. As in copywriting or songwriting, though, once you have written the words, you must still put them to music. No matter how generous the offer, your message must first be read. And to be read, it must be interesting. To be understood, it must be clear. To be trusted, it must look graphically respectable. That is, it must reflect the same quality image people have come to associate with major brand advertising.

The Need for Specialists

These are all jobs for professionals. They are no less important than a company's general advertising image, and merit creative suppliers of the same caliber. Indeed, why spend millions to build an image in mass media, only to throw it away by letting jack-of-all-trade freelancers or other nonspecialists execute your database idea.

Database execution requires a full team of professionals. As long as I've been doing this work, I still call in a professional mathematician to do the modeling and analysis, a professional researcher to conduct focus panels and interviews, and a computer systems specialist to help prepare the criteria for list processing and database management. I access the wide range of talent available in Bozell's media and production departments, plus my own staff of direct marketing planning, creative, and client service executives. Despite all this help, every database marketing project is a challenge requiring days of hard work.

The Need for Objectivity

On the other side of the fence, the marketing manager must realize that database execution is a specialty, and must listen to proposals and plans with a great degree of objectivity.

Unless such executives have a background in direct marketing, they will find every stage of a database program "not the way we do things here." Most companies are not geared to try several approaches in direct mail and see which ones work best before committing the entire budget. They are not used to working with split runs in magazines, small space in newspapers, and direct mail packages that may contain a dozen pages of text that involves, explains, assures, demonstrates and asks for an immediate response instead of a simple slogan or jingle.

I was at a Procter & Gamble final review meeting with brand managers and a group advertising manager, Ron Doornink. Our multifaceted test program just about covered a large conference room table. Ron looked at the material and said what was music to my ears. "Look, I'm not used to working with this kind of material. Tell me how you got to this, what you are trying to communicate, what the evaluation criteria are."

To his credit, he listened carefully, respected the differences in approach, and asked intelligent and relevant questions. He then made some constructive and valuable suggestions. Instead of looking down on direct marketing, he respected the differences in approach and looked for ways to make a contribution. All clients should be like this.

Five List-Building Approaches

1. Small space newspaper or magazine advertising, or on-the-street sample distribution, with a mail-in coupon for rebates or premiums. Possibly an add-on to free standing insert coupon promotions, eliminating incremental advertising expense.

2. Contest offering a prize similar to the one being sold—revealing interest in the category. Or a general travel or cash prize requiring (subject to legal exceptions) purchase of the product or response to a questionnaire.

3. Contract with a survey distributor to include your usage and brand questions, usually paying for either the space or the names produced.

4. A phone number in all national advertising, in all media, offering dealer locations. Be sure to get the inquirer's name, address and at least one useful item of data. It is amazing how often such callers are given the information—period. What a waste. Better yet, offer some sort of information or sample, to dramatically increase the number of calls. For best results, make such an offer the primary purpose of the ad, not an afterthought.

5. Mailed samples with a store coupon, or a coupon alone, marked with individual code numbers so you can tell who responded and who didn't. Even if you don't use store coupons as a purchase incentive, use one with a token amount just to identify conversion.address and at least one useful item of data. It is amazing how often such callers are given the information—period. What a waste. Better yet, offer some sort of information or a sample, to dramatically increase the number of calls. For best results, make such an offer the primary purpose of the ad, not an afterthought.

Five Database Refinement Approaches

1. Overlay your list with census tract data, available through most database management firms, to determine the characteristics of the neighborhood your customer or prospect lives in. Many people share the values and purchasing patterns of their neighbors, irrespective of differing educational backgrounds or financial situations.

2. Match your list with other individual databases that provide information that you may need for your particular product or promotional theme. Perhaps ethnicity, car ownership, occupations, interests, family configuration.

3. Develop a promotion that requires mailed-in proofs of purchase, telling you exactly which variety of your product each household is currently purchasing.

4. If you are a bank or other business with credit applications, use the information in your file to predict behavior and attitudes. Regression analysis is a necessity here, preferably comparing your file against a file representing actual purchases to determine and rank similarities.

5. The simplest of all, send a questionnaire and just ask. If so, tell them that their answers will help you send news of interest and samples or special offers from time to time. But let the direct marketing copywriters write the questionnaire, not the research department.

Conversely, we had prepared a database program for a premium cat food. Our only contact was an assistant brand manager who worried more about what his supervisor would think than whether the program would be effective. Everything was right. We had found a way to identify affluent cat owners (the owner, not the cat, being affluent). We had a knock-out way to induce multipack trial. And a terrific creative execution.

Five Winning Conquest Ideas

1. Mail coupons good for a free or discounted purchase or for free trial (such as a test drive). Be sure to use the opportunity to sell your product at the same time. It is amazing how many coupon mailings rely on the incentive alone and omit basic persuasion.

2. Mail samples, in sufficient quantities to be perceived as too valuable not to be used, with some follow-up offer to measure how many lead to a purchase. The follow-up can be a store coupon or mail-in offer.

3. Mail educational information, perhaps in the format of a magazine or brochure, to give consumers or business prospects information that will lead to the logical choice of your product or service.

4. Create a club of some type with enough practical or self-image value that someone will, sooner or later, make a purchase to become a member. This may reflect the existing interests or self-image of a market segment, adapting the product image to the interests rather than just selling the product.

5. Invite prospects to a seminar, or to view a television infomercial, or to accept a home demonstration individually or as part of a "party plan" group. In other words, use the initial contact to "sell" someone on getting even more information. This is especially valuable with office equipment (perhaps announcing a new product) or investment products.

The senior people never came to a meeting, though we made several trips across the country. Everything looked like a go. But one day the client called. "How can we be sure," he asked, "that, once we induce trial, the consumer will continue to buy our brand?"

Somewhat surprised, I blurted out, "Well, that's sort of up to the cat." I was serious, and explained my reasoning, which I thought would be obvious. "How do you know they continue when you give away a free can in a newspaper coupon?" I asked.

Five Customer Loyalty Promotions

1. Develop a catalog with an assortment of premiums available free or at savings in exchange for a collection of proofs of purchase.

2. Establish an "insiders" or "special privilege" club of your best customers, who get advance information or special service. Examples of this are hotel frequent guest plans. Despite notoriously skimpy rewards, these are still attractive because of little features like free newspapers, upgrades when available, and the avoidance of long lines for checking in or checking out.

3. Create a prestige society that is either exclusive to customers or offered at reduced prices. Include both practical benefits and self-image symbols, perhaps plaques, decals, stickers, or similar identification.

4. Establish an apparently personal relationship, with personal letters thanking customers for their business, announcing product changes, Christmas cards, birthday greetings, and the like. Treat each customer as if he or she were the only one. Assign service representatives that a customer can call or write to by name.

5. Provide extra conveniences that have a secondary purpose of increasing consumption: accessories, storage containers, usage suggestions. For example, make weekend trip suggestions for leisure customers of car rental, provide automatic delivery service for a bulky product like laser paper, give special operating advice such as the secret short-cuts Sega provides to those on its mailing list.

"Oh, we don't have to know in that case," he answered, "because we've always done it this way." This project never went to completion, and the brand is still giving away discount coupons in newspaper supplements, as they always have. I calculated that they have wasted over $10 million in the last three years because "they never did it this way."

Motivating Salespeople
and Retailers

Establish a lead generation program, and make the leads available only to full-line retailers, or to salespeople who maintain a minimum productivity level. This serves both as a motivation for your best sales producers and a convenience for purchasers, who will be directed to the most knowledgeable and well-stocked sources.

Also, if you offer a contest or gifts to the public, be sure to let your own retailers and sales personnel participate in a special promotion of their own. Involvement and motivation methods apply to everyone at every stage of the distribution system.

Extension into Mass Media

Most database promotions start with direct mail, both for building the database and using it. However, the same principles can be used in mass media as well.

Some of the largest databases have been built with booklet or sample offers on television, which should be bought at direct response rates. (It is a wasteful extravagance to be entitled to direct response preemptable rates and not use them.) However, such offers are best designed with the generation of phone calls as the objective, not a secondary add-on. (See my book, *Direct Marketing: Strategy/Planning/Execution*, for details on some of the critical differences.)

Newspapers and magazines are important name-building tools, but require a different approach to media planning. On one, hand-tipped-on or bound-in response cards are very productive. On another, a high-frequency campaign with small space advertising can bring in thousands of names at a very economical cost.

One emerging tool is *selective binding*, in magazines. This is a logical extension of the proliferation of regional and demographic editions, such as *McCall's Silver* for older readers or magazine editions for doctors or students.

This new method allows different advertisements to be inserted into different individual issues of the several participating magazines. For instance, a multibrand liquor advertiser can advertise its gin in one copy and its bourbon in another, depending on available data based on scoring its own database against the subscription list of the magazine.

Of course this method, like other database applications, is an imperfect one. The ideal use of selective binding would require a total match of the client database and the magazine's list. In practice, many of the subscribers would get an insert based on actual data about their household. Others would receive inserts selected with decreasing precision, based on less precisely applicable household data or on geographic data.

As of this writing, selective binding requires highly selective applications. The method is more suited to catalogs and book or record club announcements, where the selection can be based on specific preferences. In catalogs the preferences are based on past purchases or on list sources, in book clubs, by the "division" or stated preferences, as well as actual purchases.

For our client, Minolta copiers, we used an interesting variation—bound-in cards with the subscriber's own name and the address of the nearest dealer.

Cooperative Database Promotions

Often the economic feasibility ogre can be overcome by sharing costs or data with other, noncompetitive companies. This is particularly effective if the shared promotions are mutually supportive.

For example, a Weight Watchers promotion I managed was designed to reactivate former members. To make the arithmetic work, we sold participations to Weight Watchers frozen food licensees and to Weight Watchers magazine.

A multibrand Quaker Oats promotion featured varied-value coupons depending on the available data about the individual recipient. Even with all their brands, the mailing required additional manufacturer participation to be effective.

Most retailers get financial assistance for all or part of their direct mail efforts by asking for advertising allowances in return for featuring a manufacturer's products or brand name. American Express often shares the expense of travel and dining promotions if their card is featured. And some manufacturers or distributors have been successful at getting retailers to "buy into" database programs with either cash payments or purchase commitments.

New Product Introduction

The week I was finishing this chapter I was called into a meeting to discuss a major pharmaceutical manufacturer's plans to introduce a product in a new category for them. The product was a fairly general one, of value to any household with children in a certain age range. Use of competing brands was not a factor, for every parent used one product or another for the purpose. As a new product, 100 percent of the market was "conquest" and no selection was needed. The brand name was to be a new one, so there was no line extension possibility. But the nature of the product clearly indicated that sampling could be effective.

The client was going to test the viability of the product the way "they've always done it" (a ridiculous objection, because it automatically eliminates consideration of anything new). In this case, the "true faith" was based on television as the only possible promotion method. A proposed television commercial was to be shown to about 800 people in eight cities, who would eventually, be asked if they would buy the product. The go/no-go decision to introduce this product was to be based solely on this research process.

We argued that it was very possible, based on work with other clients, that the television approach could be a failure but that the product could be effectively launched with sampling. It had a unique format, attractive benefits, and filled a parental care need that was both practical and emotional.

After much discussion we were finally able to put together a database sampling recommendation. The approach in this kind of situation is well-established for database marketers.

1. Take the known market parameters, in this case all households with children of a certain age. For this product, there were no obvious income or other characteristics that could also be predetermined. Mail an offer of a sample to a cross-section of this list, maybe 25,000 households.

2. Between 5000 and 10,000 people will respond. Match this list to outside characteristics—interests, occupation or other data. Determine how the respondents differ from the nonrespondents and to what extent, and identify exactly how many names are worth mailing to. You may work with individual characteristics revealing tendencies to be "new triers" or to be buyers of other brands with parallel positioning to yours in areas such as price, convenience, strength, and so on, even though the other brands are in different categories. In this case, we recommended a Claritas cluster matching, since greater penetration was required than we could get with specific individual characteristics.

3. Preparing a forecast of sales potential requires one more factor: How many users of the product will like it well enough to use it again—the "conversion factor"? Some companies establish this with a parallel research project: distributing samples in one retail store and measuring how many of the sample recipients come back to try it.

4. An alternate I prefer, if you have the time and there is already retail distribution, is to send out samples to the entire initial list, enclosing a store coupon coded to determine who makes a purchase. This way your refined list consists not just of sample requestors but of purchasers, and the national roll-out can be planned accordingly. For a new product, this approach

can be done in the retail trading zones of two or three retail stores, well in advance of national distribution.

It may seem as if there are only a limited number of options, but this would not be an accurate conclusion. All promotions require some type of reward or recognition, or both. All communications in any media are improved to the extent that they can be made personal, local, and relevant. All list planning, like any media planning, is only as accurate as the data that is available on both the media and the customer.

Within these broad strokes, the creative process offers an infinite variety of options. Everything is changeable—the offer, the creative presentation, even the means and format of the communication itself. In subsequent chapters you will see many examples of the same tactical abstractions discussed in this chapter. But they look entirely different. Each product or service, each brand personality, each list or media—requires fresh and unique approaches. The creative options are limitless.

But only some will be successful while others will be embarrassing failures. The difference depends on the art and science of selecting the correct option for each situation.

10

Advocacy Solicitations

The basic overview of database marketing presumes that there is a hierarchy of relationships between a company and its various customers and prospects. This concept is usually expressed as a ladder.

The lowest rung is a *suspect*, as in possible customers. The next is a *prospect*, as in probable customers, often those who have identified themselves by asking for information or otherwise responding to some kind of advertising. Then there is the *buyer*, meaning anyone who tries the product or service once. The person or company who buys more than once is a *customer*—the heart of any business. It is the customer who regards your brand as his or her own, who trusts you and provides not only the largest portion of your present volume but also, if your company is like most, all of your profits.

For most businesses, the marketing process can be looked at as transforming suspects to prospects to buyers to customers. And indeed that is the heart of the database marketing process. But, particularly for companies who want to make full use of this direct marketing tool, it doesn't end there. There is still another rung on the ladder—the *advocate*.

Turning Customers
into Advocates

In theory, word of mouth is the most powerful form of advertising. That's why advertising for exceptional products and services seems always to be more effective than the same budget expended on routine products or services. Encouraging that word of mouth is the final stage in relationship marketing.

To some extent word of mouth will occur naturally. An advocacy program cannot create it if there is no justification for it. What it can do is accelerate the rate at which the news travels. Today's marketing pressures are too immediate to wait years for the news of the better mousetrap to spread. By that time today's equivalent of ye olde general store would have given up the shelf space to something else, perhaps to one of the dozen imitators that would be sure to emerge.

Several approaches have been developed to accomplish this acceleration of word of mouth. Many of them have been proven over years in the mail order business; others are unique to other marketing situations.

Get-a-Friend

The grand daddy of advocacy programs has been called *get-a-friend* (GAF) or *member-get-member* (MGM). When I ran a correspondence school's marketing program, we offered tuition credits for students whose recommendations resulted in other enrollments. When I ran a record club, we offered free records to members who referred other members.

As I go through my mail, my J. Crew catalog tells me that "We'll send free catalogs to you or your friends" and provides a phone number and two spaces on my order envelope. My statement from Hyatt's frequent guest program tells me I can now "earn up to 2000 Gold Passport bonus points, just for encouraging friends and associates to join Gold Passport and stay at Hyatt."

Look in your mailbox and see how many offers like these you can find. And you can presume that they are popular because they work! There is nothing extraordinary about this. The only surprise is that so few general advertisers have attempted to develop programs using this strategy. The few who have tried report very high response rates. As simple an offer as "To send a sample of this product to a friend, call . . ." can turn out to be the most cost-effective promotion of all for certain categories of products.

One interesting lesson is that customers tend to recommend customers just like themselves—for better or worse. That's why it is sometimes better to reserve this type of promotion for known repeat customers rather than make it available to any buyer. For instance, if you are selling magazine subscriptions, issuing credit cards, or writing insurance, it is risky to make a GAF offer to new orders until you know the likelihood of their renewing, paying, or being good risks. In such cases it is safer to make the offers later in the customer relationship, and only to those customers who are the most profitable. Profitable customers will refer others like themselves.

Friends and Family

One of the most inspired applications of the advocacy theory is MCI's Friends and Family plan, a scheme to provide discounts to MCI customers and to frequently called friends who also use MCI's long-distance telephone services.

Originally promoted to MCI customers only, it proved so effective that it was offered in general media and served as a conquest promotion as well. Reportedly, millions switched to MCI as a result of this simple idea. GTE's Sprint joined the bandwagon with a similar offer. And AT&T fought back by running television commercials suggesting that "friends" referred by MCI subscribers would resent being bothered by MCI telemarketers.

In some ways this type of promotion is related to so-called "third-party marketing" where products are offered to credit card holders or accounts of another firm. For instance, consider CompUCard offering its travel service to Citibank credit card holders. The implication is that the services are specially priced or exclusively available to Citibank customers. It is only one step from this to suggesting that customers, because of the relationship, can extend the offer to others. Or that customers, because of their special relationship to the manufacturer or retailer, can extend a courtesy to friends.

As in every other creative endeavor, once the principle of an idea is abstracted, new applications come naturally. By the time this book is actually printed, this concept will probably spawn many other equally imaginative and effective promotions.

Gift Giving

Another way to build on present relationships to create new ones is to encourage the giving of your product or service as a gift. A gift is more than just another sale; it is a form of sampling that in effect creates new buyers who may continue to be customers on their own.

Most magazines send their present subscribers special offers to encourage them to give the magazine as Christmas gifts. When the gift subscription expires, the customers are solicited to subscribe on their own. Again the mail order business has established the technique, and the rest of the marketing world is just beginning to figure out how to adapt it.

Omaha Steaks built its whole business on individual and personal gifts, leading to year-round purchases by satisfied gift recipients. But why isn't Shadybrook Farms encouraging buyers to give their turkeys as gifts? Or, for that matter, the distributors of fine wines and liqueurs? Or shirts and neckties? All it takes is a simple on-pack tag, possibly offering a gift catalog or special gift service. But it takes more than that. It requires the willingness to try something other than "the way we've always done it."

Part-Time Sales

Another application from the direct marketing business is the idea of soliciting particularly enthusiastic customers to become sporadic, incidental salespersons. Repeat customers are sometimes invited to "make money for your club, school, church" by selling the product about which they are evidently enthusiastic.

Obviously such an application is not practical for most retail-distributed products. It lends itself more to products or services that are sold direct to the consumer. However, if you agree with my premise that all products should use all distribution channels, this may eventually apply to every business. For instance, a manufacturer of pantyhose could easily solicit its best customers, working women, to take orders in their own offices or among neighbors. The same could apply to cosmetic products, fashions, jewelry, or leather goods.

The buyer of an educational videotape, freshly imbued with a new inspirational message or a new interpersonal skill, is usually genuinely enthusiastic, and can do a better selling job than the most skilled copywriter. All that is needed is the suggestion and the motivation—if not as part of the tape then as a follow-up letter to be sent later.

One of my friends, Larry Rosenthal, owns the company that sells the Link Responder personal emergency system. This basically consists of a remote control pendant, a receiver/relay phone unit, and an ongoing monitor service manned by people trained to call ambulances, neighbors, or whatever is appropriate. Because most buyers are genuinely enthusiastic about the system, one of the most effective marketing tools is an offer (sent three months after the service starts) of three months' free monitoring (worth about $60), if a friend they refer installs the system.

Even without financial motivation, enthusiastic customers can be your best sales force. But it helps to make it easy to turn that enthusiasm into sales. One method is to simply ask for a list of names and addresses of friends who should receive information about the product, mentioning the current buyer's name as the source. Another is to provide extra copies of an order form or information summary.

Endorsements

The least tangible sales support may well be the most valuable. I am referring to the simple, old-fashioned testimonial. Statements from satisfied users have always been one of the most effective elements of direct marketing copy.

For one packaged goods application, we increased the response rate to a database program by more than 50 percent, just by adding testimonials and photographs of real users. In this case, we had to demonstrate downscale acceptability to counter the perception that the program was only for affluent families. Where it would have been impossible to explain in words that the product was "for poor folks too," photographs of real people in modest homes communicated the message perfectly. In addition, we had so many testimonials to choose from that we were able to vary the ones used—matching the mailings sent to each state with the testimonials from the state.

What's the best way to get testimonials? Ask for comments. But knowing whom to ask is the key, and that's another use of a good database. If you have a record of multiple or long-time users of your product, it is relatively simple to solicit comments and opinions, and then solicit permission and photographs of those whose statements are the most usable.

Advocacy programs are still a relatively unexplored edge of the database explosion. For now, most companies are developing their capabilities to conquer competitive users, develop basic customer loyalties, and use their lists for cross-sell, trade-up, and line extensions. But as databases grow and the number of satisfied long-term users becomes significant, there will be more opportunity not only to recognize the loyalty of a firm's best and most profitable customers, but also to enlist them as allies in the marketing war.

11
Managing
a Database

By now I hope you have accepted the point that database management is a complex marketing science that demands professionalism in all its applications.

Just as computer firms should not attempt to offer creative services, advertising agencies should not maintain their own computer services. It has long been recognized that when an advertising agency has an investment in printing presses or media, there is a loss of objectivity that is a disservice to its clients. The solution has been to offer a partnership with such suppliers, and particularly with computer professionals.

Over the years I have worked with several, depending on the needs of my clients. One of the most creative and versatile has been a Long Island company called MBS/Multimode, which provides data entry, data management, and the whole range of computer sorts, overlays, merges, purges, addressing and production of personal letters. I am grateful to Stanley Braunstein, President of MBS, for the research and preparation of the remainder of this chapter.

The Database Process

The premise of this Database Management chapter is very simple. As businesses grow, marketing departments have a need to gather data, use the data, and keep it in a central location.

Major corporations use systems to run their core business. These systems are designed to run the business, not to gather data for marketing databases. Invariably this data has been collected across many systems that were not thought to be related when they were started. Eventually someone realizes that there is a lot of related data in these systems.

Because of this evolutionary process, needed information will not reside as a single file or data set; it will be contained in multiple data sets that have to be combined into a single cohesive format that is easy to access and maintain.

The database creation process combines these data sets into useful marketing records. The primary incentives for creating such a database are:

- To protect an investment (your customers).

- To control the information explosion by summarizing the knowledge about your customers obtained from multiple and diverse sources.

- To gain a full understanding of the strengths and weaknesses of the business.

- To evaluate fully current and past product lines and catalogs.

- To grow the business.

It is important that the marketing database be in the hands of the marketers. It should not be part of other systems. And it should not have to compete for resources with billing, payroll, inventory, or order processing.

A Typical Marketing Database

Here are some basic definitions pertinent to a database.

Field, the most elementary piece of data

Record, a collection of fields

File, a collection of like records

Database, a collection of files

Data carried on a database is stored logically, gathered field by field. Most databases are set up to carry primary fields as well as secondary fields if the data is available. In the direct marketing industry, the usual database would contain the following elements:

Primary Global Elements

Name

Address

City, state, ZIP

Source code

Original date

Original dollars

Purchase history

Secondary Detail Elements

Transaction date

Transaction dollar

Transaction source code

Purchase quantity

Global Detail Elements

Status flags

Mailable

Bad debt

Credit limit

Demographics

Alternate addresses

Typical Data Sets in a Marketing Database

Typically, there is a mélange of data sets to handle in the building process. Some are direct response files, some represent different forms of customer activity, and some are compiled data sets. Examples of these data sets follow:

Typical Data Sets

- A series of catalog files created from a mother file
- The mail order offspring of a retail giant
- The associated credit card file
- Retail sales slips and warranty cards
- Order processing files
- Third-party credit card data
- Inquiry names gathered from promotions
- Internal business files that reflect activities outside the core business, such as special sale lists or salesperson's files
- Demographic overlays.

Much of the data contained on these data sets is redundant, and all of it is kept together on separate files in different key field sequences. This is a problem common to the information explosion.

The amount of data you choose to keep determines the true size of the database. The term *database* does not dictate a specific file size; it simply means a collection of files. Databases range in size from several thousand to millions of records. Effective databases contain accurate, complete, and timely information.

The structure that you decide to create and use depends on the marketing application. This chapter will deal with helping you understand what you need to know to make database management decisions.

Database Development

A database can be structured and sequenced using one of the following methods:

- Sequential with fixed-length records

- Sequential with variable-length records
- Relational, on-line, or on-line real-time

Each of these methodologies has pros and cons associated with them. Therefore, the database designer must be able to recognize the conditions that exist in the development environment and pick a solution appropriate to the established goals and priorities.

Remember, because a file is called a database does not mean that it is on-line, real-time, and relational in structure. Databases can be maintained in simple sequential structure or sophisticated indexed relational structure.

Sequential Files

First of all, we must understand that *sequential* means in sequence by a key field. Key fields can be last name, social security number, account number, date, or something else. It is the most common method of housing information within an organization.

The following criteria should be considered in making the decision to create a sequential file, either fixed-length or variable-length. Variable records are capable of holding more data.

1. *The organization is just beginning.*
2. *There is a lack of data.* When organizations are just starting or even when they have existed for a while, there may not be enough data to create a sophisticated database.
3. *Timeliness is not critical.* Many organizations get caught up in the idea of instant access to data, but if you're not in customer service, airline reservations, or running a bank ATM system, figure out what is an acceptable timeframe for most of your responses and work towards that goal.
4. *The data is static.* If the data doesn't change often, then a set of good reports will work very well for most situations.
5. *There is a lack of funds.* It is expensive to build and maintain an on-line, real-time database system.

The major disadvantages of sequential file processing are that:

1. All records must usually be read and compared in order to process data.
2. Changes of format, or the need to add data create programming projects. Programming projects are usually costly and time-consuming.
3. It is difficult to query the data quickly.

Relational Database

This type of database can be used to combine data from multiple files that have been kept in several different sequences.

Before relational database systems existed, varied customer activity could not easily be combined. Most software systems handled activity in single sequence mode, based upon one key field. The difference in key fields made it impossible for standard sequential systems to discern the transactions as coming from the same person or household without several passes. Multiple file passes made the processing cycle long and expensive.

Now with relational database platforms the technology has caught up. Data from various customer actions, or from external activities such as orders, inquiries, cash payments and charge payments can be handled, no matter what the key field is. The information can be consolidated into a single database record for a given customer.

Consider a relational database when the following conditions exist.

1. *There is need for quick access.* You must respond to a customer immediately, as banks, airlines, customer service, overnight promotions, and hot product sellers must do.
2. *Diverse data is housed across multiple files with multiple key fields.* Traditional sequential file structures cannot deal with that type of data.

3. *The data is dynamic and voluminous.* Constant changes require a need for quick access and flexibility. Sequential files are not flexible.

4. *The volume of marketing activity is heavy.* If there are multiple requests every day for planning and execution, then sequential file processing is too time-consuming.

5. *Cost is not an issue.*

The major disadvantages of a relational database are:

1. *Its cost.* Costs are two to three times greater than a sequential file processing environment.

2. *Selecting a high volume of records will result in a long turn-around time frame.*

Now that we have an understanding of how the data will exist on the database and the options available for storing the data, we are ready to get started.

How to Get Started

You need to understand the three major parts of Database Management:

1. *Working with people.* The computer is just a tool. Data is part of the processing environment. The people who create the environment are very important, as are communications with these people. Input from everyone who works within the computer environment must be considered as the database is being built. The results of the database are judged by people.

2. *Handling the data.* There must be a thorough understanding of each field on the database. Each must have a clearly defined purpose.

3. *Using a system.* There must be a thorough understanding of how the system will work by all personnel involved with the database environment. If the system is not understood, then the data created, extracted, and used will be incorrect.

A Team Approach

The first thing to do is to pick a team.

Because of the way traditional data processing environments exist, with system responsibility split into groups, it is important that the marketing database be built by a team, and that team be considered a partnership. The team should consist of the users (marketing and management), operations (responsible for running the system), the database designer (a technical person), and a translator (someone who understands systems plus the overall business of the company).

This partnership will work on developing the specifications of the required database within the framework of a system be maintained either on a sophisticated database platform or a simple sequential file. Whatever the decision, the software is nothing more than a skeleton that must be fleshed out by the team. Database software is only a foundation to build on. Each member must understand his or her role within the constraints of building the system. The marketing/operations people must not let the technical person confine the scope of the system, while the technician must strive to keep the system practical, efficient, and user-friendly.

Set Team Goals

Once the team is in place, a set of realistic marketing goals must be established. Then the goals should be reviewed to see if they make sense and are achievable. Some realistic goals might be:

1. Generate sales or increase sales.

2. Enhance your customer relations. We want to know what stock is available or when was the product shipped. Be able to answer customer questions.

3. Analyze your business. Where do your sales come from, what are people buying, who is buying? Where do they live as opposed to where they buy?

4. Develop the ability to create marketing plans and strategies.

5. Have data available by means of a personal computer.

Without realistic goals, you won't be able to identify the data needed to achieve the goals.

Once the goals are locked in, you can concentrate on finding and selecting the usable data. This usually entails:

- Data gathering.
- Functional purpose of the data.
- Data reconciliations.

Gathering the Data

When you start thinking about gathering information, consider any data set that can provide information. Don't review the data in terms of what you think exists; find out what information is available to you. Think in terms of data that will help: Remember your set of goals. If the goal is sales, then let's create the best set of records from a promotional standpoint. If it's customer service, then all the shipping information, inquiries, returns, correspondence, and related data should be marked on the files.

When information is housed on many files, you can be sure the file formats will be different. There will be different key fields, such as account number or matchcode. The information carried on each file may represent the same data, but at the field level the formats will not be compatible. Sorting this out is a learning experience, a sort of touch and feel process that allows the database builder and the database user to gain a better understanding of what the information represents and how best to handle it. Here are the steps involved when preparing to sort out the data:

1. List all the data elements available for inclusion in the database.

2. Identify the source (field location) of each data element.

3. Specify the format of each data element.

4. Identify the key field assigned to each file.

5. Plan an audit trail for the reconciliation phase.

6. Identify the primary characteristics of each data element.

7. Determine the extent and completeness of product codes and other critical data.

8. Consider the geographical clustering of ZIP codes.

9. Ascertain the availability of mailing history and other types of potentially useful client files.

Functional Purpose of the Data

The functional purpose of the data identifies the reason for keeping a piece of data. Is it necessary for analysis, selection, mailing, and/or modeling? Make sure it is not redundant. If it is, remember to reconcile it.

During the functional review of the data, do the following:

1. Specify the objective for each data element.

2. Make sure you have the appropriate historical data for analysis.

3. Make sure you can profile—products, dollars, states, ZIP codes, demographics.

4. Look for data to help you forecast, primarily dates and dollars.

5. Make sure you can develop appropriate percentages. Data relationships are more important than pure numbers.

6. Decide on the life span of the data—how long should we keep it? For instance, some retail stores generate 10 million transactions per year. Do we need five years' worth or three years' worth?

7. Establish the priority of the data.
   - Store of preference versus store of residence?
   - MOB (mail order buyer) supersedes retail buyer?
   - Current dollars versus average dollars versus lifetime dollars?
   - Scores versus RFM (recency, frequency, monetary value)?

8. How often will data be used—daily, weekly, monthly?

9. Should the outputs be on on-line screens or in hard copy reports?

Reconciliation

After you have located the data and decided which data you are going to use, you can start on the reconciliation phase. There is *always* a reconciliation phase. You must be able to plan the consolidation of data so that you can effectively build the database.

At the beginning of the consolidation process, you should address the primary levels of consolidation.

- Data
- Customer

Data Consolidation

Data consolidation is easier to deal with because there are fewer variations. A date is a date, whether it is January 1, 1990 or 1/1/90, and the Ralph Lauren department is Ralph Lauren even if we call it RL. Tables for cross-reference purposes may be needed to equate data fields to one another.

Data Tables

There are many times within the same organization that a piece of data has a different identifier. Think of it as Robert and Bob or Elizabeth and Betty. When you build the database, you use only one identifier. There must be a standard. Table 11.1 shows the different input variations and the selected standard to be used in

Table 11.1. Data Substitution

	Department Number Data Table			
	File A	File B	File C	Database
Department	123	456	XYZ	123
	345	224	YAB	224
	678	928	ZAQ	ZAQ
	402	637	ADR	402
	833	029	HYT	833

the database. When the data is found, the standard is substituted so that the output field is correct and consistent.

Customer Consolidation

In addition to data consolidation, we must have a methodology for assembling the information about a given customer. Customer recognition is at the heart of the data collection process. Because the database is a tool for communication with people, whatever we design and implement must allow us to correctly identify and reach the customers. You must, therefore, assemble all the pieces of information pertinent to a given customer in his/her record and save the desired variation of the customer's pertinent information. This process is complicated because we must do it across many data sets and it should be done at two levels:

1. Create the customer records.
2. Create the household records.

Customer records that contain information from files using the same account number are easy to combine. Sometimes customers have multiple account numbers; you must then find another way to consolidate. In this situation, matchcodes are often used for the consolidation process. A *matchcode* is the synthesizing of the name and address elements. After you have figured out how to consolidate, you must decide when to consolidate. In some systems, account records are maintained throughout the processing cycle, and collapsed to the household for selection purposes. In other systems, records are collapsed early in the cycle. Sometimes households are never created. The real goal of consolidation is to produce the best possible customer records.

Customer recognition and household recognition can only be accomplished by using sophisticated merge/purge software. Merge/purge software routines are not included with any traditional data base software. You will have to create them or purchase them. An understanding of the nuances of this discipline is absolutely essential in the creation of a meaningful, useful database system.

When you start looking at names and addresses, you have to be prepared to make the decisions associated with duplication identification. This is not something to be left to a canned software package. It takes many hours of manual review before one feels comfortable with the householding routines.

Small pieces of data like apartment numbers or middle initials can become a factor in the process. None of this is an exact science; it is an art form. You have to decide on the level of overkill or underkill that is acceptable to your organization. Which of the examples in Table 11.2 is a match? Your guess is as good as mine. A decision has to be made.

In addition, besides the many data sets and the need for merging/purging, you will find that the data being passed to you from the different data collection systems is deficient. For instance, all records do not carry the complete name and address information needed for your merge/purge system, they just carry an account number, customer number, or matchcode. So a linkage table will have to be built.

When you build this table, conceptually, it is in multiple sequences. The sequence of the table allows you to find the appropriate master key needed to combine the data. Table 11.3 is a series of key fields linking all key fields to the associated data sets. An

Table 11.2. Duplicate Records

		Name and Address Comparison			
Name	Care of	Street Address	City	State	Zip
Sari A Jones		123 E Main St	Huntington	NY	11746
Mrs Robert Jones		123 Main St E Apt 3	Huntington Sta	NY	11746
David Wallace III		805 Longmeadow St	Longmeadow	MA	01106
M F Wallace		850 Longmeadow St	Longmeadow	MA	01106
Marilyn Petrizzo		9 Sheetbriar Lane	Oceanside	NY	11572
Marilyn H. Getrizzo		9 Sheet Briar Ln	Oceanside	NY	11572
Gertrude Davis		P O Box 92, Terry Lane	Hauppauge	NY	11788
Gertrude Davis		Terry Lane, Box 2	Hauppauge	NY	11788
Mary Fields		P O Box 126	S Hadley	MA	01075
Mary Fields		18 Kenlee Terrace	South Hadley	MA	01075

Table 11.3. Account Number/Matchcode Index

Account Number Index	
Account Numbers	Matchcode
123-45-6789	11746-HNTM-673-BRGHT
132-28-3918	11510-JKSN-92*-MPL**
133-98-8372	10292-BCHW-236-LCSTR
214-12-3748	11050-MLLR-506-LK***
436-65-3462	10570-WSHN-1**-WNTGH
475-32-4871	10292-BCHW-236-LCSTR
520-77-2344	10025-GNN*-515-SNNY*

examination of Table 11.3 shows how the linkages between the different data sets can be accomplished. Information in account number sequence is applied by account number. When information is in matchcode sequence, we can search our table for the proper account number then use the account number to apply the information to the system. Once all of the information is applied, collapsing to customer level can be achieved.

The consolidated records will contain detail purchase activity with dates and dollars for every purchase. This type of record provides the complete history of the customer to the database marketer. It allows you to select the proper customers for a given promotion and provides the basis for analyzing the results of a given promotion. The level of data collapsing depends on the complexity of usage or selection methodology. For speedy inquiries, summary fields can be created from the detail fields, or you may choose to search through all the detail fields while developing accumulators as needed.

Once the data sets have been reconciled and consolidated, the fun begins—the database is ready for use.

Uses of the Database

The primary uses of the database are to:

- View records.
- Produce reports.

- Identify records or segments.
- Analyze data.

View Records

The consolidated records represent a database of customers complete with all their activity. The collected history of a customer can be viewed on-line, real-time if necessary or in some printed form. The record in Table 11.4 shows exactly what is contained on the database. In that table, you can see:

A. *The name and address data of the customer.* It probably came from the credit application or the most recent order.

B. *Some customer level status flags.* This is information normally developed through customer communications or the data-appending process.

C. *Original order data from the order processing system.*

D. *Summary data.* This is developed from the detail transactions. It provides a way to access customer type without extensive data searches.

E. *The transaction detail.* This is a complete purchase history.

We can now take these complete, individual records and use them for marketing/management and customer service purposes.

The data shown in the table is internal to our organization, but sometimes external data may be added to the database. Enhancements can be an important part of database marketing. However, you can never really be sure as to the accuracy of the enhanced data. It may be stale. Someone who had a Mercedes three years ago may be driving a Ford today. Therefore, you should rely on data captured through your system more than enhanced data, but you must be prepared to house enhancements on your database.

From these base records, you can respond to customer queries, generate reports, and develop your marketing strategies.

Table 11.4. Complete Customer Record

COMPLETE CUSTOMER RECORD

NAME	MRS GERTRUDE DAVIS	CLIENT ACCT	190045
CARE OF		DNM FLAG –	
STREET	24 RIVER RD #324		DNR FLAG –·· B
CITY	PEPPERELL	OTHER FLAG –	
STATE	MA ZIP 01463	DEMO CODE –	1034
ORIG DATE	870519 FIRST		
ORIG DOLLAR	$44.00 ORDER	·· C	
ORIG SOURCE	M144		

TRANS SUMMARY

MAIL/PHONE: BOTH	TYPE	REC DATE	CUM	DOLLARS	FREQ
CHARGE CARDS: MVA	MOB	890823		$324.00	3
·· D	MOB	870519		$44.00	1

TRANSACTION DETAIL

TYPE	TRANS DATE	DOLLARS	SOURCE	MAIL PHONE	CASH CHARGE	STYLE	DOLLARS	CLASS	LS	SIZE
MOB	890823	$186.00	A410	P	CHARGE	CK		07	V	4
RETAIL	890402	$70.00	A410	P	CHARGE	SS		07	V	4
RETAIL	881218	$68.00	B541	M	CASH	AT		05	S	4
SALE	870519	$44.00	M144	M	CHARGE	BK		03	S	4

TOTAL TRANSACTIONS = 4

Reports

No matter what type of database you choose to build, you will need a set of reports (hard copy or screen) to help you manage the system and make the proper decisions. The team will have to be the designers of the report package. Database software systems do not produce the reports. If you get a canned system, then be prepared either to settle for its report package with some modifications, or pay a lot for customizing to meet your specific needs. These reports must be generated at two periods, what we call up-front or back-end. Tables 11.5 and 11.6 present two examples of up-front reporting.

The up-front reports should provide you with an historical picture of customers on your database. Up-front reports are a profile of the database. For example, Table 11.5 shows customers by date of most recent purchase spread across several different dollar ranges. Table 11.6 represents customers by state from different purchase categories.

Back-end reports are used for analyzing prospects after completion, hence the term back-end. See Response Analysis, Table 11.12 (page 136) These must be included in any database system to ensure the integrity of the promotions developed through the database. If you have no back-end reporting, then there is no way of measuring the effectiveness of the selection methodology used by the database system.

When attempting to create a report package from database records, always be cognizant of the amount of information that can be produced. The information will fall into two broad categories: actionable and informational.

Table 11.5. Customer Profile

CUSTOMER PROFILE BY DOLLARS BY RECENCY DATE							
Recency Date	Total	0-0	1-49	50-99	100-149	150-199	200-299
1992	8,434	32	1,437	1,548	1,069	928	1,154
1991	20,765	843	3,708	4,151	2,806	1,746	2,593
1990	12,263	23	2,582	2,870	1,952	1,238	1,492
1989	5,267	7	1,964	1,285	625	477	414
1988	4,743	612	1,358	1,059	555	338	373
Prior	166,264	2,923	105,746	35,651	11,639	5,567	2,532
Total	217,736	4,440	116,795	46,564	18,646	10,294	8,558

Table 11.6. State and Sectional Center Facility (SCF) Counts

STATE	SCF RANGE	TOTAL	RETAIL	MAIL ORDER	SALE	INQUIRY
AK	995-999	956	868	14	3	71
AL	350-369	3176	2796	82	7	291
AR	716-729	1698	1536	44	2	116
AZ	850-869	3103	2787	49	7	260
CA	900-966	31,230	28,179	629	59	2363
CO	800-819	4566	4234	99	6	227
CT	060-069	6529	5872	217	17	423
DC	200-205	19,292	1930	11,825	3396	2141
DE	197-199	1362	1206	60	8	88

Informational Data. Informational data is purely information. This type of reporting is activity-based, not customer-based. It will indicate what departments customers buy from, or what stores they frequent, or how many purchases they make. Therefore, one customer will be counted many times. This is correct for sales and inventory reporting, but not desirable for promotional planning.

Invariably, when you build a database from multiple data sets, combinations of events occur. You will find that customers have purchased from more than one entity in the organization. (Look at Table 11.4, Complete Customer Record.) When counting the number of purchases made at the organizational level, the total will exceed the number of people on the database because the customers have purchased in more than one entity. The information provided must be available at three levels: individual, gross, and net. Table 11.6 shows the actionable data associated with the appropriate informational data so that you can see how the priority selections affect the results.

Actionable Data. Only net data is truly actionable, and the most important reports will need logic in them that is unique to your business.

The primary purpose of database technology is to allow us to get at a given record quickly or at a small set of records quickly. Most database marketers have extended the rules somewhat by using database technology to find large groups of meaningful records.

These two reports—informational and actionable—represent the same customers. Table 11.7 indicates the total purchase across departments. Therefore, a customer is counted more than once.

Table 11.7. Informational Data

CUSTOMERS BY DEPARTMENT					
—LIFETIME DOLLARS ACROSS ALL DEPARTMENTS—					
Department	1-50	51-100	101-250	251-500	500 Plus	Total
Shoes	878	577	962	602	458	3477
Dresses	1311	227	807	623	435	3403
Coats	859	692	973	503	298	3325
Hats	664	572	904	516	354	3010
Gross Total	3712	2068	3646	2244	1545	13,215

Table 11.8 represents net counts by combination, a customer is counted only one time.

We select records by tying our segmentation methodologies to the actionable reports created. In essence, these reports function as the audit trail for checking our selection results.

Identify Records or Segments

The system must be flexible enough to support all the popular selection methodologies:

- RFM (recency, frequency, monetary value)
- PRFM (product, recency, frequency, monetary value)

Table 11.8. Actionable Data

CUSTOMERS AT ALL DEPARTMENT COMBINATIONS					
—LIFETIME DOLLARS ACROSS ALL DEPARTMENTS—					
Dept. Combinations	1-50	51-100	101-250	251-500	500 Plus	Total
Shoes	808	458	607	264	144	2281
Dresses	1150	124	460	300	131	2165
Shoes-Dresses	2	11	75	54	71	213
Coats	630	509	490	112	26	1767
Shoes-Coats	34	48	111	92	60	345
Dresses-Coats	132	64	147	114	88	545
Shoes-Dresses-Coats	1	0	13	28	34	76
Hats	543	413	433	110	56	1555
Shoes-Hats	33	60	147	122	97	459
Dresses-Hats	26	28	103	85	59	301
Shoes-Dresses-Hats	0	0	9	42	52	103
Coats-Hats	62	71	212	157	90	592
Net Total	3421	1786	2807	1480	908	10,402

- Modeling
- Scoring

All these can be produced from the basic customer record using the collected data: retail, MOB (mail order buyer), television, credit, etc.

Again, the database software does not contain segmentation modules, you have to write them. These have to be developed in conjunction with the database user. The basis for these modules should be the actionable information previously reported to the marketers.

We do this by creating selection templates that will allow our users to enter the parameters which ultimately pick the appropriate customers for a given promotion. These templates can be created for any methodology.

The template in Table 11.9 allows the user to select from a wide variety of customer attributes. These attributes identify the criteria necessary to pick the appropriate customers for a given promotion or report. Template methodology works for large selections and small selections. It also works with scores, RFM (recency, frequency, monetary), or single data elements. Templates should be designed with the user in mind. Templates should also be set up to handle a range of items, not single elements. You want to be able to get as much done as possible with a single entry. Users who have to deal with many entries are not happy.

Table 11.9. Selection Template

IDENTIFIER ___BS___	BUYER TYPE ___1___	(1-5)
RECENCY DATE RANGE	LOW - _890128_	HIGH - _891217_
(YYMMDD)		
LIFE TIME DOLLAR RANGE	LOW - _100_	HIGH - _500_
MINIMUM LIFE TIME PURCHASES	TOTAL - _2_	
SEX CODE ___M___ (M,F,U)		
ORDER MODE ___P___ (M = MALE, P = PHONE)		
PAYMENT TYPE ___Y___ (X = CASH, Y = CHARGE)	CHARGE CARD __	
A_ (A,V,M,O)		
ZIP RANGE: _11500_ TO _12700_ STATE ___NY___		
PRODUCT SELECTS: MERCHANDISE CLASS _03_ LIFE STYLE _V_ SIZE _4_		

Targeting Models. A targeting model is a method of selecting better customers for a given promotion using a scoring algorithm or one of the popular regression techniques. These techniques are becoming more and more popular because of their accuracy and because of the information explosion. The volume of data housed on many databases has made it extremely complex and cumbersome to select records using data elements in traditional fashion. There are just too many comparisons. A model makes it easier to discern the distinguishing characteristics of your past, present, and profitable customers.

Modeling systems are not part of database systems; they are used in conjunction with a database system, like merge/purge software. These systems offer a way to simplify handling the data, consolidating a customer's activity to a numeric value. These values can be ranked from high to low, assigned to centiles, duodeciles, or deciles, then used for selection purposes. Counts developed in this manner are 100-percent accurate, which is what the planners want and need. Plus, the selection methodology is simple since one is picking prospects by looking at a single value.

Any target model will put to work your customer knowledge (the database record) by:

1. Finding the most responsive customers.

2. Eschewing less responsive customers.

3. Potentially reducing promotional costs.

These factors mean an increase in profitability.

Types of Targeting Models

Simple RFM models. Target customers in simple situations when neither product category differences nor lifestyles are important.

Refined RFM models. Target customers when product category differences are important.

Cross-purchase models (propensity to buy models). Target customers for product category specific promotions based on customers' cross-purchasing patterns.

Zip code selection models. Target customers and select names in areas of high current customer incidence.

Overall lifestyle models. Target customers and select names based on lifestyle commitments embodied in neighborhood choice and residential location.

Product category geodemographic models. Target those with specific lifestyle needs.

Different entities have different selection needs. Department stores tend to do many specialized small promotions, while catalogs promote to larger universes. Whatever the promotion philosophy, there should be reports generated that support it. Therefore, each customer must be used in the selection scheme in the appropriate priority for the particular product.

Actual Purchase versus Propensity to Buy. By analyzing purchase patterns of a customer across several different types of transactions it is possible to establish patterns of buying behavior. These relationships can be classified as the *Propensity to buy.* These product affinity models represent a more efficient and sophisticated approach to finding net customers.

We can use this information to prospect for new customers in different departments or to send out mailings with custom messages.

When you have good product data, you can develop models like the propensity to buy model shown in Table 11.10. Notice that consumers tend to gather in clusters. Basically this means that a consumer who buys in one of the cluster departments will buy in another of the cluster departments. Here you can see distinct clusters—such as men's, children's, women's, miscellaneous.

When you create this type of model, you score customers within several targets or groups, as in Table 11.11. This type of scoring methodology allows everyone to better manage all the data. Counts can be developed to put customers into deciles, pentiles, centiles or whatever.

Table 11.10. Propensity to Buy

UPSCALE DEPARTMENT STORE

Back-End Reports/Response Analysis. No system would be complete without some form of response analysis. Response reports are the basis for recognizing how well any given promotion performed. And performance is the basis for future planning.

Response Analysis

Response analysis is a must in any database marketing environment. It ensures the integrity of the selection methodology by

Table 11.11. Customer Scoring

Target Group Sales Index	Cumulative Customers	Cumulative Percentage	Centile	Decile	
91-100	16,424	6.3%	93.7%	9	Deciles 9, 8 (Potentially
81-90	47,750	18.3%	81.7%	8	most responsive
71-80	83,222	32.0%	68.0%	7	customers)
61-70	103,057	39.6%	60.4%	6	Deciles 9, 8, 7, 6
51-60	130,121	50.0%	50.0%	5	(100,000 piece
41-50	156,983	60.3%	39.7%	4	mailing)
31-40	182,803	70.2%	29.8%	3	

Table 11.12. Response Analysis

RESPONSE ANALYSIS
CODE 067 01-12 MONTHS AUGUST TO JULY

Zip Code	City Town	Quantity Mailed	Response Pct.	Customer Count	No. Of Trans	Total Dollars	Avg $$ Per Cust.	Dollars/ Book
07405	Kinnelon	1,025	1.95%	20	53	$25,000	$1,250	$24.39
07421	W Milford	78	1.28%	1	1	$ 20	$ 20	$ 0.26
07430	Mahwah	678	1.47%	10	10	$10,000	$1,000	$14.75
07436	Oakland	425	1.18%	5	14	$ 3,500	$ 700	$ 8.24
07450	Ridgewood	2,334	2.14%	50	72	$22,300	$ 446	$ 9.55
07456	Ringwood	102	1.96%	2	2	$ 550	$ 275	$ 5.39
07465	Wanaque	278	1.80%	5	10	$ 1,500	$ 300	$ 5.40
07470	Wayne	2,099	1.67%	35	48	$ 9,000	$ 257	$ 4.29
07666	Teaneck	1,756	0.68%	12	15	$ 8,000	$ 667	$ 4.56
	Totals	8,775	1.60%	140	225	$79,870	$ 571	9.10

measuring the response rates of the promoted segments of your database. These techniques allow you to hone in constantly on your most responsive customers, while eliminating the least responsive segments from your promotions.

If this type of analysis is not done, then there can be no effective decision making process when using the database for developing promotions. Obviously, the lack of an effective tracking system severely limits the capability of the database system.

Closing the Loops

The dedication of users is needed to post data back to the system. Senior management quite often is concerned with the marketing effort making the sale, but not with feeding the database. This is particularly true when a sales force is involved. When data is needed from a sales force, such as stockbrokers, it is often difficult to get. There must be a commitment to keeping the database current. The database designers must recognize any reluctance to feed the database and provide a simple mechanism to the users to keep the system updated. You can create turnaround documents or high-tech scannable media for this purpose.

If there is no built-in response vehicle, the database will not be advised as to whether the transaction loop was closed. Also, negative feedback does not often reach the database.

Conclusion

A properly designed database will allow you to better reach and maintain your customers, thereby enhancing your investments. It must be considered an integral part of your business. Data collection decisions cannot be an afterthought. They must be mandated throughout the entire organizational structure. Without this type of commitment, any gains made during the design and implementation of the database will quickly erode.

In essence, never consider your database a finished product. Treat it like a child. It has to have room to grow and mature. With maturity comes business growth.

12
Database Mathematics

Throughout this book we have discussed media analysis, offer analysis, regression analysis, economic modeling.

Once all the great ideas are put on paper, they have to survive the reality test of economic modeling. This does not forecast results but, instead, merely adds up the premises of costs and response rates and margins to determine the reasonableness of the plan. Some ideas don't add up even with the most optimistic assumptions.

Once the plan is underway regression analysis can in some cases tell us who to mail to at the outset. In all cases, it can tell us who is worth mailing to again. A common fallacy is to look at a "test" on the basis of overall results. Wrong! The purpose of a test is to identify some combination of list, offer, and creative approach that together can achieve the desired goals.

These processes require the best mathematical talent available. While there are a dozen or so qualified analysts, the one I have worked with most closely on recent projects is John Banslaben.

John is the principal statistical marketing consultant and Vice President for Database America Analytic Services, also known as DBA-AS. Based in the New York area, DBA-AS develops state-of-the-art regression based name selection models for house files and rental list files, as well as customer purchasing affinity models (factor and cluster analyses) and other advanced analyses for numerous top 100 direct marketing companies. Additionally, DBA develops customized in-house modeling systems at the client's site and has created an automated regression modeling computer system for direct mail marketers. Mr. Banslaben has earned a B.S. degree with honors from SUNY Stony Brook and a masters degree in Mathematics and a second masters degree in Applied Statistics from Columbia University.

John has been kind enough to offer to write this chapter, as he did a similar chapter in "The Direct Marketing Handbook," and as he does on many of the plans my agency recommends to clients. This chapter, from this point on, is his contribution, which I gratefully accept and endorse.

On July 20, 1969 Neil Armstrong became the first man to walk on the moon; Richard Nixon was president; and pioneer companies like *Reader's Digest* were successfully testing and using advanced statistical techniques called discriminant analysis and regression analysis to model and identify the best customers for future promotions. Over the next 20 plus years we have seen the computer revolution fuel what has become known as database marketing. Today, the typical direct mail company has already invested at some level in building a customer database and is poised to move ahead with advanced database marketing technologies.

To obtain a glimpse of where the direct mail community will be 20 years from now, well into the twenty-first century, we have only to look at where the pioneer database companies are today. They have invested significantly in both building and maintaining the highest quality databases and the advanced modeling detectors including regression analysis, factor analysis and cluster analysis. Their impressive performance in name selection, new product development and many other marketing applications portend an exciting new era for database marketing over the next 20 years.

Increased sales are generated from acquiring new customers, retaining and upselling current customers and reactivating old customers. Focus on optimizing each stage of the customer's life cycle has evolved several different database marketing techniques.

One of the first uses of advanced statistical modeling being used by direct mail modelers was by *Reader's Digest* in the late 1960s. Using discriminant analysis a basic predictive model was developed to optimize response to a music promotion. Subsequently, throughout the 1970s the techniques became increasingly sophisticated progressing from modeling to segment names by product return rates, bad debt rates and deliverability rates. An expected profit was computed for each list segment based on its predicted response, return, bad debt and deliverability rates.

Predictive modeling applications expanded, providing the ability to determine the optimum number of bills to send a customer as well as the resulting final bad debt rates and hence the corporate reserves required to cover the costs of poor performing accounts. Focus on implementation issues led the way to validation studies, which in turn revealed the percent reduction in gains achieved in going from the analysis sample to the rollout sample. Such reliability studies progressed to develop formulas for maximum achievable gains and measures of variability, which aided the marketing manager in risk management.

As the database elements available for modeling grew, so did the natural desire to cost-justify the incremental value of utilizing new information sources such as promotional data, surveys, and sweepstakes. Multiple models were developed which conditionally included this data so that separate gains charts could be compared, in order to assess the incremental contribution of each source for identification of added profit.

The 1980s saw growth in two areas of statistical marketing. First, predictive models based on zip code level demographics grew in number, extending to census tract and census block demographic-based models. While modeling at the finer geographic level made sense, reliability of results was lower due to fewer names at these levels. Hence mixture models evolved which optimally combined actual customer penetration rates with zip code, census tract and census block results.

The second area to develop in the 1980s was the utilization of a customer's product purchasing history to group products according to the customer's propensity or affinity to purchase multiple products from the same group. Initially product migration matrices were formed which evolved into the more sophisticated factor analytic product purchasing affinity studies. A single predictive model was more efficiently developed for a whole class of products.

The average scores for the whole customer file on these generic models were used as whole list quality indicators for the various product groups. Further applications based on these product groupings led to clustering customers and included product positioning, selectronic binding, optimal product selection within a mail slot, new product development of similar products, efficient welcome wagon offers and survey questionnaire design, to name but a few.

The 1990s is proving to be a decade where the technologies that evolved over the past 20 plus years are finding their way from the elite direct marketing company's "think tanks" to a very diverse direct marketing community. Computer service bureaus are teaming up with high-tech consultants in providing a new level of service previously not available to all direct marketers.

A fundamental benefit derived from database marketing is the ability to target distinctive groups of consumers with unique characteristics including buying behaviors, attitudes and demographics. The state-of-the-art marketer uses these consumer group definitions and profiles to optimally manage future promotions. A customized promotional strategy will effectively match product, offer, number of mailings, and directed messages with each consumer group. This translates into an improved bottom line in both the short term, due to higher customer responsiveness, and long term, due to improved customer loyalty.

Here are five basic levels of instruction in basic database targeting with predictive modeling:

1. How to identify which promotions would benefit from regression modeling

2. What database elements should be included in the model

3. First-level data analysis—univariate

4. Second-level data analysis—multivariate

5. Integrating regression models into a marketing plan

These five steps are followed by an overview of future development in regression modeling. The majority of examples and illustrations in this chapter focus on regression models that predict response rate for customer mailings. However, references to the use of regression models to predict other performance data (such as dollar sales per M), and on noncustomer files, (such as rental lists), are included.

Step 1: How to Identify Promotions Best Suited for Regression Modeling

The first step in creating a regression model is to identify which direct marketing promotions will significantly benefit from this type of quantitative analysis. In order to produce a regression model that will generate a high cost/benefit ratio the mailing should:

- Meet a minimum sample size criteria.
- Have a whole list response rate that is relatively near to the break-even response rate.
- Have a *suitable snapshot* of the customer record available.
- Have significant rollout potential.

Here are these issues discussed in further detail.

- *Minimum sample size criteria.* In order to produce consistent results, the mailing should contain a large enough number of names and a response rate that generates at least 1000 orders or responses. For example, an offer with a 4- percent response rate would require a test mailing of 25,000 names. In contrast, an offer with a 0.10-percent response rate would need 1,000,000 names to generate 1000 responders. Although successful regression models have been developed with fewer names, samples that meet this criteria have generally been proven to produce more reliable results.

- *Whole list response rate to break-even response rate.* A second requirement for the test mailing is that the total response rate (or $/M) for the whole list should be relatively near the break-even response rate (or $/M). Regression modeling will not usually improve an already highly successful promotion or list, nor will it magically improve an extremely nonresponsive list, nor an unappealing offer. It is therefore important to consider carefully the relationship between the whole list response rate and the break even response rate. Since regression models typically produce gains near the 50-percent level when selecting half of the list, it is suggested that the target mailing selected for analysis have a break-even response rate (or $/M) that is 50 percent higher or 50 percent lower than the whole list response rate (or $/M). For example, a promotion with a 4-percent response rate would be a good candidate for regression modeling if the break-even response rate was between 2 and 6 percent.

- *Suitable snapshot.* A third requirement for selecting the optimum sample is to save a *snapshot* of the customer's marketing database record as it looked at the time of the current promotion and marry the responses to this promotion later, just as in a typical RFM analysis which is conducted on how the customer looked at the time of name selection. Therefore it may be necessary for the marketer to make plans to save this information from a future test mailing if it is not available from previous test promotions. It may also be possible to analyze a past mailing for which responses have already been received.

- *Have significant rollout potential.* The marketer must next consider whether a test mailing has rollout potential in sufficient quantities to justify development costs of a regression model. Alternatively, if a single mailing does not possess rollout potential, a generic model could be developed by selecting one or more test mailings which are representative of future mailings. A generic model is a model which is applicable to a class of promotions whose responders possess similar discriminating characteristics.

To form an analysis sample for developing a generic model it is necessary first to combine several promotions that are representative of the several products that define the generic group. Each individual product promotion must meet the previously established minimum sample size requirement. This requirement may be somewhat relaxed if the products defining the generic group are closely related in terms of their respective buyer profiles, based on prior knowledge. A response grouping of products based on the customer's characteristics is optimally developed using the statistical procedures known as factor or cluster analysis to conduct what is known as a product purchasing affinity study. Care should be taken in evaluating the applicability of the resulting regression model by determining that the profiles of the high responders from the test sample match those of the high responders in the rollout promotion.

Step 2: What Database Elements Should Be Included in a Model

The clues to determining which customer will respond to a future promotion are contained in the wealth of information about that customer on the marketing database. The value of the data elements on the marketing database comes into play when segmenting the high responders from the low responders. Virtually any piece of information available on the database about a customer is a candidate for inclusion in a regression modeling analysis.

In general, information about the customer's previous purchases, such as RFM (recency, frequency, and monetary value), have the highest discriminatory value in segmenting the best customers from the worst. Next in order of significance in segmenting the customer file are other individual characteristics including promotional history and individual demographics. This would be followed in order of priority by the "in-house" demographics such as the customer penetration rate by zip code, and finally, zip code level demographics. However, the discriminatory value of the data will vary not only by the product offer, but also by the list segment being analyzed.

The RFM information plays a much less significant role in identifying customers in the one-time buyer list segment than in the multibuyer list segment. The reason is that the multibuyer list segment, which is defined as the list of customers that have purchased at least twice, contains more of the important historic information on previous customer purchases than does the one-time buyer list. The predictors of response that are more significant than RFM for the one-time buyer list segment include the original source of the name, individual and area demographic enhancements, especially age, income, sex, and single versus multiple family dwelling unit, along with survey questionnaire responses and in- house demographics.

The question that often arises is: What additional value to the mailing will regression models contribute over and above RFM selection? Regression's contribution over and above RFM is, for the most part, determined by: (1) the availability of regression variables that discriminate response beyond the RFM variables; and, (2) the reduction of variability in the RFM response estimate due to data analysis methods employed by using regression modeling. The additional value regression models contribute over RFM as detailed:

1. *Regression variables beyond RFM.* The marketing database contains data elements in addition to RFM which significantly predict response as determined by the statistical technique known as Response Cross Tabs (see Step 3—Univariate Analysis). A regression model will outperform RFM by an amount that is proportional to the unique contribution of these additional data elements. The marketing database may include well over a hundred data elements that have the potential to segment, beyond RFM, the best from the poorest performing names and may include information from the following data classes:

   - *Previous product purchasing history:* Names in the same RFM cell that have already purchased product A may be more likely to purchase product B. The response relationships between two products at a time are studied in a response cross tab report while more than two products are best studied in a product purchasing analysis using the statistical methods known as factor and cluster analyses.

   - *Prior promotional history:* Number of promotions since last order, average number of orders per promotion, etc.

The better prospects have fewer promotions since their last order and also a higher average number of orders per promotion.

- *Survey questionnaire response data*: Responses to product related preferences and demographic information such as age and income may indicate high responsiveness to a specific promotion.
- *Sweepstakes response data*: Both yes and no responses indicate a degree of direct mail responsiveness and may add to the discriminatory value of the regression model.
- *Address data*: Title (relates to sex and life style), date of last address change and number of address changes (relates to mail responsiveness and deliverability), and address type (relates to urban versus rural, and dwelling type).
- *Acquisition date*: Date entered on the database and original list source of the first order.
- *In-house demographics*: Customer penetration and response rates by zip code. These variables become more reliable and valuable as the absolute number of customers in a zip code increase, and also as the number of names that were exposed to the promotion in the zip code increases.
- *Individual and area demographics (zip code, census tract and census block level)*: Age, income, sex, education, magazine penetration, etc. The census tract and census block level data define a finer level of geographic detail and may have a greater amount of variability in response estimates. These finer levels are consequently used to augment, not replace, the zip code level demographics.
- *Geographic location*: Include especially for climatically seasonal products. Examples include state, average temperature, rainfall, and latitude and longitude.
- *Method of previous orders*: Cash or charge (related to income), telephone or mail (related to presence of children).

2. *The contribution in value of regression modeling over traditional RFM name selection.* This is also a result of the methods used to analyze the data. Traditional RFM analysts must make a trade-off between using smaller RFM cells with fewer names and greater discrimination in response versus larger

RFM cells with a greater number of names and less discrimination in response. This tradeoff is illustrated by considering the RFM cell that contains 1000 names that have ordered in the past six months, and responded to the current promotion at a 3.0 percent response rate (30 orders). A higher level of discrimination is attained by redefining the RFM cell into six separate RFM cells containing those names that had recency values of one, two, three, four, five, and six months, respectively. However, the six new RFM cells now contain fewer names, and therefore the response rate for each new RFM cell is less reliable than the original RFM cell definition. See Table 12.1.

Regression based modeling addresses this problem by looking at each of the new RFM cell definitions at the finest, most detailed level simultaneously, and modeling the trends from this data, extracting the maximum segmentation power in the most reliable manner.

Table 12.1. Sample RFM Cell Definitions

Currency of last order	Frequency or order	Cumulative monetary value
0-6 months	2 or more	$200 plus
0-6 months	2 or more	$100-$200
0-6 months	2 or more	$50-$75
0-6 months	2 or more	$25-$50
0-6 months	2 or more	$1-$25
0-6 months	1	$200 plus
0-6 months	1	$100-$200
0-6 months	1	$50-$75
0-6 months	1	$25-$50
0-6 months	1	$1-$25
6-12 months	2 or more	$200 plus
6-12 months	2 or more	$100-$200
6-12 months	2 or more	$50-$75
6-12 months	2 or more	$25-$50
6-12 months	2 or more	$1-$25
6-12 months	1	$200 plus
6-12 months	1	$100-$200
6-12 months	1	$50-$75
6-12 months	1	$25-$50
6-12 months	1	$1-$25

Step 3: The Univariate (One-Variable-at-a-Time) Analyses

Response Cross Tabs

The report known as the *response cross tabs* or *cross tabs* is a univariate or one-variable-at-a-time analysis of the elements on the customer database. The response cross tabs are the fundamental means for reviewing the detailed relationships between the performance variables such as response, and the predictor variables, including RFM, to determine which variables should be input into the regression variable selection program. The response cross tabs also provide the marketing manager with a detailed understanding of the characteristics that differentiate their best and poorest customers and is used in developing optimum marketing strategies.

Like a profile analysis (where counts are given but not response rates for each group of names), the response cross tabs include recoding the data in order that each reporting cell contains a fixed number of names. For example, if each reporting cell or row contained 5 percent of the sample, then the response cross tabs would include twenty rows, plus a row for totals. The response cross tabs go beyond the standard profile analysis in that they illustrate, for each variable, the response, sales, and other performance information as well as means for data from key variables (such as RFM, age, and income) for each reporting cell (see Table 12.2).

Illustrative data plots showing response and other performance data versus each regression variable have proven to be instrumental in assisting the marketer to easily understand the output. These plots may also include various transformations of the data, such as the log of the response rate, in order to evaluate the benefits of using these transformations later in the regression modeling.

Prior to developing the response cross tabs it is very important that the statistical analyst conduct a thorough audit of the test sample to ensure that the sample was properly composed. A review of a sample of customer records, along with a comparison of means for all database elements and response rates for known list codes, is essential.

The marketing manager reviews the response cross tab report and the data plots or graphs along with the statistician, in order to identify which variables should be candidates for inclusion into a regression model. To identify which variables will be recoded and used in the next phase of model development, the variables are placed into three groups: (1) variables whose response rate is as predicted from previous experience; (2) variables with either no response relationship or one that is contrary to previous experience; and (3) new variables with new, previously unknown response relationships.

1. The first group contains those variables whose response relationship is well known and show the expected response relationship in the response cross tabs (as per the marketing manager's previous knowledge). This might include RFM, related products purchased, survey questions checked and the basic age, sex and income demographic variables about which the marketer has extensive experience.

2. The second group is composed of those variables that show either no relationship to response or are not consistent with known response relationships. These variables are dropped from further consideration for this particular analysis.

3. The third group contains the remaining variables which may contribute significantly to the regression model's ability to segment the file's best from poorest responders. However, their

Table 12.2. Sample Response Cross-Tab Report

Number of pro-motions since last order	Mail quantity	Orders	Response rate (%)	Response index	Pull ($/M)	Pull index	Pay (%)	Pay index
0	10,000	500	5.0	167	$1250	192	95	112
1	10,000	400	4.0	133	$ 900	138	90	106
2	10,000	300	3.0	100	$ 600	92	85	100
3-5	10,000	200	2.0	67	$ 350	53	80	94
6+	10,000	100	1.0	33	$ 150	23	75	88
Total	50,000	1500	3.0	100	$ 650	100	85	100

response relationships are not well-known to the marketing manager. In regard to the marketer's strategy, a conservative approach is to set these variables aside until additional corroborative evidence is available from response cross tabs on other test samples, in order to maintain a maxium reliability for the model's application to future promotions.

Variable Interactions

An interaction between two variables is a relationship that affects response. When such a relationship occurs, it must be incorporated into the regression model with special coding. An example of an interaction would be if a product generated a high response to both older men and younger women and a low response to younger men and older women. This example would result in a flat response relationship between older and younger people in general, and between males and females in general. Thus the response relationship would exist only in the interaction of age and sex. An interaction may also exist when the individual variables (age, sex) have response relationships.

There are several ways to identify these interactions including two-dimensional response cross tabs and Chaid analyses. Once the interactions have been identified, their effects are then included into the regression model by, for example, creating new variables that are the product of the original variables.

Sales	Sales per order	Average recency (months)	Average number of orders	Average monetary value	Average age (years)	Average income
$12,500	$25.0	4	5	$50	50	$100,000
$ 9,000	$22.5	9	4	$40	40	$ 75,000
$ 6,000	$20.0	12	3	$30	35	$ 40,000
$ 3,500	$17.5	15	2	$20	30	$ 35,000
$ 1,500	$15.0	20	1	$10	20	$ 25,000
$32,500	$21.7	12	3	$30	35	$ 55,000

Variable Recoding

The response cross tabs contain plots or graphs which illustrate the relationships between the customer's characteristics such as RFM and the response rate as previously described in the section on response cross tabs. These relationships are used to determine how to recode or transform the data in each record.

After selecting the individual database elements that predict response in the response cross tabs, the next step is to develop the best recoding program for the data, prior to regression modeling. For each variable, the response cross tabs with response plots will indicate either: (1) a group of names with equal response rates that should be combined (20 to 25 and 26 to 30 age groups); (2) linear response rate relationships (low responding low income versus high responding high income); and/or (3) nonlinear or curved response rate relationships. The subsequent recoding is of a more technical nature requiring discussion in detail.

1. The first method of recoding is to create a new *dummy* or *indicator variable* for each value of the variable that has shown a significant difference in response via response cross tabs. For example, if the respective response rates of customers with one, two, three or more previous purchases was 2, 3, and 3 percent then the two and three plus groups would be combined and a dummy variable would be created that had a value of one if the customer had only one previous purchase and a value of zero otherwise. A second dummy variable would be created that had a value of one if the customer had two or three or more previous purchases and a value of zero otherwise. The effect of the dummy variables is to model very closely the subgroup response rates. Dummy variables, like RFM cells, are defined so as to strike a balance between defining a large subgroup which reduced the variables' power to discriminate high responders from low responders, versus, defining a small subgroup which maximizes discriminatory power but increases variability and hence reduces reliability.

    A minimum is established for the number of names permitted to define the smallest dummy variable subgroup by empirically analyzing the relationship between response and cell size. A plot of the response rates by sample size across all variables will indicate a sample size at which the reliability of the data is maximized. This is the point where the variability of the response rates stabilize for larger samples but increases for smaller sample sizes.

2. The second method of recoding is to identify in the response cross tabs those variables exhibiting two or more strictly linear response relationships, for example, an inverted V-shaped response curve (low and high income groups are low responders, middle income group are high responders). These variables should be split into two or more *Splines* (lines or curves) or separate variables for input into the regression modeling algorithm.

3. The final group of transformations deal with attempting to create a linear response relationship from a nonlinear one. This class of transformations includes using several mathematical operations on either the independent predictor variables or dependent response variables and may give rise to new forms of analyses such as a log-linear type logit modeling. A typical example of variables that may become linear upon applying such a log transformation are the strongly curved relationships between the response rate and the RFM variables.

The main area of caution in using these types of transformations is that the nonlinear response relationship needs to be very consistent from mailing to mailing and therefore several response cross tab reports need to be compared across several promotions in order to avoid a biased fit of the model.

Step 4: Multivariate Regression Class Analyses

Regression analysis selects the best set of variables to create a set of coefficients or weights which are then multiplied by the value of the respective regression variables. Next the resultant products are totalled to produce a single score for each customer that will predict the response rate or whatever performance variable is being modeled. This regression score is the basis for selecting names from the customer database for future mailings.

Simply stated, regression analysis reviews the complete record of each individual customer and combs the data to select the best names for each promotion. The final resulting regression model may be viewed as a score card whereon each important piece of information is assigned a weight or score which reflects its importance in predicting response. (See Table 12.3.)

Stepwise Regression

The regression coefficients or weights are computed by a stepwise method which looks at the correlations between all of the recoded predictor variables and the dependent response variables. The stepwise regression algorithm begins by selecting the variable that has the highest correlation with response. Next, it *subtracts out* of the response rate the predictive value of the first variable and

Table 12.3. A Simplified Two-Variable Scorecard with File Distribution

Variable name	Level	Regression score	4/89 Test sample distrib. of names (%)	4/90 Master file distrib. of names (%)	Increase or difference (%)
Recency	0-3 months	500	20	22	+ 2
	4-6 months	390	15	18	+ 3
	7-9 months	290	15	16	+ 1
	10-12 months	180	10	10	0
	13-15 months	125	15	15	0
	16-18 months	95	10	8	− 2
	19-24 months	75	5	4	− 1
	25+ months	25	10	7	− 3
Number of promotions since last order	0	500	15	25	+10
	1	435	15	20	+ 5
	2	330	30	30	0
	3-5	200	20	15	− 5
	6+	25	25	10	−10

selects the second most important variable having the highest correlation with the adjusted response rate. This continues on until a predetermined level of significance, called the alpha level (which measures the statistical significance of the new weights being nonzero), is no longer attained.

The precise meaning of the term *subtracts out* used in the previous paragraph is defined as follows. In effect, at each step in stepwise regression a predicted response is generated and subtracted from the actual response rate to form an adjusted response rate. In each subsequent step the variable that is chosen next is the one with the highest correlation to this adjusted response variable.

If only a single predictor such as frequency were being used to predict the response rate then the resultant regression model would be akin to fitting a straight line using a ruler on a piece of paper. A better fit using our ruler model would be attained using a logarithmic transformation of the frequency variable since this latter form has a "linear" relationship with the response variable.

The final regression model is next reviewed for statistical reliability and to be certain that the weights for the variables follow a logical consistency with past experiences. If the sign of the coefficient is negative but should be positive (as the number of previous products purchased increases so does the response rate and therefore a positive coefficient is expected), the usual reason is that two or more predictors are highly correlated in which case the statistician will consider dropping one of these codependent variables from the model.

Several variations of regression methodology exist such as discriminant analysis, latent root regression, ridge regression and especially logistic regression, probit regression, and arc-sine regression. The most mentionable attribute of the latter three is that they all constrain the predicted value to have a value between zero and one. This has significance when either fewer than 25 percent of the list or more than 75 percent of the list are being selected, otherwise the difference in segmentation is minimal.

Break-Even Regression

A new regression procedure which is called break-even regression is a method to improve the accuracy of predicting response rate for customers near the break-even response rate level. It is the names that respond at a rate near break-even where increased sensitivity in the regression model is most beneficial since the names that respond at a rate significantly above break-even are going to be mailed whether they score a little higher or lower, and conversely, the names that respond at a rate significantly below break-even will not be selected for promotions even if their score changes a little.

The break-even regression method is a two state regression methodology. The first stage is to develop the regression model as described in the previous section. The next step is to determine the regression score level at which customers respond at a rate equal to break-even. The gains chart, described in the next section, is used to determine this score level.

The difference between the regression score level that corresponds to the group of customers responding at a break-even rate (say 0.04) and the original regression score (SCORE) is then computed for each individual customer. A second regression model is then developed using a weighted least squares algorithm wherein the weights are inversely proportional to the distance from break-even. An example would be to weight each customer by $1/(SCORE - 0.04)$.

Thus the customers that are near break-even will make a much greater contribution to the regression weights than the names that are significantly above or below break-even. However the names not near break-even will still contribute, although to a diminishing degree. This results in a regression model that is most accurate in predicting the customer's response rate near the break-even level and therefore selects the group of customers with the greatest overall response rate.

The Gains Chart Report

The regression model's performance is measured by the increased response rate or gains achieved over the whole list pull when selecting the top score names. Such performance is illustrated in a gains charts report (see Table 12.4.) and data plots. The gains chart is similar to a response cross tab of the resultant regression model score.

The sample, which now contains a score from the regression model, is sorted by score from high to low and divided into buckets or groups with an equal number of names in each bucket. Then the response data is computed for each bucket. As in the response cross tabs, a plot of the response rates by high to low regression score is very instructive in showing the amount of segmentation achieved in the results.

The gains charts is used to examine several customer characteristics of each group of names as defined by subsequent regression score ranges. As in the response cross tabs, in addition to mail quantity, number of orders, response rate, response index, total dollars, dollars per thousand mailed or pull, pull index, average dollars per order and other response characteristics, the gains chart report also contains the average RFM values, and any other available descriptive statistic such as age, sex and income. This cell profiling information is very useful both to corroborate that the best names are being selected in an RFM-, Age-, Sex- and Income-sense and to illustrate to the marketing manager the profile of the customers that are being selected.

The marketing manager uses the gains chart report to determine the cut-off level or the score level above which names will be selected for the promotion. The production scoring program will produce a report of how many names fall into each score group. A second report will monitor the occurrences of any distributional shifts in the customer database for the key regression variables that might cause an upward or downward shift in the scoring of these names.

Step 5: How to Integrate Regression Models into a Marketing Plan

After the regression model has been developed, the next step is to integrate it into the marketing plan. The goal is to establish a

Table 12.4. Sample Gains Chart Report

Regression score range	Mail quantity	Orders	Response rate (%)	Response index	Pull ($/M)	Pull index	Pay ($)	Pay index
0.050-Max.	10,000	500	5.00	182	$1,250	207	95	112
0.045-0.049	10,000	450	4.00	164	$1,080	179	95	112
0.040-0.044	10,000	400	4.00	145	$ 920	152	90	106
0.035-0.039	10,000	350	3.00	127	$ 770	127	90	106
0.030-0.034	10,000	300	3.00	109	$ 630	104	85	100
0.025-0.029	10,000	250	2.00	91	$ 500	83	85	100
0.020-0.024	10,000	200	2.00	73	$ 380	63	80	94
0.015-0.019	10,000	150	1.00	55	$ 270	45	80	94
0.010-0.014	10,000	100	1.00	36	$ 170	28	75	88
Min.-0.009	10,000	50	0.50	18	$ 80	13	75	88
Total	100,000	2,750	2.75	100	$ 605	100	85	100

smooth transition between the current name selection technique, (usually an RFM based selection), and name selection using regression models. By using the regression models to successively add and suppress names to the RFM selection, the marketing manager can lead up to a total replacement of RFM with regression models in a controlled manner.

Initially, the marketing manager will begin with a standard RFM selection of names for a particular promotion and key the names according to their respective RFM cell definitions as was done in the past. Next, the regression model is applied to the names that fail the selection via RFM. The highest scoring (using regression) names in this group that are above the break-even score level are added to the mailing and keyed according to regression model score ranges, from best to worst, resulting in an increase in the mail volume. The subsequent step is for the marketing manager to apply the regression model to the names that were initially selected using RFM (passes). The lowest scoring names in this group that are below the break-even score level are targeted to be suppressed from the mailing.

This method allows the marketing manager to specify fully the quantity of names to be added and suppressed via the regression model and to monitor the results in a manner that allows a comparison with those from previous mailings. This method will

Sales	Sales per order	Average recency (months)	Average frequency (#orders)	Average monetary value	Average age (years)	Average income
$12,500	$25	4	8.0	$25.0	50	$100,000
$10,800	$24	5	7.0	$23.0	50	$ 90,000
$ 9,200	$23	9	6.0	$22.0	40	75,000
$ 7,700	$22	10	5.0	$21.0	40	50,000
$ 6,300	$21	12	5.0	$20.0	35	40,000
$ 5,000	$20	13	4.0	$19.0	35	40,000
$ 3,800	$19	15	4.0	$18.0	30	35,000
$ 2,700	$18	18	3.0	$17.0	30	35,000
$ 1,700	$17	20	2.0	$16.0	20	25,000
$ 800	$16	24	1.0	$15.0	20	25,000
$60,500	$22	13	4.5	$19.6	35	50,771

allow the marketing manager to make a smooth transition from the RFM analysis, for which results are available from many past mailings, to the ultimate goal which is to select names by using the regression models exclusively.

Checks and Controls

It is important to establish a set of checks and controls to ensure the quality of the names selected, using any name selection methodology including regression models. The checks and controls system for regression models is used both to ensure the reliable application of scoring the model and to monitor any changes or shifts in the characteristics, in the customer file that could affect the name selection.

The scoring of the regression model is usually accomplished in the main production program that selects the names for mailing using a native language such as Cobol. To ensure that the recode definitions and model coefficients are correctly applied, a comparison needs to be made between the Cobol program and the original code used to develop the model, for example, SAS (statistical analysis system). A sample of names (for example, 10 percent) is selected from the master file, (often from the previous months' selection tapes), and scored using both the Cobol and SAS programs. First, 200 or so names are compared name by name to identify any inconsistencies and correct them. Next, the total sample is scored and distributed or grouped into twenty buckets based on predetermined regression score levels and the counts between the Cobol and SAS program are compared. Any discrepancies between these counts are completely reconciled by a comparison of the values for each variable in the model using the Cobol and SAS programs.

Once the Cobol scoring program has been validated, the next step is to evaluate whether the characteristics of the customer file have shifted significantly from the time that names were selected for the test promotion used in development of the model, to the time that names were selected for the current promotion. The most important customer characteristics to compare for this purpose are those that are included in the regression model. The means report (see Table 12.3), generated for this comparison, contains the following information for each variable included in the model or set of models:

1. The variable name, for example, customers whose most recent purchase was in the past three months

2. The number and percent of people with this particular characteristic at the time names were selected for test promotion used in development of the model

3. The number and percent of people with this particular characteristic at the time names were selected for the promotion that is currently being scored

4. The coefficients or weights applied to customers with each respective characteristic

The marketing manager uses this means report to identify whether any distributional shifts of the customer's characteristics occurred and the degree to which they may impact the name selection process. The variables that have larger coefficients and large distributional shift will have the largest impact on how the names score.

A monthly house census report includes counts and percents for the most important variables on the house file. It is a useful resource for the marketing manager trying to gain an understanding of the long term distributional shifts on the customer file.

What's New on the Horizon: Methodologies and Applications

New Methodology

Typically, the best customer models are able to achieve gains equal to 200 percent above break-even for the best 10 percent of the file, and 50 percent above break-even for the best half of the file. The theoretical maximum gain for selecting the best 10 percent is 900 percent above break-even versus a theoretical maximum of 100 percent above break-even for the best half of the list. It is therefore obvious that much more improvement is theoretically possible in selecting names. The newer statistical methodologies will improve the gains in response rate for the best names. Here enumerated, hereafter detailed are these methodologies: (1) Improved use of ordinal variables, (2) Enhanced weighting function for the break-even regression, and (3) Advances in artificial intelligence.

1. *Ordinal variables*: Variables are classified as either nominal, ordinal or interval. Nominal variables are simple labels of different categories such as male versus female, whereas ordinal variables also allow an ordering into higher and lower groups such as social classes. Interval variables in addition to the characteristics of ordinal variables also give a measure of the distance between categories such as age or income.

   Current regression modeling algorithms accommodate nominal and interval variables very well but ordinal variables must be adapted to a nominal or interval form resulting in a loss of information. A statistical modeling procedure which accommodates all three types of variables (known as alternating least squares) is now available in a SAS procedure called PROC TRANSREG and should result in a significant increase in segmentation potential.

2. *Enhanced break-even regression*: Empirical research as to the optimal parametric form of the weighting function in the break-even regression will improve its performance. The weighting function determines the degree to which each name contributes to the final model. For example, should names near break-even contribute, two, three or four times as much as the names that are twice as far from break-even?

3. *Artificial intelligence*: Advances in the areas of artical intelligence do not equate with improvements in statistical modeling methodologies, however, they will simplify the modeling process and allow for industry wide quality standards to be implemented, although this is an ambitious goal.

New Applications

The application of regression models may be extended from selecting the highest responding names to selecting the most deliverable, highest dollars per order, highest pay, lowest returning, lowest bad debting names and ultimately the highest lifetime value names. Regression models developed for predicting deliverability, pay, returns, and bad debts tend to be very generic, that is, independent of the product being promoted. Therefore, new response model scores may be combined with standard, generic deliverability, pay, return, and bad debt scores to form an expected profit score for name selection. In general, it is possible to identify the best names using:

1. *Deliverability model.* Identify up to 15 percent of the list that is twice as undeliverable as the whole list.

2. *Bad debt model.* Identify up to 10 percent of the list bad debting four times the average.

3. *Returns model.* Identify up to 25 percent of the list returning three times the average.

4. *Zip code based model:* Identify up to 10 percent of a rented list pulling 80 percent above average via zip code and/or census tract and census block based demographic models.

Additional applications proven successful for regression models include predicting how many bills to mail before sending the account to a collection agency, projecting final reserves from as early as second billing, and projecting final intake from as little as two weeks of intake.

Summary

The benefits and rewards of learning how to use regression models are well worth the effort. Regression models are proving again and again to be not only more accurate than RFM but also more manageable by providing the marketing manager with a single ranking of all names from the best to the worst performers along with a high level of detail on their characteristics. The keys to establishing a solid regression modeling program are selecting the right promotion, developing a good model, and rolling out with the appropriate checks and controls.

Regression modeling begins with the appropriate definition of the analysis sample. It is essential to save a snapshot of the customer file as it looks at the time names are selected for the promotion in order to develop the best models. The targeted sample should also meet certain sample size and response rate level considerations in order to ensure maximum success. The subsequent steps toward developing and successfully implementing regression models, whether using mainframe computers, minicomputers or personal computers, are well defined. Even the advanced statistical methods employed have become increasingly understandable for a growing number of marketing managers.

13

Improving Database Return on Investment

This is another approach to financial modeling and analysis, using the lifetime value method. It is interesting in that it not only lists ways of determining return on investment (ROI) but also lists specific suggestions for improving it.

Just one section of a very comprehensive document entitled *Managing Database Marketing Technology for Success* published by the Direct Marketing Association, the text consists of a study conducted by Deloitte & Touche. I recommend it for those engaged in financial modeling and analysis. The full report, based on roundtable discussions and in-depth interviews with practitioners, runs over 100 pages. To order a copy, write the Direct Marketing Association at 11 West 42nd Street, New York, NY 10036.

How to Calculate and Improve
Database Return on Investment

After addressing the strategic and tactical concerns of a database marketing plan, the manager proposing the system may have to develop a traditional return-on-investment (ROI) analysis. Unfortunately, experience dictates that traditional, objective ROI analysis is difficult to perform due to the many hard-to-quantify benefits associated with database marketing systems.

These benefits are difficult to quantify since many of them are not known until after the system is in place. With many other computerized information systems, however, the processing improvement is known before purchase. Database marketing systems, though, offer "what if" analytical capabilities that have to be utilized intelligently by the user. (Just having the technology will not provide any benefit.) A single targeted idea, developed because data was available to the marketer, could provide a dramatic increase in sales which can pay for the system several times over.

Most of the database marketing systems implemented by study participants were installed and implemented with either no financial justification or with cursory estimates of perceived benefits. As one participant indicated:

> Part of the justification for investing in a databse is its ability to bond customers, sell the marketer's culture, improve its image and [provide] other intangibles.

To be more succinct, one marketing manager who oversaw the installation of a multi-million dollar database marketing system indicated:

> We did it on a "leap-of-faith." We got approval to go ahead without any financials. Senior management thought [financial justification] was an impossible task.

These same ROI justification themes were echoed by the comments of a large service bureau executive, who said:

> Not many companies start out talking about ROI. We actually bring it up first. It's like pulling teeth to set up a process to measure ROI.

However, according to some experts, excessive reliance on traditional ROI analysis can prevent firms from fully exploiting promising new technologies, and it may even retard the development of advanced systems that have the capability to sustain long-term competitive positions.

The following basic analysis framework was developed to help in structuring a complete ROI model. For the purposes of this report, a catalog operation was selected as an example. This framework should be modified and extended by the reader, as appropriate, to suit other database marketing situations.

One of a catalog company's most valuable and unique assets is its customer list, since few catalogers manufacture products, and their fixed assets, such as office space and equipment, are commodities. The other major significant asset a cataloger has, the merchandising selection team, walks out the door each day.

The most actuarially sound way of valuing the list asset is to model each customer's discounted cash flow, or lifetime value (LTV), to the firm. The amount of the LTV represents the net payments, or return on investment, from each customer. It includes the customer acquisition costs, promotion costs, product costs and product payments (including interest, if any). Any LTV analysis must include changing purchase amounts, purchase frequency, list aging and other traditional parameters.

The database marketing system, the backbone of many relationship marketing programs, seeks to increase the value of the customer list by increasing the list size via better selection of names from outside sources while building stronger affinity about the company in the minds of current customers. In addition, these programs also try to promote more frequent and repetitive purchases from existing list members.

Thus, the ROI of the marketing database is the discounted, or present value of:

$$\frac{\text{Change in total customer LTV}}{\text{(Database marketing expenses } - \text{ cost savings)}}$$

over a defined period of time—say, five years.

In firms where LTV is harder to calculate, but where revenues can be attributed to the marketing database, the ROI should be calculated using the net present value of database marketing cash flows: database marketing costs (a negative), incremental revenues and incremental cost savings. Alternative ROI strategies are discussed at the end of this section for businesses such as packaged goods companies, which have more difficulty associating specific customer sales with database marketing initiatives.

The framework classifies individual ROI components into three parts: cost reduction, revenue enhancement and economic value created by process improvements. Each of these components has *hard*, or quantifiable dollar benefits, as well as *soft*, or qualitative or indirect benefits. After each of the components is presented, methods for determining the quantifiable benefits are illustrated. The valuation of the qualitative benefits is left to the reader based on the reader's corporate circumstances and values.

The framework relies heavily on the assumption that any database marketing development process begins with a test implementation to provide actual values to quantify benefits in order to validate ROI assumptions.

As Fig 13.1 indicates, there are three major areas of benefits when considering a database marketing system. Each of them and their components will be discussed below.

ROI Step 1: Cost Reductions

Net Reduction in Mailings

This can be divided into two components, where applicable: first, a reduction in the total amount of mail (promotions, letters, catalogs, etc.) and the associated printing costs; second, a further reduction of the mailing which can be attributed to a disciplined mail rationalization plan.

Reductions in the volume of mail come from a targeting policy that evolves from nth name, or random selections to Recency/Frequency/Monetary value (RFM) analysis—through selection models based on external demographic and psychographic data using regression analysis, to selections made from models based on actual customer transaction information augmented with other external information. The goal is to reduce the number of pieces mailed and to increase profits by reducing printing and postage expenses and sending promotions to customers with higher-predicted response rates. Alternatively, returns can be increased by keeping the mail volume the

Main Components

Cost Reductions:

Net Reduction in Mailing = Change in Number Mailed ×
(Mail + Print Costs per Piece)

Loyalty Reward Rationalization = Change in Subsidy to Pre-existing
Loyal Customers

Building a Marketing Information Asset = Change in Data Collection/
Analysis Costs

Reducing Customer Acquisition Costs = Reduction in "Trial" List Rentals

Revenue Enhancements:

Increased Revenue = Change in Response Rate × Average Product Net Margin

Increased Average Purchase Amount = Change in Average × Average Net Margin

List Rental Income $= \left(\dfrac{\text{Database Size}}{1,000}\right) \times \left(\dfrac{\text{Net Revenue}}{1,000}\right) \times$ Rental Frequency

Miscellaneous Indirect Benefits = Leverage, Employee Empowerment,
Improved Advertising Decisions

Process Improvements:

Increased Revenue = Net Additional Mailings × Average Response Rate ×
Net Margin

Figure 13.1. Marketing database ROI.

same and by mailing promotions to a larger number of targeted customers (if they can be economically determined).

It is important to note that the majority of interviewees indicated that selection and predictive models built from internal customer transaction data (coupled with customer-provided demographic information) generally produced results superior to models built from external psychographic and lifestyle information purchased from third-party data providers. The same interviewees indicated that they first optimize the models built with internal data before adding refinements using external data.

After the selected group has been determined, mailing costs can be saved even further by adhering to a strict marginal cost/marginal revenue analysis. In this scenario, the marketer first determines the total actual cost of the *entire* offering (printing, mailing and all fully loaded direct and indirect costs for the product) via an activity-based costing (ABC) analysis. ABC seeks to assign, via rigorous analysis, an exact dollar amount to each activity in the value chain of an organization to uncover the true cost drivers.

Once the marginal cost of the product, offering or mailing is known, the database marketer should select all names — starting with the best customer — that have an expected marginal revenue greater than the marginal cost of the promotion.

The best and quickest method to determine mail cost savings is to employ a service bureau or a modeling consultant on a one-time, trial basis. Using the same file of customers, the current in- house selection process is run on a randomly selected sub-list of half of the names, while the service bureau or consultant performs a more advanced, rigorous modeling on the other half. The difference in the number of names selected, multiplied by the per-piece printing and mailing costs, can be determined and placed into the ROI calculation.

A modified version of the above analysis can also be utilized to determine the benefit of augmenting traditional RFM analysis (performed either in-house or at a service bureau) with more advanced regression, logit, neural network or fractal analysis.

Loyalty Reward Program Rationalization

Promotional analysis offers a discount coupon to all customers (via newspaper advertisements or freestanding inserts). Another type of analysis segments an offer, or reward, to customers based on population groups with similar attributes. However, both of these analyses ignore the differences in consumption and behavior between specific individuals while at the same time subsidizing loyal customers. As a result, a promotion offering one free $30 product for every ten $30 products consumed will reward all current customers, regardless of their purchase patterns, in the same manner as potential customers. But, this type of program does not motivate occasional customers to become regular customers. Database marketing systems that track individual transactions for each customer have the capability to tailor reward and promotional programs individually to specific customers in order to motivate an occasional customer to become a steady customer.

Building a Marketing Information Asset

An on-line database gives users instant access to a pool of the most relevant market research a company can have: its own customers. For example, a mail-order company contemplating opening its first retail store can analyze its customers' locations and spending habits in an ad hoc fashion to help decide where to situate the store. Or, a packaged goods manufacturer can scan all past customer orders for affinity sales—products purchased together—to identify merchandising and packaging trends.

As part of the database design, allow traditional market research data, such as answers to survey and product purchase questionnaires, to be linked to individual customers. In many companies, the detailed information content of the original customer-level data is lost when the marketing research department summarizes large customer bases into trends, averages and percent change. As one database marketing executive commented:

> Many companies have excellent detailed market research data, but it tends to sit in boxes.

By allowing database marketers to associate market research responses directly with each customer, specialized promotions can be planned. For example, customers who are dissatisfied with a given product can be identified and offered a discount on a "new-and-improved" version. Or, a letter of thanks for past patronage—acknowledging input into product design—can go a long way toward retaining a dissatisfied customer.

A customer database, when augmented by extensive, internally collected research data, can be used to quickly generate market research charts and graphs — to support product conceptualization, design and marketing — instead of more expensive one-on-one consumer panels. Consumer panels can cost up to $500 per interviewee and require long analysis lead times. Database marketing activities in this area will serve to reduce costs normally associated with focus groups and research tabulation.

Reducing Customer Acquisition Costs

Many direct marketers with no database marketing system capability repeatedly purchase lists of outside names, merge them with house lists and track the results in an effort to find the "best" types of prospects. However, with improved modeling and segmentation, many direct marketers have found that they can become more specific when requesting outside lists, thus reducing the costs of customer acquisition and the number of iterations required to increase the size of the house list.

ROI Step 2: Revenue Enhancements

Increased Revenue

The correlation between selection accuracy and response rate improvement, while it usually exists, varies from product to product and from company to company. While the short-term goal of a database marketing program is lift—or response improvement—the strategic long-term goal must be to improve the relationship, or affinity, between consumer and seller. Thus, the direct and quantifiable benefit of database marketing is the increased lift associated with targeted offerings.

The best method for determining the exact change in response rate is to utilize the selected list produced in step one (cost reductions) and track the difference in response rates with an offering made to this targeted group versus the offering made to the control group. The improved response rate should be multiplied by the net margin that the product or promotion provides to the company and inserted into the ROI calculation.

Increased Average Purchase Amount

Over time, as customer selection improves and regular customers become more accustomed to purchasing products via direct marketing, the average purchase amount may increase (depending on the offer). An example might be a catalog buyer of specialty hardware and tools who first buys a screwdriver and later a table saw after being won over by consistently high service and quality.

At the time of preliminary ROI calculations, a plug—or working value—for this number may be the historical increase in average purchase amounts over time. During the test implementation phase, actual data should be collected and analyzed, where appropriate, to see how improved selection affects average purchase amounts over the same time period. This percentage, when multiplied by the new response rate, should be inserted into the ROI calculation.

List Rental Income

Having a marketing database that can quickly select groups of customers based on a series of attributes can allow a direct marketer to rent customer lists to firms—to increase revenue directly attributed to the database marketing system.

In order to quantify the value of this income, marketers are advised to work with list brokers in order to understand the rate per thousand that their data can command, given the projected attributes that will be stored in the database. (Most lists sell for $40 to $100 per thousand names and some specialized lists command $200 per thousand.) In addition, the broker should be able to estimate the number of times per year the list can be rented. The total revenue stream derived, is then:

$$\left(\frac{\text{Database Size}}{1,000} \right) \times \text{Net Revenue per 1,000} \times \text{Rental Frequency}$$

Thus, a one million name list renting only once at a cost of $60 per thousand will generate $60,000 in revenue.

Miscellaneous Indirect Benefits

The following indirect and qualitative benefits of database marketing systems were all suggested by the study participants:

- *Leverage*: A database marketing system allows a company to leverage its lists to develop new offerings and products, or compensate for seasonal effects on revenue. For example, a general home products marketer can select all customers who have puchased garden equipment in order to jump-start a new gardening offer.

  Another example cited by one database marketer was the development of complementary catalogs: one for winter products, and another for summer products — with the processing spread across a single database marketing system. Previously, the company had only one product line, and its revenue was very cyclical.

- *The impact of employee empowerment*: Some panelists indicated that on-line access to information contained in a database marketing system allowed marketing employees to provide information more quickly while also allowing merchandising employees to perform faster and more repetitive testing. As a result, these employees felt more professional and were able to be more creative.

- *Improved advertising decisions*: By collecting and coding the newspapers, magazines and journals read by customers, the marketing database can be turned into a media-buying decision analysis tool. Instead of a single mass market campaign, for example, the database might point out that three smaller, directed campaigns would be more effective in reaching different groups of customers. This is a use of database marketing systems mentioned only by a few of those interviewed.

ROI Step 3: Process Improvement

Increased Revenue

While nearly all of the study participants suggested calculating ROI using the parameters in step 1 (cost reduction) and step 2 (revenue enhancements), very few of them calculated the value (either in increased revenues or decreased operating costs) of the change in operational processing resulting from database marketing.

One large direct marketer pointed out: "We used to take four months to decide on merchandise and to select the names to mail. If we can now perform the same operation in half the time, that means twice as many mailings."

The key point in this manager's organization was that product merchants could get answers—via terminals on their desks and ad hoc querying software—to questions such as, "Did we sell more coats when they were placed adjacent to the order blank or when they were on the back cover?" in four minutes instead of four days. Previously, the same request would have been sent to the information systems group where programmers would create a unique, or "disposable," program and the user would wait for the response. Specific areas where process speed-up occurs include:

- Merchandise selection based on historical sales
- Promotion analysis
- Market research analysis
- Pricing analysis
- Customer identification

It is up to the marketers themselves to determine their firms' individual process improvement benefits and the amount of time that can be saved by having on-line access to historical promotion, pricing, response and sales data. The end result of this evaluation process should be a determination of the net increase in mailings per year, which is multiplied by the new average response rate and the net margin contribution to quantify the dollar benefit of faster processing.

Alternative ROI Constructs

Nonrevenue-Based Metrics

An often-cited comment by the study participants was that long-term (three-to-five year) database marketing programs are often hindered by a focus on short-term revenue and profitability analysis by senior management. This is particularly an issue when database marketing programs are used for market research, affinity building and sales-force lead generation, and not to directly sell a product or service.

In these cases, the consensus opinion was to evaluate the success of the databases by using quantitative measures other than revenue. These metrics include new lead generation (and associated cost reductions), membership in affinity clubs, better targeting of promotions, increased product trials, increased brand conversion, increased list rentals or general advertising reductions.

By setting primary targets such as customer or household counts, upper management will have a quantifiable and agreed-upon criteria by which to judge the early success of the database when revenues are hard to attribute to database marketing activities.

Internal Charge-Back Systems

When it is difficult to justify a database marketing system on revenue increases or cost savings, an alternative ROI construct is needed. One alternative is to establish internal charges for production services such as lead generation and tracking, label generation for sales and marketing promotions, as well as market analysis and reporting. Many organizations interviewed employed this technique, and the responsible database marketing managers indicated that this method accomplishes several goals:

- *Distributes database marketing costs to several groups*: When funded from multiple budgets, the system does not fall under a single, corporate budget that is easier to "kill" than scaling back the database marketing budgets of many departments that have grown reliant upon fast and easy processing of labels and reports.

- *Fosters "what if" analysis*: A minority of firms indicated they did not charge users, regardless of department, for performing queries to help select customers. The only charge occurred when the users requested a mailing or letter to be sent. This approach does not penalize users for their curiosity and encourages repeated testing. The only down-side to this policy is that users could overwhelm a computer if ad hoc queries that require significant computer resources are not controlled.

Increased "Hit" Percentages in Business-to-Business Direct Marketing

In the business-to-business segmet of direct marketing, the goal is to reduce the number of items mailed to people who do not influence the buying decision. In companies where direct marketing is used for lead generation, the verification of better targeting of mailing due to more advanced selection techniques can be accomplished via the use of telephone follow-up studies.

By simply asking the question, "Did you receive the catalog and are you the person responsible for making buying decisions?" database marketers can determine their before and after hit percentages. Using historical sales conversion percentages, database marketers can value the amount of revenue directly attributable to increased hits and compare that figure with alternate costs for creating the same level of lift.

Present Database Marketing Expenses as a Percentage of the Total Marketing Budget

Due to their technical nature, database marketing expenses are often viewed in comparison to overall corporate information technology purchases at organizations that have not historically performed direct marketing (such as packaged goods firms). When viewed in this way, many databases quickly become a dominant percentage of the information systems budget.

Many of the study participants indicated that their database marketing budgets—some in the millions of dollars—were presented in comparison to overall general marketing budgets. In addition, money was appropriated from the marketing budget and not from the information technology department budget. When presented this way, the marketing database is usually a very small part (perhaps only 1 or 2 percent) of the general marketing budget and thus becomes a more palatable expense.

Factor Increasing Computer Load and Associated Costs into Database ROI

Estimates of the costs of in-house database marketing activities should include future computer central processing unit (CPU) upgrades and disk drive purchases as the database grows. As one catalog database manager pointedly remarked:

> Database marketing is like a narcotic. The demands increase as users get used to getting answers quickly.

As part of the project plan, the following estimates need to be made: the starting database size; its growth over time, and the disk drives required to store the entire database each year. Since purchases of additional computers and disk drives can sometimes take up to six months, there must be planning up-front to proactively acquire additional hardware and build that into expectations about the total system cost.

14

Competitive Research

Although there are many systems for tracking competitive advertising, pricing, and sales, few companies routinely track database marketing programs. Many marketers see these programs as low-impact. In other words, because they are so highly targeted, they think they can't possibly have a dramatic effect on their short term volume. As you have seen in the preceding chapters, they are mistaken. Conventional tracking sources do not capture these programs because they run across multiple media and are not coded as being response-producing. Those conventional sources currently available include:

1. Leading National Advertisers (LNA) for media dollars and spending patterns by market doesn't isolate budgets or timing of direct response television.

2. PIB/ACB measures magazine dollar spending—and separately, the creative themes. But finding which ads are response-oriented is time-consuming and tedious.

3. Promotion tracking services are a comprehensive record of conventional promotion activity and dollar spending projections (SummaryScan, IRI Promoscan, Sunflower Group AdTracking Service); but again they don't distinguish many

response- producing programs (e.g., companies asking for name address blocks in coupons.)

4. Direct mail by definition tends to be highly targeted and fractionated, and most worrisome to the marketer, it is the least susceptible to tracking, although there are services attempting to do so.

But the need to track increases as more companies experiment and roll out programs. "What you don't know can hurt you" will become the watchword. For example, how can Coca Cola estimate the long term effect of Pepsi Cola's targeted sampling of a full case of Diet Pepsi to known Diet Coke users in April 1992? These kinds of large-scale targeted marketing efforts are likely to continue.

How to track is the difficulty; the reality is no one can adequately track all that's occurring because of the inherent private nature of much of the communications. Once consumer product companies recognize that DBM is more than simply an add-on to consumer promotion, recognition of the need to track will increase.

How to Begin—Collecting Information

Magazines. What magazines do your competitors usually use? Answer that and you're halfway home. Use conventional sources such as PIB to identify and get yourself and others in the company on the *comp* list.

Monitor them routinely; designate a person to be responsible for routine scanning. Don't waste time on the articles; the drill here is to look only for the ads. And then to respond to them.

As a next step, select and scan several additional books that you or a competitor might experiment with (for example, if using *Bon Appetit*, check *Eating Well*; if using *Reader's Digest*, check *Modern Maturity* and *Prevention*).

Look for variations in offers or creative execution in the same magazine or one versus another. This suggests that testing is taking place prior to a planned larger-scale database campaign (such as straight ad versus ad with bind-in card, free booklet versus free product sample offer). Current examples include Warner-Lambert's Lubriderm and Kraft General Foods' Gevalia Kaffe.

Direct Response Television (DR TV). Watch, watch, and watch more. Get your people attuned to the kind of commercials you're talking about. Many staffers don't even notice commercials with an 800 number free sample offer at the end. It is important to write down the exact 800 number, call it when the spot is viewed, and note the date, time, and on what station it ran. If you see more than one phone number, it is probably an indication that media or other testing is in progress. Responding to these offers is also cheapest and easiest, usually requiring no expense.

DR TV commercials run less frequently than the brand's conventional spots. They run more often in first and third quarters because it's more efficient than second and fourth; better availabilities are offered even at low direct response rates. They run as spot television or on cable stations in selected markets, and so are hard to pick up. You must ask for help from local company representatives (regional sales people, plant personnel, R&D group).

Remember that LNA only records the brand and dollars spent by market, not whether it's an 800 number commercial. It's quite difficult to estimate how much of the spot TV budget is being spent on DR TV. However, it is possible to monitor this activity in creative terms by asking one of the commercial monitoring services (Ad-Bank, Radio-TV Reports) to provide any competitor's 800 number commercials. In addition to seeing and evaluating the execution, you can learn where it ran and when.

Free-Standing Inserts (FSI). These Sunday newspaper coupon sections are heavily used for ongoing consumer promotion by many consumer products. The three key vehicles are Valassis, Product Movers, and Quad Marketing. FSIs are increasingly being used for data collection. Sweepstakes, mail-in offers, cash rebate offers, recipe books—all are being used. Many of these offers are captured by the promotion tracking services; screening and analysis are tedious but worthwhile and indeed essential.

John Cummings & Partners, a consulting company specializing in this field, indicates that FSIs are the primary vehicle for name gathering. It's not enough to know that your competitor ran an FSI nationally. It's possible they ran several test variations and have generated an additional one million names—of your users.

DowBrands did just that in August 1992 when they tested a competitive user brand-switching program in FSIs on not just one, but two of their key brands (Ziploc Bags and Spray 'n Wash) in different markets. They announced to competitive users that they could begin to receive a free newsletter without any obligation to purchase the DowBrands products. How many of their competitors do you believe noted this activity?

Direct Mail. The most inexact medium to track comprehensively. One excellent source is the *Who's Mailing What* newsletter. They use a network of correspondents around the country to capture a wide range of mail activity. It's carefully coded and·categorized as to size, number of creative elements, new or repeat program, and so on.

The basic step to learn more about competitive activity in this medium is to *seed* your name on your competitors' database. Do so by filling out the name/address block in their coupon, carefully noting the date. Respond also to any sweepstakes program. Take any opportunity to complete data collection questionnaires in your categories.

Tracking Competitive Programs

Seeding Names Smartly. It's not enough to simply seed your name. If you do it often enough, you'll quickly learn that you must use different code names. The reason for this is it's the only way to distinguish between sources acquiring your name—by FSI versus mail versus TV, and so on. And it's not enough to use different names; you must carefully record which name is used. It is important to have others in the organization do the same so that you get different names and addresses in the database.

Responding to Offers. Although the first mail-in offer will be fulfilled promptly, the next mailing you receive (if any) from the manufacturer indicates their interest in beginning a more substantive bonding, or relationship marketing program. Follow-up mailings sometimes require more feedback from the consumer. For example, Kraft General Foods' Miracle Whip Cooks Recipe Exchange program asked the consumer what their favorite Miracle Whip hot recipe is (involvement). You'll have to respond here with more than a fake first name. It takes time, but it's necessary because it's the only way you can get at the underlying rationale for the bonding strategy.

An Ongoing Process. The relationship marketer's goal is to communicate on an ongoing basis. To successfully track activity implies staying with it in order to mimic what the "real" consumer is experiencing. It is not sufficient to monitor on a project, or "ad hoc," basis.

Role of the Agency. Most agencies are very sensitive to the competitive situation of their clients' businesses. Advertising agencies have historically tracked copy and media expenditures, as well as the performance of network television buys. However, the normal focus of the direct response agency is to maximize response rates, cost-per-order, and profitability of the client's product or service. However, as database marketing programs become a more integral part of a brand's total marketing effort, all DR agencies will need to become more familiar with the competition's activities. Their clients will demand it, in the same way the ad agencies routinely provide this service.

Institutionalize the Process. The key to tracking database marketing is making a commitment to do it and sticking with it. Always be vigilant, and seek support and information from the widest array of resources. Know that it's hard work—in fact, often a thankless task. The net is that you've got to do it, or else sooner or later you'll find yourself surprised with a mysterious share loss.

A New Way to Track
DBM Activity

If the process of tracking these programs appears daunting or complicated, there is another solution. Specialized tracking services have been established to meet the largely unfilled need. One excellent source I use and recommend is *DBM/scan*™ (6 Blair Road, Armonk, NY 10504) which specializes in packaged goods DBM program tracking. Begun in 1991, DBM/scan has built a computerized database of over 2500 programs run by over 275 companies. It provides a quarterly review of activity across multiple media, i.e., magazines, free-standing inserts, DR TV, on-packs, and direct mail. Customized category reports are also available, and particularly valuable when launching a new product or for agencies taking on a new database client. Reports are provided to subscribers in hard copy and data disk formats. It is a very broad-based file, useful for cross-category comparisons and measuring the evolution and progress of company and category activity. I could not have written this book without access to this service. Many of the database programs presented in the next section were provided by DBM/scan.

Interpreting Packaged Goods DBM

Tracking of packaged goods activity is particularly difficult because DBM is but one tool in their arsenal of weapons. How do you determine from an analysis of a conventional promotion program whether one of its goals was active data collection—as opposed to getting names as a by-product of the effort, to be fulfilled quickly, then merely forgotten?

John Cummings & Partners, which developed the DBM/scan tracking service, has developed a set of "leading indicators" that help to determine how serious companies are in their DBM efforts. While no one of these is sufficient to predict a company's true intentions, they form a powerful set of factors that, taken together, can predict what's really going on:

DBM/Scan Leading Indicators of Company Interest

Program Characteristics

- Number of loyalty programs as percent of total activity

- Number of multimedia programs
- Number of repeat programs

Sophistication of Data Collection

- Percent company activity collecting name/address plus versus total file
- Household-coded mailings/programs
- In-coupon data collection
- Coupon copy "To be considered for future offers . . ."

General

- Trend of number of divisions and brands running programs
- Trend of number of DBM programs running by quarter
- Use of DBM programs on new product launches
- Level of internal, dedicated staffing

The method of analysis is to compare the incidence of these factors in the total DBM/scan file to their incidence in the relevant companies. Shown in Table 14.1 are the results of such an analysis where two similarly sized household and personal products companies are compared. Clearly, Company "A" is a more serious experimenter in database marketing!

The objective of competitive research is not to copy what others are doing, but to evaluate the activity in this field so that it can be incorporated into overall planning. It is also necessary to watch

Table 14.1. Comparison of Leading Indicators

Evaluation element	Company A	Company B
Loyalty programs	Above average	Below average
New products using DBM	Above average	Above average
Multimedia DBM programs	Above average	Below average
In-coupon data collection	Yes	No
Household-coded coupons	Yes	No
Collecting name/address plus	Above average	Below average
Dedicated DBM staff	Yes	No
Quarterly program trend	Up	Up

what others do in order to establish the base line of present activity, so that your database promotion will be designed to exceed it. Database marketing is an evolving specialty. While the ordinary approaches are still effective for most businesses, just as ordinary direct mail once was, the future will require creativity and flair to get maximum impact.

Table 14.2. DBM/scan Top 25 Product Categories

Rank	Product category	Number of programs
1	Multibrand programs	113
2	Cold juices/drinks/beverages	94
3	Cigarettes	93
4	Pet food	74
5	Toys	66
6	Disposable diapers	54
7	Cheese	50
8	Cereals	49
9	Liquor	43
10	Sauces/gravies	42
11	Fresh meats/poultry/fish	41
11	Coffee/tea	41
11	Diet products	41
14	Feminine hygiene products	38
15	Analgesics	36
16	Salad dressings	34
16	Candy	34
18	Hosiery/bras	32
19	Baby food/infant formula	31
19	Lotions/creams	31
21	Beer	29
22	Shelf-stable main meals	28
23	Fragrances	25
24	Bar and liquid soaps	23
24	Baby care products	23
25	Baking needs	21
25	Shampoo	21

Based on 1827 cases in database as of September 2, 1992.

Table 14.3. DBM/scan Top 25 Companies

Rank	Company	Number of Programs
1	Kraft General Foods	146
2	Procter & Gamble	104
3	Johnson & Johnson	50
4	Nestle USA	44
5	Quaker Oats	40
6	Philip Morris	38
6	Hasbro	38
8	Sara Lee	37
9	S.C. Johnson & Son	36
10	Ralston Purina	32
11	Nabisco Brands	31
11	Kimberly-Clark	31
13	H.J. Heinz	30
14	Bristol-Myers Squibb	27
15	Seagram	23
16	Hershey Foods	22
16	Borden	22
16	Mars	22
19	American Tobacco Company	21
19	R.J. Reynolds	21
19	Campbell Soup	21
22	Colgate Palmolive	19
22	Pillsbury	19
22	Gerber Products	19
22	Scott Paper	19
22	Warner-Lambert	19

Based on 1827 cases in database as of September 2, 1992.

Figure 15.1. Database marketing mix in the marketing mix.

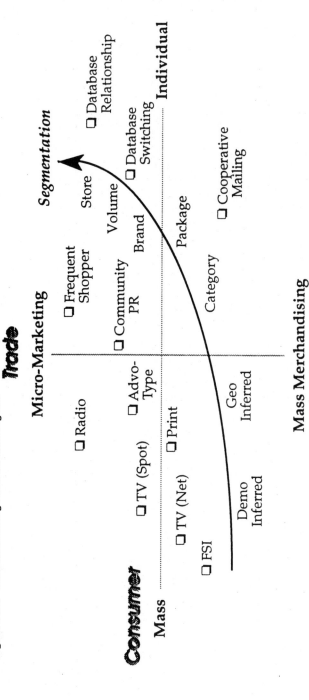

15

Consumer Applications

In the previous chapters database marketing has been discussed in theory and principle. Eventually it all adds up to writing a plan, determining costs, forecasting results, and then, designing and executing advertising or mailings to make it all work. Add to this the need to follow through to assure flawless handling of responses, storage of data, and whatever is needed to close the sale.

This chapter deals with consumer applications. The examples range from packaged goods to automotive to travel and could include virtually any kind of product where the arithmetic comes out right. As discussed in an earlier chapter, the applicability depends on the value of the retained or acquired customer, offset by the costs of acquiring the name, maintaining the file, and communicating with the person represented by the file.

As many database programs are highly influenced by the computer or management information systems (MIS) executives instead of, or as well as, the marketing department, many companies approach database marketing as if it was just another systems project. The intention of this chapter is to demonstrate, by example, that successful programs require strategic innovation, tactical diligence, and bold creativity—all rooted in a knowledge of the direct marketing experiences which are and always will be the foundation of this new marketing technology.

The need for creativity is constant, regardless of the product or service, regardless of whether the objective is trial, conquest or consumer loyalty. What are the elements of creativity that make a difference? That is not the purpose of this book, but of broader-based books, including my own, dealing with the many creative and positioning strategies proven effective in the wider worlds of direct marketing and mass advertising.

The Marketing Mix

Target Base Marketing's chart (Fig. 15.1, page 188) addresses how database marketing fits in the marketing mix of Consumer Packaged Goods (CPG) firms. The key message is that improved understanding of a company's markets through segmentation can lead to application of more targeted strategies and tactics in both trade and consumer marketing. With this foundation, the role of database marketing becomes clearer vis a vis other elements in the marketing mix.

Today most major CPG firms market along two dimensions: trade and consumer, also known as *push* versus *pull*. Along either dimension there is an evolution describing more effective, or at least more targeted, marketing strategies.

Trade marketing views the retail store as the place where the marketing action is—where most resources should be spent. The goal is movement of product to retailer, sometimes through irresistible incentives, and forcing the retailer to move it to the consumer. As a result, increases in spending on slotting allowances, discounts, bill-backs, merchandising and displays can be expected. This *push* marketing can become more effective and efficient depending on a company's ability to target spending and focus tactics on where they will do the most good. In short, trade marketing strategy depends on understanding where the business is, how to avoid waste and what tactics to use to maximize opportunity. The more a company succeeds in this, the more they move away from being a mass-merchandiser to being a micromarketer.

In similar fashion, consumer marketing encompasses a myriad of tactics, each designed to reach some level of audience. On one end of this spectrum is *mass marketing* where the goal is the broadest exposure of the message. On the other end is *individualized marketing* which includes the ability to establish and maintain loyalty based on a relationship with an individual consumer. The key reason CPG firms now drive towards individualized marketing is to improve the focus of spending on where it will do the most good: the best prospects, heaviest users, etc. This focus creates efficiencies via targeting in a hyper-segmented, dynamic consumer marketplace and effectiveness via personalized, value-added relevant marketing messages and promotions.

Most CPG firms want *the ability* to be an individualized consumer marketer and micromarketer. We emphasize *the ability* because it is not imperative—or even desirable—for *all* marketing resources to be spent on either end of the *push* or *pull* spectrum. For example, distribution support would be limited, and perhaps opportunity lost, without some degree of mass merchandising; new products and new propositions would get limited exposure and, perhaps, credibility without some level of mass marketing.

What is necessary is having a balanced marketing mix with the ability to apply the right resources to the right strategic need.

The defining factor of all elements in the marketing mix is segmentation. Improving the understanding of the segments that define and drive one's business is critical to adopting and applying any marketing tactic. For example, segmentation is the way to target *push* and *pull* tactics, eventually evolving beyond just aggregate geographic and demographic definitions. In fact, the final stage in segmentation is identifying key opportunities by households, getting all relevant defining information about them, including the stores they shop.

The only marketing tactic capable of delivering action on this level of segmentation is *database marketing*. Database marketing belongs in the marketing mix as an essential tool, provided by segmentation and critical to achieving a full balance of resources directed at trade and consumer marketing dimensions.

Some Applications

While I have categorized these examples by objective and product, I suggest the reader examine all of them, for each has some interesting lesson that can apply to other situations as well.

Advertiser: United Artists Theaters
Objective: Customer Loyalty

United Artists has been testing a frequent movie-goer program in fifteen theaters. Movie-goers are issued a scannable card which records each time a patron buys a ticket at one of their theaters.

The theater chain records not only the number of tickets purchased, but also which types of movies, days of the week, and showing times. Incentives are offered such as free popcorn or soft drinks, or preferred seating.

The database allows the theater to send promotions to those most likely to be interested in a given type of motion picture. For popular pictures that are sold out at peak times, they can promote to those card holders who are likely to attend those showings that are not sold out. This is equivalent to airline and hotel programs designed to fill empty seats.

Advertiser: Time-Warner
Objective: Advertising Sales

This promotion was built around selling automobiles, but its real objective was selling advertising.

Time, Fortune, and *Sports Illustrated* put together a combined advertising and database program which they offered to their automobile accounts.

The packages began with advertising in their magazines offering one of several kits. Each compiled information about a price or style category of participating automobile brands. Called *The Time-Life Information Place for New Car Buyers,* it was offered to prospects who would call an 800 number and were willing to pay a nominal price of about $3.95 for the kit. Each kit included worksheets, brochures, and a videocassette demonstrating up to ten automobiles in the category. The names of local dealers for each participating car were also provided.

During the phone call, present car ownership and timing information was solicited. In addition to providing information to consumers, the database information was to be supplied to each automobile company for their own follow-up.

This type of promotion could be applied to any product category, and offered by any media—even local newspapers on behalf of local dealers. In this case there is added value because of the presumed objectivity of the well-known publishing company sponsoring the information service.

Advertiser: **Chrysler Dealers**
Objective: **Customer Loyalty**

Once an automobile dealer knows a customer's name, one use of the resulting database is to support dealer's service departments. Especially as the car gets older, owners often get their automobiles maintained by local, independent mechanics.

This self-mailer was sent to owner's of Chrysler cars one year old or older. The theme was a Fun in the Sun Sweepstakes, offering "a Florida vacation filled with fantasy and fun." The letter invited the owner to "bring your entry form into (Dealer Name), compare it to the number located on the sweepstakes display," and so on. It went on to say "There's no better time to bring your (Year Car Model) to us for service." The letter was further personalized with a specific service offer, the name of the service manager, and the hours the particular dealer was open.

Other personalization included the entry form, a full page of customized conveniences and services unique to the particular dealer, and four separate coupons offering specific services—in this case wheel bearing repack, wheel alignment, oil and filter change, and charging system service. Each coupon repeated the dealer name and phone number as well as unique identification codes.

While this offer relates to automobiles, I have classified it as retail because the concept is applicable to any type of chain store maintaining a record of its customer purchases. I do not know if the coupons in this mailing varied according to the age and make of the car, to reflect service patterns, but it could have. The same concept can be applied to any type of purchase that lends itself to either service or related sale.

Advertiser: **Oldsmobile**
Objective: **Conquest**

Many automobile companies add a line to their general advertising to the effect "Call this tollfree 800 number for a free brochure." But it almost seems that art directors vie to find new ways to deemphasize this kind of offer. Perhaps there is a *Hide the Offer* award being given somewhere.

Those calling are often sent the basic car brochure for the particular model being advertised, even though it may not turn out to be the model most likely to appeal. Other companies, particularly Oldsmobile, Mazda, and Nissan, have taken the idea of "integrated advertising" more seriously. Instead of hiding the offer of a brochure, they have made it as interesting and as prominent as possible.

In this example, a four-page advertisement took on the competition with the headline: "The Oldsmobile Achieva Went 100,000 Miles Against Honda Accord and Toyota Camry and Out-Performed Them in a Real-World Test." Support in the ad was a chart prepared by an independent testing service comparing operating costs. But that was just the beginning. One-third of a page was devoted to this: "Need further proof? One phone call gets you more detailed test results, plus a video documenting the test—Free. 1-800-523-TEST." Art directors please note: The phone number was in type one half-inch high!

To take it a step further, there was also a bound-in business reply card with the same offer. Both the card and phone operators asked about age, make, and model of current automobile as well as the critical "When do you plan on purchasing your next new vehicle?" This offer was also a key part of television spots for this automobile, with the report illustrated and a phone number provided to order it. The spots I saw did not mention the videotape.

Every respondent received not only the videotape and other mailings, but also a phone call from the local dealer—one right away asking if the video was received, and another at the time indicated by the prospect. The "test results" included an offer of a free oil change, "while you are taking a test drive."

You can bet that this was a successful plan, because it is a repeat of the method used to first introduce this model a year earlier, which also used a phone number and a bound-in card. One very important improvement: the earlier version invited calls only between 8 a.m. and 7 p.m. EST weekdays; the later ad invited calls anytime.

I don't know if direct mail was used also, but the offer lent itself to mailing to owners of specific cars. Buick is reported to have mailed videotapes directly to selected prospects, but I doubt that would be as cost effective as a two-step process: first offering it, then sending the costlier follow-up only to those who request it.

Advertiser: **Bristol-Myers Squibb (Nuprin)**
Objective: **Trial**

If your brand does not have the dominant share in the market, even mass media can offer "conquest" opportunities, for the simple reason that most respondents to an offer will be using a competitive product. However, as the message is not directed specifically to users of another brand, the objective is generally considered to be *trial*. Using a direct marketing term, it is a *front-end* program, while consumer loyalty or usage increase would be called *back-end*.

The Nuprin Challenge pulled out all the stops, with information (*Pain Relief Guide*), sampling (8 tablets), a sweepstakes (worth $20,000), a $1 store coupon to track conversion and, of course, a questionnaire.

First tested in a single market, Tampa, the program eventually ran in 100 markets with an intensive multimedia schedule–free-standing inserts in local papers, television spots with an 800 number, and solo and co-op direct mail.

The *Pain Relief Guide* was tested against a first aid kit as well as other creative executions. The result was a real winner for the company if not the contest entrants. Over 500,000 people responded, answering the questionnaire with information about symptoms and lifestyle to facilitate future promotions. And, according to subsequent research, 80 percent of those calling the tollfree 800 number had been users of Tylenol, the competitive product.

Advertiser: Ronzoni
Objective: Customer Loyalty

To many consumers pasta is a commodity, to be purchased more on price than on flavor or nutrition. So, how does one of the leading brands, a subsidiary of General Foods Corporation, get buyers to stick with their brand despite competitive discounting and bargain-priced house brands?

They launched the Ronzoni Sono Buoni Club, a membership program which offered "great savings, recipes, party ideas, contests" in return for proofs of purchase of Ronzoni products.

"I'm enclosing 4 Ronzoni UPC symbols, " the coupon read, "for two 25¢ bonus coupons and 3 issues of your newsletter." Those who responded by a certain date were to receive a free bonus of a "special pasta cooking tips booklet."

One interesting offer twist was a trial membership. "Your club sounds like fun, but I'd like a trial issue of your newsletter first" (for 1 UPC symbol). "If I join, I'll send the required number of Ronzoni proofs later."

The Newsletter itself was only four pages, but crammed with consumer goodies: recipes, contests, and free or price-reduced items such as a pasta plate, colander, bread basket, grater, and a cookbook. The two-tier system was used. For instance, a $29 value ceramic bread basket was available free for 30 proofs or for only $16.50 with 2 proofs.

The most interesting part of the offer, in my opinion, was omitted from the ads announcing the program—the newsletter's stories about the history of pasta, the origin of sauces, the reason for varied pasta shapes. This intangible material would have attracted me faster than 50¢ worth of coupons.

Advertiser: **Price-Choppers**
Objective: **Database Building**

In New England, the Price Chopper supermarkets have a typical but very effective method of building a database and encouraging consumer loyalty: their *Advantage Club* is offered in their stores with a prenumbered *Instant Membership Card.*

Store patrons see *Advantage Specials* in circulars and throughout the stores. These special prices or cents-off offers, the kind of coupon specials most stores would offer to anyone who brings in or picks up a coupon, can be obtained here only by members. But *instant membership* is available at the check-out counter, just for filling out an application.

In their case the application is burdened with credit information (employer address, driver's license number, and the like) needed to provide access to video rentals. But they do find room to ask how many people reside in the home, ages of children, and about special dietary needs.

I probably also would have inquired about types of products purchased, typical purchase amount and frequency of shopping, as well as day of the week and time. It would also be helpful to know if the consumer buys generic or house brands. It's also possible that this data is collected automatically from the checkout counter data.

This program is particularly interesting because it is applicable to any retail business where the names of customers would be valuable. For instance, it could be used by restaurants, department stores, garden supply stores, barber shops—any business where the names and addresses of customers are not usually available.

Advertiser: **Avis Car Rental**
Objective: **Consumer Loyalty**

Most people think of the car rental business as a national marketing problem. The truth is that it is very local, with very different pricing and demand situations in different markets.

For Avis Car Rental's New York stations, where many families find it more convenient not to own a car but to rent one when needed, summer is a highly competitive period. Avis looked up the names of summer renters and sent them automatic memberships in a program called *Summer Rent Control.*

Members who carried this membership card were entitled to special rates, upgrades, and other privileges (with extra motivation provided for the season's first rental and for later multiple ones), especially those that extended into mid-week.

The initial mailing included not only a letter, various certificates and the membership card, but a second "Pass-Along Card" to be given to a friend. As this program has been repeated for several years and imitated by at least one competitor, it is obviously effective for Avis.

Advertiser: **Budweiser**
Objective: **Database Building**

"Play Bud Summer Games and You Could Win Big!" said the headline of this full-page, full-color sweepstakes advertisement in national media, specifically *Sports Illustrated, People, Time* and *Entertainment Weekly,* as well as co-op Sunday newspaper inserts in selected markets.

Tying in with the Olympics, the ad included an Official Game Ticket, which listed six-digit numbers for each of gold, silver, and bronze competitions. The reader was asked to take the ticket to a dealer and compare the numbers with a display. If the number matched, they could win one of five gold-colored Jeep Cherokees, one of 500 silver-colored Trek mountain bikes, or one of 250,000 bronze Bud Dry Olympic pins, featuring their brand name.

Similar contests, with different prizes, were offered tying in with Memorial Day, July 4th, and Labor Day. In addition, one prize was common to all the contests—a grand prize of $1 million in gold, to be awarded based on a drawing.

What's the catch? Just a straightforward database questionnaire, asking name, phone, birthdate, sex, "Brands you drink regularly" and "In a typical week, how many beers do you drink?" What can they do with this database? You can use your own imagination. The uses are almost unlimited, for conquest, for loyalty programs, for cross-sell (Eagle snacks?), and for new brand introductions.

Advertiser: **Wyeth-Ayerst**
Objective: **Customer Loyalty**

There are few product categories as difficult as that of prescription drugs, where the end user cannot make a purchase without the sanction and cooperation of a doctor. To sell the doctor you have to overcome his or her resistance to the mountains of mail sent not just for medical products but for every type of investment and personal purchase as well.

What if you could write the doctor about a specific patient, referring to a specific ailment? That would get the doctor's attention, not just on behalf of the one patient but for all those patients with a similar ailment.

The ailment in this case is Premarin, an estrogen tablet for women going through menopause. Anticipating the eventual availability of this type of medication in generic form, the manufacturer needed a way to promote loyalty to the established brand. The incentive to patients is a free six-times-a-year magazine called *Seasons* especially for women who need this medication.

The magazine is effectively described in both emotional and practical terms. "Yes, we're older. But we're also more self-confident. Our relationships are changing—and we have more time to explore them . . . ." "Separate the myths from the facts." "Tasty concoctions from famous spas." "Rx for aging muscles." "Rita Moreno's menopause relief." And so on. And so on.

Not only do they capture the subscriber's name and address, but a secondary offer of a health information card provides a reason to gather more statistical data: physician's name and phone, pharmacy's name and phone, symptoms, and more—all to be personalized on your card.

Responding to industry concern's about the privacy issue, this advertiser advises the respondent of how the information will be used and discloses whether it will be made available to others. (This issue is discussed further in the final chapter of this book.)

Evidently the brochure was distributed in pharmacies and doctors' offices, and also appears to have been mailed to women in affected age ranges.

Advertiser: **Neiman Marcus**
Objective: **Customer Loyalty**

When your best customers are people who can, and do, buy whatever they want anywhere in the world, how do you keep them making most of their purchases at home?

Neiman Marcus solved this problem by creating the *InCircle,* a membership club with very tangible rewards for frequent purchasers. Presented as "a special way of saying 'thank you' to our best customers," it automatically enrolls anyone who applies for and uses a Neiman Marcus charge card, but the membership card is not sent until the customer has reached a level of 3000 points (purchased dollars).

At this initial level they get rewards such as a quarterly newsletter, free gift wrapping, and a complimentary cookbook or magazine subscription. Other services include private store shopping evenings, for members only, reservation services, and a travel assistance plan.

At 7500 points, members get gifts such as Waterford Crystal (shipped twice a year), hams, turkeys and more cookbooks. At 15,000, add fine wines and sterling silver gift items. At 45,000 points, they can enjoy a week in Hawaii or the Caribbean at a luxury resort. And the list goes on, up to 10 days at a famous German spa or on the French Riviera, at 250,000 points. For 500,000 points (Mrs. Marcos' shoe budget perhaps, or new wardrobes for all of the Emir of Kuwait's wives?), they offer "a series of rare international excursions that will intrigue the senses and delight the imagination."

Advertiser: **Ramada Inn**
Objective: **Conquest**

Can a database promotion be used as part of a head to head competitive promotion? Ramada did just that in advertisements and mailings with this headline: "2000 reasons why Ramada's Business Card is better than Holiday's."

The main reasons were 2000 points for signing up. But the points were usable not only for free hotel rooms, which most frequent travelers get enough of, but also for over 10,000 merchandise items in the Service Merchandise catalog. Holiday Inn's comparable card was

usable only for a limited list of selected merchandise. A car rental offer
(rent one day and get another one free) was an added sweetener.

Advertiser: **Bristol-Myers (Nuprin)**
Objective: **Conquest**

One of the classic consumer conquest programs was Bristol-Myers'
Nuprin Challenge campaign directed specifically at Tylenol users.
Sixty-second spots in 100 markets offered a *Pain Relief Guide* and
samples. Those who responded received the tablets and a brochure,
plus a $1 coupon redeemable at stores. This particular coupon did
not, for some reason, include individually trackable coupons, but
a separate questionnaire was enclosed which asked database questions while entering the respondent in a $20,000 sweepstakes.
   Here are the questions:

1. For what kind of pain did you use Nuprin?
2. What pain reliever have you used most often?
3. Age and gender.
4. How many adults? Children?
5. In which of the following activities (golf, biking, and the like) do
   you participate regularly?
6. How often do you participate in sports activities or exercise?
7. In which of the following hobbies/interests (cooking, traveling,
   and so on) do you frequently participate?

   The television spots featured a former Tylenol user who switched
on a doctor's recommendation. It has been reported that 80
percent of the 500,000 callers were former Tylenol users.

Advertiser: **Kraft General Foods**
Objective: **Customer Loyalty**

One of the longest lasting customer loyalty programs aimed at
children is the Kool Aid *Wacky Warehouse* program.

Basically a catalog of unique (that is, "wacky") gifts for kids, it offers the items free or at lower than retail prices in return for proofs of purchase. The offer of the brochure has been aimed right at children as well as parents, using comic books, co-op mail, and direct mail and Saturday morning television.

The program has been kept fresh by updating the catalog twice a year and adding new items, such as Nintendo and Sega games, travel radios, Swatch watches, and (offered on a local basis), tickets—to zoos, baseball stadiums, and other entertainments.

Some cross-brand promotion is evident in recent inclusion of this offer in other Kraft Macaroni and Cheese and other KGF products.

Advertiser: **Virginia Slims**
Objective: **Conversion/Loyalty**

A highly targeted brand is Virginia Slims, aimed at women smokers with an independent, contemporary self-image. "You've come a long way baby" is their now classic advertising theme, and the companion direct marketing programs are no exception.

National advertising in women's magazines and Sunday supplements offers *The Book of Days*, a unique specially designed appointment calendar with holidays, advice and inspirational quotes especially designed for women who share the Virginia Slims self-image.

Any coupon redeemer who tries Virginia Slims, evidenced by precoded or by fill-in coupons, also receives an invitation to join the "Virginia Slims Club," in a circular which plays on the word *Club* by visually presenting it as very chic nightspot.

The personalized message tells the story:

> Go ahead, open that door. Step across the threshold. And get ready to have a great time when you join the Virginia Slims Club.
>
> There are no rules, no obligations, no dues. It will never cost you a cent. As a Superslims smoker, all you have to do is check the enclosed reply card and return it within 30 days.
>
> Then take a front-row table. After you respond, we'll be back with exciting offers on fashions and accessories, on next year's edition of the Virginia Slims *Book of Days*, and on special events

in your area. For starters, there's a coupon for valuable savings on any style pack or carton of . . . .

The coupon was pre-coded, offering $1 off on three packs or a carton.

Advertiser: **Merit Cigarettes**
Objective: **Conversion/Loyalty**

Another tobacco brand with an active program to convert triers to users is Merit. The DBM/scan service turned up two very different programs, each of them with the same obvious objective.

One was a self-mailer sent to Merit triers, offering a custom-designed lightweight travel bag with several attractive new features, a $30 value, free with proofs of purchase (POPs) from five cartons of Merit. The personalized message explained that the offer was "our way of saluting you for discovering the combination of good taste and low tar . . . ." To help get the recipient started on saving their five carton POPs, a $2 coupon was also enclosed.

Another more complex offer dramatized the *lightness* image of this brand with a *Lighter Side* promotion. A guide to *America's Lighter Side* described curious celebrations throughout the year, including the Maine Lobster Festival, a Texas Chilympiad, a Duck-Calling Contest. Readers were invited to send in photographs to "Picture a Place" wackier than those listed in the guide. Still another element was an offer of free travel gifts for various UPC codes.

Advertiser: **Dow Brands**
Objective: **Conquest/Usage Increase**

Here's how one company built a list of competitive users in a category that was not available through outside sources.

Dow makes ZipLoc storage bags, a product that generally has more uses than most households take advantage of. Dow created a newsletter called *All Zipped Up: The Woman's Guide to Creative Household Management.* It offered "expert advice, helpful hints and secret strategies to help the busy woman maintain control of her kitchen, her household, her life!" Not inconspicuous in the descriptive copy was "maximizing the freshness and taste of your family's meals."

The newsletter was directed specifically to users of the two leading competitors, although users of any brand of zippered bags were eligible. "If you use either of these to help manage your busy household . . . then help yourself to this free newsletter." An added appeal was a bonus offer for responding by a certain date, a handy storage bag organizer.

Questions asked referred strictly to usage:

1. Have you used any storage bags in the last six months?

2. How many per month?

3. Which brands?

4. Of your last 10 purchases, how many were our brand?

5. What are the numbers on the bar code on your usual brand?

While these questions might help to prove the effectiveness of this program, it does little to help the marketing effort. One question which would be a selling statement in itself, as well as a way of guiding the newsletter's editorial content, would have been to list uses of storage bags and ask which the respondent already uses them for.

These are just a samples of some interesting database promotions, from the hundreds that take place every year. There is a wide range of uses and objectives. The point of this chapter is that the attractiveness to the consumer (and consequently the effectiveness) of a database promotion is vitally dependent on creativity—in the offer, the presentation, and in the basic concept itself.

16

Business-to-Business Applications

Business-to-business (BTB) database marketing has its own set of challenges and opportunities, but contrary to popular opinion it is not immune to the do's and don'ts of consumer marketing.

As in consumer products marketing, it is most effective when it adheres to the response-multiplying lessons of the direct marketing field, while still respecting the taste levels of contemporary communication.

Some practitioners have the attitude that BTB is a less difficult aspect of marketing. In fact, the opposite is true. BTB is more difficult and requires more detailed planning than many consumer programs. So, what are the differences?

The Problem with Business Lists

The state of business mailing lists is primitive, compared to consumer lists. Yes, there are ample lists of companies, sorted in every which way by SIC (Standard Industrial Classification) categories and subcategories. But these very complete lists of businesses usually require title addressing as names of individuals may not be consistently available, or if they are, are often not accurate.

The U.S. Census reports that 13 million people have executive, technical, or professional responsibilities. But even the largest multiproduct publishing companies have fewer than two million individual executives by name.

Dun & Bradstreet does offer names of presidents, chief financial officers, and a scattering of other officers. Some magazines and directory publishers provide pretty good lists of executives in specific industries. For some specialties, especially computers, compilers can offer substantial quantities of prospects.

If you are selling a universal product such as telephone services, air express, office supplies, or machines, database programs can be conducted with existing lists by addressing the president of the company by name or other officials by title. But this is not really database marketing, as it has developed.

A true database program would provide both selectivity and relevance. Most existing lists do not tell what products or services the company presently uses or, more importantly, who in the company initiates the purchase of your product or service, who influences it, and who approves it.

For instance, if you are selling printing and have some new format capabilities, you can get lists of advertising agencies and send me, as many do, mailings to make me aware of your company's name. Maybe I'll pass it on to my production manager but then maybe I won't. Some production managers are identified in some lists but most are not. But that's not all. In order to sell a format you also have to make the art directors aware of it so that they can suggest it on the next appropriate project.

Most available mailing lists have no depth at all. The orders may come from the production or purchasing manager but the buying decision is initiated elsewhere in the company. This type of situation exists in almost every field. Suppliers of building materials should be reaching architects as well as builders. Office service and equipment decisions are often initiated by an administrative assistant, though authorized by more senior executives.

Even the Direct Marketing Association faces this dilemma. Announcements of its excellent educational courses are sent to senior executives like myself, rather than to the middle and junior managers who are the more probable attendees. But even this association's database doesn't distinguish between approvers and initiators.

Database Building

If the problem with business mail is that it is too often sent to the wrong people, or not to the right ones, then the need for companies to build their own unique databases is just as important in business-to-business marketing as in any other field.

Therefore building the database must be considered an objective in itself when planning marketing programs. Data request cards should be enclosed in every communication, accompanied by appropriate motivators to send them in.

Magazine, newspaper, or even television advertising should include offers that require not just name and address of the requestor, but information about purchasing responsibilities, brand usage, and others influencing the decision-making process in the company.

Because of the high lifetime value of most BTB propositions, usually much more substantial offers and communications are affordable.

- Some companies use dimensional mailings, sometimes including gifts or gift offers, asking the president's secretary or others for information to enhance their files.

- Many use telemarketing banks. Phone operators call and ask the switchboard operator such obvious questions as "Who is in charge of . . . ?" Often they will talk to several people in each firm to get the information they need.

- Companies with ample sales forces can often compile the information from their saleperson's notes, but it is amazing how often such information remains decentralized.

- Advertisements in trade magazines can offer information, appraisals, samples (just as consumer database promotions do), in order to identify new entrants to the market.

Inquiry Generation
and Conversion

The historic alternative still used by many businesses is to spend fortunes on enlarging its sales force to canvass prospective customers, usually by phone, to find buyers for its products.

The problem is that the nature of selling has changed, and buyers will give repeat business to companies and sales representatives that can help them handle their increasingly complex responsibilities. Accordingly today's sales representative must be a consultant, a technician, a troubleshooter. The catch is that it is exactly this kind of professional who is usually least effective at making cold calls to strangers.

It's wasteful to have a professional representative or counselor doing prospecting when they can be much more effective building the volume of present customers or converting inquiries from new ones. Prospecting is best done by direct marketing, using ads, mail or a separate telemarketing department.

And, to be effective, inquiries should have information and be from executives who know enough so that the lead is a serious one. In *Direct Marketing: Strategy/Planning/Execution* I discuss the inverse relationship between quality and quantity of leads, and how this is influenced by the amount of information provided and requested.

The same steps are needed to convert an inquiry as in consumer marketing. The mailed answer to the inquiry should be personal, prompt, and relevant, independent of the sales contact which should also be as prompt as possible.

One example of the correct way to handle such inquiries is that used by the Xerox Corporation. They were the first to create a client task force concept which they call *Team Xerox*. This consisted of a marketing or sales representative who would manage the sales process plus a product manager, a specialist who knows the client's business, and a service or training representative. IBM and many other companies have also adopted this sales structure. Inquirers get very specific responses and proposals, usually created and customized from word processing master files.

Customer Loyalty

At seminars and workshops for business-to-business marketers, I am often asked how the concept of customer loyalty programs applies. This question is understandable, for it would be inappropriate to ask customers to have employees save some sort of proof of purchase in order to get free gifts or win vacation trips.

However, some marketers do offer personal or business gifts in return for business purchases. For instance, while most stationery suppliers offer corporate discounts for volume purchases, others will offer specific gifts in return for a specific size order.

Once when I inquired about why my agency had bought so many boxes of an inferior ball point pen, I discovered that a portable TV set was part of the deal. That office manager soon had plenty of time to watch the set—at home. Yet such offers are effective. Often they are made less obvious by offering items which have dual use in the office or home, such as a desk clock or briefcase.

On a quieter basis, many companies use travel and entertainment as a reward for customer loyalty, usually on an individual basis by the sales representative, or as parties at industry conventions or even at customer sales meeetings. The definition of where the line is drawn between appreciation and good will on one hand, and bribery on the other, is an important subject—but for books other than this one.

A proper customer loyalty program is based around customer service, extended into tangible reminders of the expertise of the seller. By this I mean the sending of brochures, articles, bulletins, samples—information that offers news of products and applications, or references that will help the customer be more successful at his or her job.

Certainly one of the clearest examples of this approach is the creation of newsletters and even magazines, providing they are perceived as primarily helpful and of obvious value. One of the best examples of this strategy, both for building customer relationships and maintaining contact with prospective clients, is a Bozell publication, the quarterly magazine *Opinion*.

Some Applications

Unlike consumer database marketing, where anyone can get on a mailing list and where there are monitoring services as discussed previously, business-to-business examples are more difficult to obtain and less covered in the trade press. Each company tends to get mailings only in their own specialty. I invite one of my readers to make their fortune by finding a better way to monitor BTB activity. However, here are a few examples from my experiences:

Advertiser: **Pitney Bowes Postage Meters**
Objective: **Direct Sales**

Pitney Bowes is the clear leader in the postage meter field, and, because the meter portion is leased, has a virtually complete list of customers. Because every type of business, no matter what size, can use this basic piece of business equipment, they presume that anyone not on their list is a prospect.

Their basic strategy has been to sell or lease a simple inexpensive unit that is sold direct by mail. In this endeavor, it is presumed that their competitor is not another brand, but ordinary postage stamps. Therefore their copy sells against the clutter and inconvenience of stamps, as well as the image of professionalism in sending out metered letters.

I recommended a test program based on a strategy I originally developed for Polaroid's BTB sales. Instead of sending out mail to generic "business owners" I designed a program dramatizing the specific advantages of these meters to specific market segments. The Pitney Bowes application targeted doctors and real estate offices, with copy describing and illustrating the applications for these specific types of businesses.

Advertiser: **Avis Rent a Car**
Objective: **Corporate Accounts**

Like all car rental firms, Avis maintained a strong sales force calling on major national accounts, setting up corporate discounts in return for the corporation's total car rental business.

But, as with most sales forces, there were many potential accounts that were either too small or geographically inconvenient to merit sales calls.

Avis authorized a substantial program to midsized companies, selected by size, business category, and credit rating, using the D&B list. Mailings were sent to the presidents and to the chief executive officers, by name, announcing a plan where these smaller companies could, depending on volume, earn the same kind of benefits usually offered only to large corporate accounts.

The first mailing presented the highlights, but no details, which were promised in a subsequent mailing. When that second mailing arrived, it included a hand-written message on the envelope which referred to the president or CFO of the company by name: "This is the confidential proposal Mr. X is waiting for." The proposal included a computer-printed page which referred to the information known about the company as justification for their selection in being part of this new experimental program.

After three more mailings and a phone contact, the program paid for itself a dozen times over in the first year's sales. Hundreds of corporate accounts were opened and tens of thousands of new cards issued. Later the program was expanded to make similar offers to other market segments including associations, unions, clubs, and even smaller companies.

Advertiser: **GTE Business Centers**
Objective: **Product Cross-Sell**

With every business in its territories already customers, and a growing range of new products and services, it soon became inefficient to use sales representatives. For one thing the sale had to be made from product literature as there was no way to demonstrate the equipment.

Instead GTE set up showrooms where their various new phones were installed and could be demonstrated with ease. Once this conversion method was established, the problem became getting business buyers to visit the showrooms.

The initial program began with invitations and special events, then proceeded to announcements of specific products and services. GTE did not try to close the sale by phone, but instead invited inquirers to make appointments to see demonstrations at one of the business sales centers.

As with most phone companies, there was already data on each company's type of equipment and their telephone patterns. It was therefore possible to select which offers were made to which companies, and to refer to present equipment and systems when appropriate.

Database Opportunity

Some companies knowingly use larger, inefficient lists on the theory that the cost savings aren't worth the trouble. Perhaps, but they are missing the most valuable aspect of business-to-business database marketing: the ability to make messages and contacts relevant. There is far too much emphasis on selectivity and not enough on relevance, in all forms of direct marketing.

More ambitious programs can be established, preferably by publishers or list brokers, to assemble new databases that cannot only aid their own sales but also provide a valuable list rental service to other companies. As discussed in previous chapters, there are significant cost advantages in multiproduct database building (requesting data on several business fields at once).

The business marketing field desperately needs someone to distribute multiproduct questionnaires to build a commercial database that not only lists executives but provides clues as to their responsibilities. One major publishing company I consulted with considered publishing horizontal (by job title rather than industry) directories, offering free listings to those who provided information, resulting in the ultimate business list for their own trade magazines. Middle management was enthusiastic, but the president didn't understand it at all.

Some of the best lists are those compiled by controlled circulation (free) trade magazines, which require some data in order to renew or start a subscription. Unfortunately, these are almost always purely demographic in nature and designed to provide data to advertisers. These would be much more valuable if they were expanded to ask questions like these:

- What brand of copiers does your company use?
- Who selects your air express shipper?
- Are you considering moving or opening new branches?
- Do you have a corporate car rental plan? With whom?

Until this type of brand-specific, decision-maker data is available, companies will have to build and enhance their own databases, asking those questions that will be most valuable to their own marketing efforts. This opportunity is still waiting.

17

Financial Database Marketing

While consumer and packaged goods database marketing make headlines because of famous names and big budgets, nowhere is database marketing as refined and profitable as in the field of financial services marketing.

Database marketing is practically a redundant term for banks and credit card companies, brokers and mutual funds, and contemporary insurance issuers. Virtually all financial advertising is, to some extent, database building for each transaction, account, or policy is the beginning of a relationship and an opportunity for selling additional products or services. The big difference is that the application forms provide so much relevant information that cross-selling and retention activities can be targeted very accurately with highly predictable results.

Every principle discussed elsewhere in this book applies to some extent to financial marketing. It is the most challenging and in many ways most satisfying application of database theory. The only area seldom used, most likely out of a sense of professional courtesy, is conquest marketing. *Bank Marketing* magazine deals with database marketing as a routine part of bank marketing. Books such as Holtmann & Mann's *New Age of Financial Services Marketing* (Sourcebooks), which I recommend, are devoted almost exclusively to database marketing applications.

Most financial database experience is interchangeable, although there is some difference within the three basic categories:

- Retail banking (including credit cards)
- Investments (primarily stock brokers and mutual funds)
- Insurance

These services not only share common marketing techniques, but increasingly each is getting into at least one of the other's businesses. For instance I have helped introduce a money market fund for Equitable Insurance, a checking account for Merrill Lynch, insurance for Citibank, and home mortgages for Cigna insurance. Today we have the added spectacle of credit cards being offered by football teams, appliance manufacturers, department stores, and automobile companies. Where will it stop? It won't.

To some extent financial services is not an application of database marketing, but its source. Over 20 years ago a pioneering company by the name of Customer Development Corporation coined the term database marketing to describe the computerized promotion services it was developing for banks and finance companies.

At that time computers were mainframe operations producing reams of voluminous reports that piled up on windowsills. Laser printing had not been developed; so versioning required dozens of individually printed lots. Personalization was done mostly with impact-printed salutations. And, like many packaged goods and other advertisers, their clients were skeptical, maintaining a *prove it* attitude. Oddly this resulted in smaller institutions moving faster in the development of database marketing than the more cautious Goliaths, some of whom still have not caught up.

To make account data useful it had to be *householded*, that is, consolidated to match up all accounts and transactions in a single marketing unit—a challenging computer-matching exercise. The resulting database is often called a Marketing Customer Information file, and the individualized promotions using the data are sometimes called *matrix mail.* Some of the largest credit card companies today still have been unable to effectively pull together records of cards held at business addresses with those at home addresses, or cards held by different members of the same household.

Tom Lund, the founder of Customer Development Corporation, started matrix mail after noting that the personal sales efforts of branch managers resulted in widely varied levels of sales and profitability. The top 20 percent built their branches with good relationships, ongoing communications, and personal sales efforts based on knowing the customer as well as the territory.

The goal was to bring the same kind of marketing to all the branches, by finding a way to replicate the information gathering, the selection judgments, and the personal mail and phone communications. Today's database marketing, especially where it emphasizes "relationship marketing," is as close as the business world has come, so far, to achieving this goal.

Preapproval

If you have received letters that begin with "You have already been approved for . . . ," you know first-hand the power of credit bureau mailing lists. To facilitate this kind of offer the bank or other credit card issuer must have access to credit-acceptable names. These can be obtained internally or externally.

Internally such offers are a simple by-product of data available to any institution engaged in financial transactions. Banks know about balances, assets, timely repayment of loans, anything that might generate a high probability of good credit. And they know who already has one of their credit cards. However, this required that the data from all sources be linked and organized for easy comparison and analysis. Unfortunately this is not as easy as it looks.

Cross-Sell

The lessons the early pioneers learned were direct applications of mail order. The basics of recency-frequency-average sale were proven consistent in this field as well. Where traditional marketers might want to space out promotions, or concentrate on the largest number of prospects, database marketers discovered that the best prospect was someone who either bought many of the institution's services, bought one recently, or made a deposit or loan that was larger than most. Just as mail order firms target *multibuyers* and *hot line* names, the same concepts applied to financial transactions.

Some databases include 30 or 40 characteristics, but usually only a few are usable for marketing. Most new users put database marketing in the hands of analysts or computer managers who load up on data, rather than advertising personnel who tend to focus on applications. Three that often do prove valuable are age, family, and transaction type. The customer's age and family data serve often as an indicator of financial needs due to lifestyle changes. Growth accumulation is of interest to young couples, college planning to young parents, and retirement planning for older customers.

The lists can also be enhanced as discussed in previous chapters. Geoselect lists such as Prizm and Micro-vision can append data based on neighborhood characteristics, often useful for database promotions but less so for financial propositions which should rely more on individual household data. Donnelly, Metromail, Polk, MBS/Multimode, and Equifax are some of the better known companies providing such data. Most advertising agencies specializing in direct and database marketing regularly work with such suppliers. They can therefore take responsibility for coordinating these list, creative, and executional details.

The availability of data is only the beginning of the process, not the end. First of all, the data must be updated, at least monthly. The market is made up of individuals whose financial situations and, more importantly, whose attitude and confidence, change frequently. The response difference between a likely prospect and an unlikely one can be measured in multiples as high as five or ten.

Once experience has been gathered, prospects can be scored or indexed in rank order according to the probability of their purchasing a given product or service. It is then a routine matter to prepare financial models indicating the expected return on the marketing investment of different marketing decisions. These will determine which names to mail to, how often, and how much of an incentive can be afforded. This step, usually called *database research*, is the key analytical step between database compilation and database implementation.

Creative Questions

Some newcomers to the field act as if selecting the most likely prospect is the only decision to make. However, this is only one aspect, in effect the media decision. The offer and creativity deserve at least equal attention. Considering the impact on profits, cross-sell mailings are not something to relegate to freelancers or in-house staff. The creative execution of database mailings demands the highest level of direct marketing professionalism.

Here's where different strategies and styles began to emerge at different financial institutions. Some relied on inexpensive mass form-letter mailings inviting the customer to buy another type of account, take advantage of an investment opportunity, or buy another kind of insurance protection. Some used clever and colorful mailings. Others relied on very personal letters, or on quality graphic styles.

One effective cross-sell strategy is to make the prospect feel privileged, positioning the new offering as a special privilege, or accompanying it with some form of reward or recognition. But the rewards have to be believable. Special service desks or private bankers are very appealing, providing the lines really are shorter. And special low loan or brokerage rates are appealing, if they really are special.

Some institutions concentrate on product sell—each mailing or phone call making an offer for a single purpose. And some package several services into a special customer relationship or insider club privilege.

My recommendation is to do both. Create a magazine or newsletter that has value to the customer independently of the cross-sell elements. Develop specific campaigns (note I didn't say a mailing) to offer specific products to the most likely buyer. Then add the one element missing from most financial marketing, which is simply to ask the investors, depositors, or customers what their needs are. This database enhancement step (now recognized by packaged goods marketers) is the one area that many financial marketers have passed by, missing a golden opportunity.

The reason I refer to campaigns rather than a mailing is that repeat mailings, while they do not do as well as single efforts, should be considered. Often the second mailing will do two-thirds of the first, and a third mailing will do half as well. When the database is modeled, it is likely that the top 10 percent may have sufficient potential to merit all three mailings, and possibly a telemarketing effort to boot. The second 10 percent two mailings. And the third only one. (Thirty percent of the file is an average selection for many database efforts.)

Retention

An often ignored element of financial marketing is *defensive promotion*. It often costs less to prevent the loss of a customer than to gain a new one. Not enough attention is given to this type of promotion, but it is gaining usage in many other fields. One good example is American Express, which monitors usage activity among credit card holders. Here's a letter I received from them:

> We noticed that you have not been using the American Express Card as frequently as you had in the past and we would like to know if there is something we can do to better serve you . . . we have established a special, toll-free number . . . dedicated exclusively to respond to your suggestions and questions. . . .

Demarketing

A unique application in financial marketing is *demarketing*. In any business with ongoing overhead expenses, there are always some clients or customers whose volume level or service demands make them unprofitable.

One example is a free checking account. Mailings can be sent to selected customers raising the minimum balance requirements, and increasing monthly fees for those who do not qualify. Some customers raise their balances, others will cancel their accounts. Either way the bank wins.

Market-Specific Mailings

Basic direct marketing has always enabled marketers to offer products to specific segments of the general population. Certainly financial institutions have always had and made good use of lists of affluent prospects, homeowners, small business owners, chief financial officers or newly promoted executives of larger businesses, car owners, parents, and others. Newly moved families are particularly effective lists for branch-based businesses such as banks and brokerage offices.

This type of direct mail can be very effective in reaching out to attract new customers. But it can also be used to enhance a financial institution's own list by appending this type of information to it's own database.

Product Versus Prospect

Most financial institutions are organized around product lines. Banks have managers to get assets (loans) and liabilities (deposits). Brokerage firms have product managers for funds, for bonds, for stocks. Insurance companies plan separate budgets for each type of insurance, and even for varieties of insurance with the same purpose.

The lesson being learned by more and more companies of all kinds is that the most efficient database marketing is prospect-driven, not product-driven. While most database programs up to now are designed to start with a product and figure out who to sell it to, I predict that the emphasis will eventually switch to a market-driven approach. If we start with the premise that everyone is a customer for something, the state of the art will evolve to analyzing available data and making recommendations that not only sell but also render a genuine advisory service to customers.

Imagine a letter that said "We note that your investment mix is 87 percent in equity stocks; because of current market conditions many advisors suggest a more balanced portfolio with. . . ." Or try this one: "Thank you for renewing your term life policy. As a service to our customers, we are enclosing a questionnaire which you can use to list all your policies and needs. We will computer-analyze this and send you a customized recommendation to help you. . . ." As in other forms of direct marketing, the trend is to use these systems to get closer to the customer, to try to provide (on a mass basis) the kind of individual service most customers would like.

For Dean Witter, I used gummed stamps to represent not different investment products but different objectives: retirement, college, asset preservation, growth, and the like. It was an inexpensive mailing consisting of the gummed sheet of a dozen stamps, a one-page letter, and a simple reply card with the prospect identification and space to affix one stamp.

The results were the best cost per response in their history. The leads were channelled to different product groups. Some received a response with a mailed prospectus, others with calls from assigned brokers. The test was never followed up, because they could never get their product managers to pool funds again, and the product managers had control of the budgets. The ad manager who worked with me on the program soon quit out of frustration.

At one insurance client, a different strategy dramatizes the opportunity in putting the prospect first rather than the product. Their hundreds of local agents ignored a $10,000 supplemental life policy designed for seniors, yet they objected at first to the idea of the company selling it direct, using response television. The company decided to go ahead, and produced thousands of new customers, whose names were also given to the field force to contact about other insurance needs. Though the agents made no commission on the initial sale, they and the company profited greatly on new customer relationships. This company recognized the growing need to use all channels of distribution, and allocated funds to the direct insurance project based on its overall profit potential. Here are some additional case histories in financial database marketing.

Advertiser: **Major Full Service Brokerage House**
Objective: **Cross Selling Directly to Broker-Generated Clients**

Large segments of this brokerage business's IRA clients had dormant accounts where no contribution was made within the year. In addition, other segments of the client base had very low liquid assets, and did not appear to have an IRA with the company. As a result, few brokers contacted these customers to encourage them to activate their accounts, or increase their asset base.

The company took the challenge into their own hands and developed a mailing designed to motivate these low-end clients to buy directly, through the mail. A dollar cost averaging investment strategy was offered to "hook" these clients into not feeling "pinched" by investing more.

Using transactional data about several segments of the customer file, the company was able to personalize letters and applications to each of three groups. One group was encouraged to move funds from a money market earning 3 percent to a capital fund earning about 8 percent; others were asked to bring new funds into an IRA using the systematic savings strategy of dollar cost averaging.

Since clients already owned a specific fund, they knew that it was right for their investment goals (broker had recommended and transacted), could buy more of the fund easily (already had prospectus) by authorizing trade through the mail, and could start to earn more on their assets than if they were to stay in the money market fund they owned.

To further minimize any broker irritation for contacting clients directly, all applications authorizing the transfer of funds from one account type to another were encoded to be returned to each individual broker.

Overall, this mailing was a "win-win" for the company and the brokers alike.

***Advertiser:* Major Individual Life Insurance Company**
***Objective:* Relationship Building and Cross Selling**

Many of life's events as well as innumerable transactional events afford companies and sales people alike an opportunity to contact existing customers. This was the basis on which a fully automated and completely integrated communications system was built for one of the nation's top insurance companies.

Agents could simply design their own communications profile. Once a year—subject to quarterly changes—agents "told the system" what types of customers they wished to contact about what products in what communication mode. Agents could be sent a monthly listing of all customers who owned life insurance, but didn't have auto coverage with them. Or, fully lasered letters could be produced for every client whose birthday was coming up for the agent to sign and mail. Even reminders could show up on the agent's computer to contact a particular customer about a query voiced months ago, or a CD maturity date. And because the agent had control over the types and frequency of communications, he or she was more apt to follow up and close more business.

***Advertiser:* Major Direct Marketing Insurance Company**
***Objective:* Increase Premium per Thousand**

An insurance direct marketer was regularly using a credit card list, which was doing well. Mailing results, however, were beginning to plateau. They decided to test:

Clearly identifying the well-known company up front.

Having the mailing come from the company's less-known subsidiary.

Using an outer envelope with the credit card's identification on it (i.e., the affinity group from which the list was culled).

Relative to the subsidiary test cell, the first mailing produced a 62 percent lift in premium per thousand mailed; the affinity mailing produced a 45 percent lift.

Advertiser: **Direct Marketing Insurance Company** *Objective:* **Increase Premium per Thousand**

Again, using a bank credit card file, an insurance company increased its success ratio through the use of a multivariate model. But what they discovered was not just to mail to the top seven deciles those above the break-even—once or twice, but how much more premium could be produced from mailing up to five times to the top four deciles.

In addition, not only did the premium per thousand mailed increase, but the actual mailing universe was expanded simply because of the frequency.

Table 17.1 shows how this phenomena works. The mail quantity actually increased from 1 milltion to 1.3 million, and premium per thousand from the combined second through fifth mailings was higher than that produced from the first effort.

Today's top management in the financial world should reorganize their marketing departments in the same way packaged goods firms have in order to give adequate control and ample budget to the cross-brand marketing functions such as database building, enhancement, analysis, management. If results are the criteria, these database functions should certainly have as large a share of the budget as does brand-awareness general advertising.

Table 17.1. Bank Credit Card File

Dealer	1st mailing ($/M)	Expected 60% 2nd mailing ($)	Mail to B/E only ($)	Maximize Mailings to B/E ($)			
				2nd	3rd	4th	5th
1	2000	1200	1200	1200	720	430	260
2	1700	1000	1000	1000	600	360	
3	1250	750	750	750	450	270	
4	975	570	570	570	340		
5	580	340	340	340			
6	340	200	200				
7	170	100	100				
8	120	70					
9	70	40					
10	35	20					
	7240	4,290	4160	7290			
Average	$724/M	$429/M	$594/M	$729/M			
Mail	1,000,000	1,000,000	700,000	1,300,000			
Premium	$724,000	$429,000	$415,800	$947,700			
	Premium per 1000 people mailed	To full mailing B/E not acceptable	Only mail to top deciles	• Top deciles frequently every 4 weeks a contact $550 acceptable			

18
What's Next?

As is evident throughout this book, database marketing is far from a mature marketing science. Some corporations, particularly in financial services, packaged goods, and automobiles, are making major investments in building databases and achieving major marketing successes in using them. But most companies are, at this writing, still tentatively experimenting with it. Worse, others have tried half-hearted ill-planned applications and, based on disappointing results, presumed that it's not for them.

To complicate matters, database marketing is a moving target. As soon as we master one element of it someone comes up with a new marketing idea, a new method of computer personalization, or a more reliable method of mathemetical analysis or modeling. As someone who has seen the entire field of direct marketing go through the same stages, from an instinct-driven communications art to an accepted marketing science, I can predict that its mutated descendant, database marketing, will go through and survive the ordeal.

Change brings with it opportunities and problems. Like Kipling's reference to triumph and disaster, we should "treat those two imposters just the same." Perhaps a better quote would be the statement Tom Collins used often when we worked together: "Problems are opportunities in disguise." The future depends on how we deal with both.

"Privacy" Legislation

The number one threat to database marketing, and to direct marketing as well, is the pending state and federal legislation intending to restrict the use or compilation of mailing lists.

It is ironic that some of the same legislators who pander to the misguided do-gooders are the most avid users of database mail and telephoning. If such legislation is ever passed, note that Congress will probably exempt themselves, as they have from OSHA and other regulations, so that they can continue to use database methods to raise their campaign war chests and target their get-out-the-vote efforts to the various special interests in their districts.

It is also tragic that the proposed restrictions will make it harder to make mailings more selective, therefore subjecting people to more, not less, mail and phone calls. Perhaps if Congress were composed of more scientists and business people and fewer lawyers, they would understand that actions have reactions, and that natural law and human nature survive any legislation.

The opprobrium *junk mail*, when its usage is clarified, means any mailed communication that is not wanted by its recipient—not wanted because it is not relevant or has not been sent to the right household. A similar term can be applied to *junk ads* and *junk commercials* viewed by those not interested in the product category. If publishers and broadcasters realized that such restrictions could eventually apply to them as well, perhaps they would be a little slower to applaud this assault on a competitive advertising medium.

For example, consider automobile commercials on television. If you can't afford a new car, they are junk commercials and a source of irritation. But if you are considering buying a car, you switch channels looking for more auto commercials! People irritated by mail can easily get their names off the lists of all responsible direct marketers, by writing to the Direct Marketing Association. (Or they can, as thousands do, request that their name be added to more lists!)

The fact is that no mailer in his or her right mind wants to mail to people who would not be interested in their product or service. In a way, the whole development of database marketing is dedicated to reducing the amount of unwanted mail, not increasing it!

So I urge established direct marketers and newcomers alike to support industry attempts to fight such legislation, and to participate also in self-corrective steps to address those consumer concerns which are legitimate.

The Ethical Imperative

While it is easy to focus on wrong or misguided legislative restrictions, we who view database marketing as an industry in itself should recognize that these restrictions are based on some legitimate concerns. And, while we have been unable to completely rid ourselves of the scam mail order operators who badly damage the image of direct mail, we must do better in the more highly sensitive arena of database marketing.

There are three principal areas we can take steps to avert legislative interference, and which should be included in our own code of ethics.

1. Disclosure. When we ask people for their names or other information, make it clear what the names are being used for. Some manufacturer's coupons are already using language like this: "To receive promotional mailings, print name and address here." Cigarette companies go even further, with phrases such as "I am willing to receive free samples and incentive items in the mail. . . ." Those who fear that no one would reply should know that similar offers, disclosing only that information and samples may be sent from time to time, have pulled double-digit response rates for some companies.

2. Option. "Check here if you do not wish your name made available to other companies" or similar language is a simple way to assure people know that their names need not be rented out to, or exchanged with, others. It is a reasonable option and one that only a small percentage of customers will exercise.

3. Sensitivity. One would think it should not be necessary to discuss basic good taste, but unfortunately the marketing barrel has its own share of bad apples. And it is precisely to the extent that some of us have abused our freedoms that they are now threatened.

One issue is the need to respect the confidences that people have shared with us. They care what the postal carrier thinks as well as other family members who may see their mail. Therefore age-sensitive people might be more likely to open an AARP solicitation if the return address was not quite so prominent, and certainly the "Days Inn Club for People over 50" could find a better place to proclaim their objective than on the outside envelope. The Better Sex Institute has the sense to use initials, but other mailers proclaim the recipient's interests or affluence on the envelope. Such insensitivity is not only offensive, it doesn't help results.

Equally important is that good taste should be exercised in granting permission to rent a mailing list. I don't believe the list owner should be excused from responsibility when renting a list to companies who have a long history of postal and Better Business Bureau complaints. For that matter, neither should publication media nor broadcast stations, some of which amaze me by continuing to accept advertisements from companies publicly accused of deception.

Another issue is unsolicited phone calls, whether at home or office. I personally don't believe that people should be called at home where there is no prior relationship. If we don't start differentiating between solicited and unsolicited calls in our defense of telemarketing, we may soon lose the right to make any calls.

Calls to business offices are also a problem. Not a week goes by without getting three or four calls from brokerage houses, insurance agents, or real estate brokers. Most try a variety of tricks to get by the receptionist or secretary. "Tell Ed it's Bill calling" and "It's personal" are my favorite annoyances. No one respects a mailing that tricks the reader into opening the envelope (such as check enclosed); there is no reason to respect telephone salespeople who act as if they have nothing legitimate to call about.

The Universal Database

For those concerned with universal privacy, or business people looking for universal efficiency, there is a common long-range solution: the ultimate database.

Imagine a database where all the people in the country have entered a list of their interests and needs, the brands they use, the cars they drive, their tastes in fashion and furniture, their ambitions, their dreams. Imagine another where every business tells us exactly whom would be interested in each kind of product or service the company uses. With these ultimate databases, and a way to keep them up-to-date reflecting changes, no one would ever get unwanted mail or calls. And every marketer would be able to bring news of its products and services to every possible prospect.

This may be pure fantasy. But then again it might be a realizable goal. I have already had meetings with one company about creating the business version. And in some consumer product categories 40-50 percent of users have already responded to one questionnaire or another.

In some countries, even income tax data is used by the government to provide mailing lists based on family configuration and income specifications. In others, the postal system actively works with mailers to find ways to encourage the use of the mails. And here in the United States census data is already a key to geodemographic mailings.

With more and more list compilers pooling resources, and with increasing government interest and cooperation recognizing direct mailers as the postal system's largest customer, who knows? To achieve a goal, you must first state it. Consider it stated.

Interactive Communications

Another area of profound change is the development of interactive home-to-home or office-to-office communications. The changes are geometric. The evolution is dynamic. And the applications to our marketing discipline are inevitable.

Already Prodigy, TVAnswer, and CompUServe have developed hundreds of interactive programs that not only enable subscribers to get information but also to respond. They can open a bank account, pay bills, and make investments from their own homes. They can see a catalog, check availability, and place an order. They can consider vacation alternatives and book hotels and air transportation.

Cable TV is now "addressable" and permits you to order the movie you want, when you want. And new "multiple channel" configurations made possible by optical fiber networks will make hundreds of channels available, on an interactive basis.

Apple has already introduced their latest Macintosh Powerbook; with sound and motion, it offers both entertainment and a business tool anywhere. With fax, modem, or cellular hookups, it can connect with office, library, school, or broadcaster—or with the catalog or showroom of any kind of retailer, manufacturer, or service institution—to see merchandise, get specifications, and place orders. This book was largely written on planes and trains with a Mac Powerbook, which I can connect to all my office files as well as E-mail. It won't be long until we all use them, for all of our communications.

As fantastic as this all sounds it is less of a fantasy than the universal database. The technology is in place and its availability is growing. It is important that in the struggle to master the present we not lose sight of the future.

Agent Matching

This database application is one that is just as *way out* but that I've already recommended for one of my clients who maintains a large sales organization that engages in continuing relationships with clients.

In many companies, sales leads, once received by the marketer, are distributed by rotation or according to seniority or product interest. In this advanced conversion approach the prospect is not only asked about product interest but also about age, education, and interests.

This new method would have all the company's sales representatives fill out a similar questionnaire. When a lead is received, it would be computer-matched against the sales agents in the local office and ranked according to the probability that the sales representatives will relate well to the new prospect. For instance, a salesperson who has a sailboat might be assigned to a new customer who is also a sailor. Or the same with sports enthusiasts. Or with less precise matches, age and other factors can be taken into account and still produce a much better probability of relationship-building than previous methods.

Segmented Media

Another area to watch is the growing recognition by all media of the need to provide the kind of selectivity that until now has only been available in direct mail.

Addressable broadcast is only one area where a former mass media is becoming segmented or even personal. It is now possible to buy advertising in magazines where subscribers can get different versions depending on individual characteristics.

Let's say you are advertising liquor in *Time*. Those subscribers where data is available can receive advertising for the type of liquor they prefer. This type of segmentation has already taken place for automobile and packaged goods advertisers. For instance, Buick used segmented magazine inserts, selected by geodemographic clusters, to improve efficiency of their message. Higher income areas were offered the Buick Park Avenue. In suburban areas Buick station wagons were featured.

The Academic Dimension

With all of the exciting possibilities of database marketing, probably the most significant progress is arriving quietly, without fanfare. It is the infusion of the world of academia into this field until now dominated by those with practical business experience.

Over the years I have watched the Direct Marketing Educational Foundation grow in size and stature, from a training ground for new practitioners to become what it is now: an intellectual force stimulating basic and advanced education at every level. The *Journal of Direct Marketing* (Northwestern University) and the papers presented at DMEF conferences have ranged from the theoretical to the practical.

I have been surprised at the useful information being developed at universities, from analytical methods to simple research. For example, I learned from a DMEF presentation that people are more likely to buy an item in a catalog if there is a similar alternative (with higher price or fewer features) than if only one option is offered.

The database marketing organization of the future would do well to combine the talents of both worlds. For one thing, there are too few of us who have survived the rigors of this result-driven business discipline. For another, the academics bring new planning and research tools and more important a new perspective. Soon the graduates of these courses and the writers of these papers will be available to the business world. We would do well to hire them. In the meantime, it is a win-win situation to support the work of the DMEF and encourage our local universities to add basic and advanced courses in this fast-moving science of database marketing.

I encourage the reader to view this book, or any other on this subject, as only a snapshot of a discipline whose birth and growth can only be called explosive.

The underlying point I have tried to make is that database marketing is an extension of direct marketing, which is rooted in the history and experience of what was once called mail order advertising. It is not a computer science. It is not a mathematical science. Those are tools we use. But the control of planning and execution must be in the hands of marketing strategists.

As such database marketing shares direct marketing's strengths and its weaknesses. The key strength is that everything you do is measurable, and therefore every idea is testable. The weakness is the tendency to copy what others have done, sacrificing freshness and creativity for the illusion of playing it safe.

Database marketing is an idea in itself. It, and its practitioners, will prosper as long as it is led by those who make their living creating ideas.

Appendix A

Economic Value Models

If seeing is believing, then an actual demonstration of the economics of a typical direct marketing proposition should convince even the most skeptical.

The following three tables present three typical situations: a high ticket durable goods product selling for $500, a medium priced $100 durable goods item, and a $3.00 packaged goods product.

They are representative examples of a packaged goods and two durable goods assumptions, showing the potential after-tax profit over a five-year period. It assumes that the acquisition, maintenance, an ongoing relationship will continue, adding new customers and new sales from those customers over the period.

Acquisition presumes the cost of pulling together existing lists and refining them with overlays and selection. I am indebted to Jock Bickert, founder of NDL and a respected leader in this field, for permission to use them.

Acquisition cost often involves advertising in media to generate names for the database, when such names are not otherwise available. The principle is the same, and usually some combination of internal, external, and advertising-generated names will be needed. Obviously these costs will vary widely. For instance, if the entire database can be built with in-packs and free inserts in FSIs, this cost can be nominal.

Database assembly refers to the cost of acquiring the names, either renting them from a firm like NDL or the shared cost or pro-rata average cost of acquiring the names in previous name acquisition promotions. In this case it is assumed to be a rental requiring the indicated cash outlay.

Incentive is the cost of the store coupon, premium, booklet, the shared cost of a contest, or whatever.

Promotion is the cost of the initial mailing or other communication. The figure shown is the combined cost, rightfully presuming that there is an inverse relationship between them.

Database maintenance is the cost of entering and storing the name and address, basically the role of the computer fulfillment service.

Ongoing relationship management is the cost of using the name once acquired, which of course will vary depending on the type of ongoing relationship. This budget is more than adequate to support a monthly newsletter, a quarterly magazine, a premium catalog, or to subsidize some sort of membership relationship.

The figures here are not to be taken as specific examples. Obviously promotions can be designed on a lavish scale or an inexpensive one. And offers can be created that will return the investment at a slower or faster rate than indicated here.

Table A.1. Calculation of Economic Value: Packaged Goods

Assumptions

Name acquisition cost:		
Database assembly	1,000,000 names	$0.24 per name
Incentive/promotion	1,000,000 names	$1.50 per name
Total Acquisition Cost (Yr. 1)	1,000,000 names	$1.74 per name
Ongoing database costs:		
Database maintenance		$0.10 per record
On-going relationship management		$2.20 per record
Total On-going Costs (Yrs. 2-5)		$2.30 per record

Economic Value Analysis

	Year 1	Year 2	Year 3	Year 4	Year 5
Revenues:					
1. Total customers	1,000,000	1,200,000	1,400,000	1,500,000	1,600,000
2. Percentage of customers cross-sold		15.00%	16.00%	17.00%	18.00%
3. Sales price		$3	$3	$3	$3
4. Annual unit sales per customer		30	30	30	30
5. Total Revenue = (1) × (2) × (3) × (4)		$16,200,000	$20,160,000	$22,950,000	$25,920,000
Direct Costs:					
6. Name acquisition costs (assumptions)	$1,740,000	$348,000	$348,000	$174,000	$174,000
7. On-going database costs (assumptions)	$1,740,000	$2,300,000	$2,760,000	$3,220,000	$3,450,000
8. *Total Database Costs* = (6) + (7)	$1,740,000	$2,648,000	$3,108,000	$3,394,000	$3,624,000
9. Cost of goods sold 60% × (5)		$9,720,000	$12,096,000	$13,770,000	$15,552,000
10. *Total Direct Costs* = (8) + (9)	$1,740,000	$12,368,000	$15,204,000	$17,164,000	$19,176,000
Gross Profits:					
11. Gross profits = (5) − (10)	($1,740,000)	$3,832,000	$4,956,000	$5,786,000	$6,744,000
Operating Expenses:					
12. Selling G&A = 18% × (5)		$2,916,000	$3,628,800	$4,131,000	$4,665,600
13. Taxes at 34%		$311,440	$451,248	$562,700	$706,565
Net Profits:					
14. Profit After Tax = (11)-(12)-(13)	($1,740,000)	$604,560	$875,952	$1,092,300	$1,371,744
15. *Cumulative PAT*	($1,740,000)	($1,135,440)	($259,488)	$832,812	$2,204,556

Discount factor:	12%
Economic Value (NPV):	$1,024,406
Return on Investment (IRR):	36%

Table A.2. Calculation of Economic Value: Medium-Priced Durable Goods

Assumptions

Name acquisition cost:		
Database assembly	500,000 names	$0.21 per name
Incentive/promotion	500,000 names	$1.50 per name
Total Acquisition Cost (Yr. 1)	500,000 names	$1.74 per name

Ongoing database costs:	
Database maintenance	$0.08 per record
On-going relationship management	$2.25 per record
Total On-going Costs (Yrs. 2–5)	$2.33 per record

Economic Value Analysis

	Year 1	Year 2	Year 3	Year 4	Year 5
Revenues:					
1. Total customers	500,000	800,000	1,000,000	1,100,000	1,200,000
2. Percentage of customers cross-sold		5.00%	5.00%	5.00%	5.00%
3. Sales price		$100	$100	$100	$100
4. Annual unit sales per customer		2	2.25	2.5	2.5
5. Total Revenue = (1) × (2) × (3) × (4)		$8,000,000	$11,250,000	$13,750,000	$15,000,000
Direct Costs:					
6. Name acquisition costs (assumptions)	$855,000	$513,000	$342,000	$171,000	$171,000
7. On-going database costs (assumptions)	$855,000	$1,165,000	$1,864,000	$2,330,000	$2,563,000
8. Total Database Costs = (6) + (7)	$855,000	$1,678,000	$2,206,000	$2,501,000	$2,734,000
9. Cost of goods sold 60% × (5)		$4,800,000	$6,750,000	$8,250,000	$9,000,000
10. Total Direct Costs = (8) + (9)	$855,000	$6,478,000	$8,956,000	$10,751,000	$11,734,000
Gross Profits:					
11. Gross profits = (5) – (10)	($855,000)	$1,522,000	$2,294,000	$2,999,000	$3,266,000
Operating Expenses:					
12. Selling G&A = 15% × (5)	$1,200,000	$1,687,500	$2,062,500	$2,250,000	
13. Taxes at 34%	$109,480	$206,210	$318,410	$345,440	
Net Profits:					
14. Profit After Tax = (11)–(12)–(13)	($855,000)	$212,520	$400,290	$618,090	$670,560
15. Cumulative PAT	($855,000)	($642,480)	($242,190)	$375,900	$1,046,460

Discount factor:	12%
Economic Value (NPV):	$464,246
Return on Investment (IRR):	33%

©1998 National Demographics & Lifestyles

Table A.3. Calculation of Economic Value: High-Ticket Durable Goods

Assumptions

Name acquisition cost:		
Database assembly	300,000 names	$0.18 per name
Incentive/promotion	300,000 names	$2.00 per name
Total Acquisition Cost (Yr. 1)	300,000 names	$2.18 per name
Ongoing database costs:		
Database maintenance		$0.07 per record
On-going relationship management		$2.50 per record
Total On-going Costs (Yrs. 2–5)		$2.57 per record

Economic Value Analysis

	Year 1	Year 2	Year 3	Year 4	Year 5
Revenues:					
1. Total customers	300,000	550,000	750,000	950,000	1,100,000
2. Percentage of customers cross-sold		2.00%	2.25%	2.50%	2.50%
3. Sales price		$500	$500	$500	$500
4. Annual unit sales per customer		1	1	1	1
5. Total Revenue = (1) × (2) × (3) × (4)		$5,500,000	$8,437,500	$11,875,000	$18,750,000
Direct Costs:					
6. Name acquisition costs (assumptions)	$654,000	$545,000	$436,000	$436,000	$327,000
7. On-going database costs (assumptions)		$771,000	$1,413,500	$1,927,500	$2,441,500
8. Total Database Costs = (6) + (7)	$654,000	$1,316,000	$1,849,500	$2,363,500	$2,768,500
9. Cost of goods sold 60% × (5)		$3,300,000	$5,062,500	$7,125,000	$8,250,000
10. Total Direct Costs = (8) + (9)	$654,000	$4,606,000	$6,912,000	$9,488,500	$11,018,500
Gross Profits:					
11. Gross profits = (5) – (10)	($654,000)	$884,000	$1,525,500	$2,386,500	$2,731,500
12. Extended warranty profit $3.00 × new cust.	$750,000	$600,000	$600,000	$450,000	
13. Total Gross Profits = (11) + (12)	($654,000)	$1,634,000	$2,125,500	$2,986,500	
Operating Expenses:					
14. Selling, G&A = 20% × (5)		$1,100,000	$1,687,500	$2,375,000	$2,750,000
15. Taxes at 34%		$181,560	$148,920	$207,910	$146,710
Net Profits:					
Profit After Tax = (11)–(12)–(13)	($1,740,000)	$604,560	$875,952	$1,092,300	$1,371,744
Cumulative PAT	($1,740,000)	($1,135,440)	($259,488)	$832,812	$2,204,556

Discount factor:	12%
Economic Value (NPV):	$1,024,406
Return on Investment (IRR):	36%

© 1993 National Demographics & Lifestyles.

239

Statistical Projection Tables

As direct marketing has evolved into database marketing, one of the dramatic changes has been in the range of response rates that can be achieved. It stands to reason that a proposition that used to produce a 7 percent response rate can achieve 14 percent if an unproductive half of the list is eliminated. Therefore statistical validity tables which were more than adequate at a high range of 10 percent have been useless for many database programs. The fact is that we are already realizing response rates that test out in the upper range of these charts and, as always, the margins of error hold true in roll-outs.

For further explanation of these tables and how to use them, I refer the reader to my book *Direct Marketing:Strategy/Planning/ Execution*.

The tables were prepared by Lloyd Kieran a prominent direct marketing consultant operating out of Laguna Niguel, California.

Direct Mail Projection Tables

95% Confidence Level - Standard Deviation: 1.960

ANTICIPATED PERCENT RESPONSE

Sample Size (000)	.5% ±%	Variance Low	High	1.0% ±%	Variance Low	High	1.5% ±%	Variance Low	High	2.0% ±%	Variance Low	High	2.5% ±%	Variance Low	High	3.0% ±%	Variance Low	High
1.0	87.4%	.06%	.94%	61.7%	.38%	1.62%	50.2%	.75%	2.25%	43.4%	1.13%	2.87%	38.7%	1.53%	3.47%	35.2%	1.94%	4.06%
2.5	55.3%	.22%	.78%	39.0%	.61%	1.39%	31.8%	1.02%	1.98%	27.4%	1.45%	2.55%	24.5%	1.89%	3.11%	22.3%	2.33%	3.67%
5.0	39.1%	.30%	.70%	27.6%	.72%	1.28%	22.5%	1.16%	1.84%	19.4%	1.61%	2.39%	17.3%	2.07%	2.93%	15.8%	2.53%	3.47%
7.5	31.9%	.34%	.66%	22.5%	.77%	1.23%	18.3%	1.22%	1.78%	15.8%	1.68%	2.32%	14.1%	2.15%	2.85%	12.9%	2.61%	3.39%
10.0	27.6%	.36%	.64%	19.5%	.80%	1.20%	15.9%	1.26%	1.74%	13.7%	1.73%	2.27%	12.2%	2.19%	2.81%	11.1%	2.67%	3.33%
12.5	24.7%	.38%	.62%	17.4%	.83%	1.17%	14.2%	1.29%	1.71%	12.3%	1.75%	2.25%	10.9%	2.23%	2.77%	10.0%	2.70%	3.30%
15.0	22.6%	.39%	.61%	15.9%	.84%	1.16%	13.0%	1.31%	1.69%	11.2%	1.78%	2.22%	10.0%	2.25%	2.75%	9.1%	2.73%	3.27%
17.5	20.9%	.40%	.60%	14.7%	.85%	1.15%	12.0%	1.32%	1.68%	10.4%	1.79%	2.21%	9.3%	2.27%	2.73%	8.4%	2.75%	3.25%
20.0	19.6%	.40%	.60%	13.8%	.86%	1.14%	11.2%	1.33%	1.67%	9.7%	1.81%	2.19%	8.7%	2.28%	2.72%	7.9%	2.76%	3.24%
25.0	17.5%	.41%	.59%	12.3%	.88%	1.12%	10.0%	1.35%	1.65%	8.7%	1.83%	2.17%	7.7%	2.31%	2.69%	7.0%	2.79%	3.21%
30.0	16.0%	.42%	.58%	11.3%	.89%	1.11%	9.2%	1.36%	1.64%	7.9%	1.84%	2.16%	7.1%	2.32%	2.68%	6.4%	2.81%	3.19%
35.0	14.8%	.43%	.57%	10.4%	.90%	1.10%	8.5%	1.37%	1.63%	7.3%	1.85%	2.15%	6.5%	2.34%	2.66%	6.0%	2.82%	3.18%
40.0	13.8%	.43%	.57%	9.8%	.90%	1.10%	7.9%	1.38%	1.62%	6.9%	1.86%	2.14%	6.1%	2.35%	2.65%	5.6%	2.83%	3.17%
45.0	13.0%	.43%	.57%	9.2%	.91%	1.09%	7.5%	1.39%	1.61%	6.5%	1.87%	2.13%	5.8%	2.36%	2.64%	5.3%	2.84%	3.16%
50.0	12.4%	.44%	.56%	8.7%	.91%	1.09%	7.1%	1.39%	1.61%	6.1%	1.88%	2.12%	5.5%	2.36%	2.64%	5.0%	2.85%	3.15%
60.0	11.3%	.44%	.56%	8.0%	.92%	1.08%	6.5%	1.40%	1.60%	5.6%	1.89%	2.11%	5.0%	2.38%	2.62%	4.5%	2.86%	3.14%
70.0	10.5%	.45%	.55%	7.4%	.93%	1.07%	6.0%	1.41%	1.59%	5.2%	1.90%	2.10%	4.6%	2.38%	2.62%	4.2%	2.87%	3.13%
80.0	9.8%	.45%	.55%	6.9%	.93%	1.07%	5.6%	1.42%	1.58%	4.9%	1.90%	2.10%	4.3%	2.39%	2.61%	3.9%	2.88%	3.12%
90.0	9.2%	.45%	.55%	6.5%	.93%	1.07%	5.3%	1.42%	1.58%	4.6%	1.91%	2.09%	4.1%	2.40%	2.60%	3.7%	2.89%	3.11%
100.0	8.7%	.46%	.54%	6.2%	.94%	1.06%	5.0%	1.42%	1.58%	4.3%	1.91%	2.09%	3.9%	2.40%	2.60%	3.5%	2.89%	3.11%

Direct Mail Projection Tables

95% Confidence Level - Standard Deviation: 1.960

ANTICIPATED PERCENT RESPONSE

Sample Size (000)	3.5% ±%	Variance Low	High	4.0% ±%	Variance Low	High	4.5% ±%	Variance Low	High	5.0% ±%	Variance Low	High	5.5% ±%	Variance Low	High	6.0% ±%	Variance Low	High
1.0	32.5%	2.36%	4.64%	30.4%	2.79%	5.21%	28.6%	3.22%	5.78%	27.0%	3.65%	6.35%	25.7%	4.09%	6.91%	24.5%	4.53%	7.47%
2.5	20.6%	2.78%	4.22%	19.2%	3.23%	4.77%	18.1%	3.69%	5.31%	17.1%	4.15%	5.85%	16.2%	4.61%	6.39%	15.5%	5.07%	6.93%
5.0	14.6%	2.99%	4.01%	13.6%	3.46%	4.54%	12.8%	3.93%	5.07%	12.1%	4.40%	5.60%	11.5%	4.87%	6.13%	11.0%	5.34%	6.66%
7.5	11.9%	3.08%	3.92%	11.1%	3.56%	4.44%	10.4%	4.03%	4.97%	9.9%	4.51%	5.49%	9.4%	4.98%	6.02%	9.0%	5.46%	6.54%
10.0	10.3%	3.14%	3.86%	9.6%	3.62%	4.38%	9.0%	4.09%	4.91%	8.5%	4.57%	5.43%	8.1%	5.05%	5.95%	7.8%	5.53%	6.47%
12.5	9.2%	3.18%	3.82%	8.6%	3.66%	4.34%	8.1%	4.14%	4.86%	7.6%	4.62%	5.38%	7.3%	5.10%	5.90%	6.9%	5.58%	6.42%
15.0	8.4%	3.21%	3.79%	7.8%	3.69%	4.31%	7.4%	4.17%	4.83%	7.0%	4.65%	5.35%	6.6%	5.14%	5.86%	6.3%	5.62%	6.38%
17.5	7.8%	3.23%	3.77%	7.3%	3.71%	4.29%	6.8%	4.19%	4.81%	6.5%	4.68%	5.32%	6.1%	5.16%	5.84%	5.9%	5.65%	6.35%
20.0	7.3%	3.25%	3.75%	6.8%	3.73%	4.27%	6.4%	4.21%	4.79%	6.0%	4.70%	5.30%	5.7%	5.18%	5.82%	5.5%	5.67%	6.33%
25.0	6.5%	3.27%	3.73%	6.1%	3.76%	4.24%	5.7%	4.24%	4.76%	5.4%	4.73%	5.27%	5.1%	5.22%	5.78%	4.9%	5.71%	6.29%
30.0	5.9%	3.29%	3.71%	5.5%	3.78%	4.22%	5.2%	4.27%	4.73%	4.9%	4.75%	5.25%	4.7%	5.24%	5.76%	4.5%	5.73%	6.27%
35.0	5.5%	3.31%	3.69%	5.1%	3.79%	4.21%	4.8%	4.28%	4.72%	4.6%	4.77%	5.23%	4.3%	5.26%	5.74%	4.1%	5.75%	6.25%
40.0	5.1%	3.32%	3.68%	4.8%	3.81%	4.19%	4.5%	4.30%	4.70%	4.3%	4.79%	5.21%	4.1%	5.28%	5.72%	3.9%	5.77%	6.23%
45.0	4.9%	3.33%	3.67%	4.5%	3.82%	4.18%	4.3%	4.31%	4.69%	4.0%	4.80%	5.20%	3.8%	5.29%	5.71%	3.7%	5.78%	6.22%
50.0	4.6%	3.34%	3.66%	4.3%	3.83%	4.17%	4.0%	4.32%	4.68%	3.8%	4.81%	5.19%	3.6%	5.30%	5.70%	3.5%	5.79%	6.21%
60.0	4.2%	3.35%	3.65%	3.9%	3.84%	4.16%	3.7%	4.33%	4.67%	3.5%	4.83%	5.17%	3.3%	5.32%	5.68%	3.2%	5.81%	6.19%
70.0	3.9%	3.36%	3.64%	3.6%	3.85%	4.15%	3.4%	4.35%	4.65%	3.2%	4.84%	5.16%	3.1%	5.33%	5.67%	2.9%	5.82%	6.18%
80.0	3.6%	3.37%	3.63%	3.4%	3.86%	4.14%	3.2%	4.36%	4.64%	3.0%	4.85%	5.15%	2.9%	5.34%	5.66%	2.7%	5.84%	6.16%
90.0	3.4%	3.38%	3.62%	3.2%	3.87%	4.13%	3.0%	4.36%	4.64%	2.8%	4.86%	5.14%	2.7%	5.35%	5.65%	2.6%	5.84%	6.16%
100.0	3.3%	3.39%	3.61%	3.0%	3.88%	4.12%	2.9%	4.37%	4.63%	2.7%	4.86%	5.14%	2.6%	5.36%	5.64%	2.5%	5.85%	6.15%

Direct Mail Projection Tables

95% Confidence Level - Standard Deviation: 1.960

ANTICIPATED PERCENT RESPONSE

Sample Size (000)	6.5% ±%	Variance Low	High	7.0% ±%	Variance Low	High	7.5% ±%	Variance Low	High	8.0% ±%	Variance Low	High	8.5% ±%	Variance Low	High	9.0% ±%	Variance Low	High
1.0	23.5%	4.97%	8.03%	22.6%	5.42%	8.58%	21.8%	5.87%	9.13%	21.0%	6.32%	9.68%	20.3%	6.77%	10.23%	19.7%	7.23%	10.77%
2.5	14.9%	5.53%	7.47%	14.3%	6.00%	8.00%	13.8%	6.47%	8.53%	13.3%	6.94%	9.06%	12.9%	7.41%	9.59%	12.5%	7.88%	10.12%
5.0	10.5%	5.82%	7.18%	10.1%	6.29%	7.71%	9.7%	6.77%	8.23%	9.4%	7.25%	8.75%	9.1%	7.73%	9.27%	8.8%	8.21%	9.79%
7.5	8.6%	5.94%	7.06%	8.2%	6.42%	7.58%	7.9%	6.90%	8.10%	7.7%	7.39%	8.61%	7.4%	7.87%	9.13%	7.2%	8.35%	9.65%
10.0	7.4%	6.02%	6.98%	7.1%	6.50%	7.50%	6.9%	6.98%	8.02%	6.6%	7.47%	8.53%	6.4%	7.95%	9.05%	6.2%	8.44%	9.56%
12.5	6.6%	6.07%	6.93%	6.4%	6.55%	7.45%	6.2%	7.04%	7.96%	5.9%	7.52%	8.48%	5.8%	8.01%	8.99%	5.6%	8.50%	9.50%
15.0	6.1%	6.11%	6.89%	5.8%	6.59%	7.41%	5.6%	7.08%	7.92%	5.4%	7.57%	8.43%	5.3%	8.05%	8.95%	5.1%	8.54%	9.46%
17.5	5.6%	6.13%	6.87%	5.4%	6.62%	7.38%	5.2%	7.11%	7.89%	5.0%	7.60%	8.40%	4.9%	8.09%	8.91%	4.7%	8.58%	9.42%
20.0	5.3%	6.16%	6.84%	5.1%	6.65%	7.35%	4.9%	7.13%	7.87%	4.7%	7.62%	8.38%	4.5%	8.11%	8.89%	4.4%	8.60%	9.40%
25.0	4.7%	6.19%	6.81%	4.5%	6.68%	7.32%	4.4%	7.17%	7.83%	4.2%	7.66%	8.34%	4.1%	8.15%	8.85%	3.9%	8.65%	9.35%
30.0	4.3%	6.22%	6.78%	4.1%	6.71%	7.29%	4.0%	7.20%	7.80%	3.8%	7.69%	8.31%	3.7%	8.18%	8.82%	3.6%	8.68%	9.32%
35.0	4.0%	6.24%	6.76%	3.8%	6.73%	7.27%	3.7%	7.22%	7.78%	3.6%	7.72%	8.28%	3.4%	8.21%	8.79%	3.3%	8.70%	9.30%
40.0	3.7%	6.26%	6.74%	3.6%	6.75%	7.25%	3.4%	7.24%	7.76%	3.3%	7.73%	8.27%	3.2%	8.23%	8.77%	3.1%	8.72%	9.28%
45.0	3.5%	6.27%	6.73%	3.4%	6.76%	7.24%	3.2%	7.26%	7.74%	3.1%	7.75%	8.25%	3.0%	8.24%	8.76%	2.9%	8.74%	9.26%
50.0	3.3%	6.28%	6.72%	3.2%	6.78%	7.22%	3.1%	7.27%	7.73%	3.0%	7.76%	8.24%	2.9%	8.26%	8.74%	2.8%	8.75%	9.25%
60.0	3.0%	6.30%	6.70%	2.9%	6.80%	7.20%	2.8%	7.29%	7.71%	2.7%	7.78%	8.22%	2.6%	8.28%	8.72%	2.5%	8.77%	9.23%
70.0	2.8%	6.32%	6.68%	2.7%	6.81%	7.19%	2.6%	7.30%	7.70%	2.5%	7.80%	8.20%	2.4%	8.29%	8.71%	2.4%	8.79%	9.21%
80.0	2.6%	6.33%	6.67%	2.5%	6.82%	7.18%	2.4%	7.32%	7.68%	2.3%	7.81%	8.19%	2.3%	8.31%	8.69%	2.2%	8.80%	9.20%
90.0	2.5%	6.34%	6.66%	2.4%	6.83%	7.17%	2.3%	7.33%	7.67%	2.2%	7.82%	8.18%	2.1%	8.32%	8.68%	2.1%	8.81%	9.19%
100.0	2.4%	6.35%	6.65%	2.3%	6.84%	7.16%	2.2%	7.34%	7.66%	2.1%	7.83%	8.17%	2.0%	8.33%	8.67%	2.0%	8.82%	9.18%

Direct Mail Projection Tables

95% Confidence Level - Standard Deviation: 1.960

ANTICIPATED PERCENT RESPONSE

Sample Size (000)	9.5% ±%	Variance Low	High	10.0% ±%	Variance Low	High	10.5% ±%	Variance Low	High	11.0% ±%	Variance Low	High	11.5% ±%	Variance Low	High	12.0% ±%	Variance Low	High
1.0	19.1%	7.68%	11.32%	18.6%	8.14%	11.86%	18.1%	8.60%	12.40%	17.6%	9.06%	12.94%	17.2%	9.52%	13.48%	16.8%	9.99%	14.01%
2.5	12.1%	8.35%	10.65%	11.8%	8.82%	11.18%	11.4%	9.30%	11.70%	11.2%	9.77%	12.23%	10.9%	10.25%	12.75%	10.6%	10.73%	13.27%
5.0	8.6%	8.69%	10.31%	8.3%	9.17%	10.83%	8.1%	9.65%	11.35%	7.9%	10.13%	11.87%	7.7%	10.62%	12.38%	7.5%	11.10%	12.90%
7.5	7.0%	8.84%	10.16%	6.8%	9.32%	10.68%	6.6%	9.81%	11.19%	6.4%	10.29%	11.71%	6.3%	10.78%	12.22%	6.1%	11.26%	12.74%
10.0	6.0%	8.93%	10.07%	5.9%	9.41%	10.59%	5.7%	9.90%	11.10%	5.6%	10.39%	11.61%	5.4%	10.87%	12.13%	5.3%	11.36%	12.64%
12.5	5.4%	8.99%	10.01%	5.3%	9.47%	10.53%	5.1%	9.96%	11.04%	5.0%	10.45%	11.55%	4.9%	10.94%	12.06%	4.7%	11.43%	12.57%
15.0	4.9%	9.03%	9.97%	4.8%	9.52%	10.48%	4.7%	10.01%	10.99%	4.6%	10.50%	11.50%	4.4%	10.99%	12.01%	4.3%	11.48%	12.52%
17.5	4.6%	9.07%	9.93%	4.4%	9.56%	10.44%	4.3%	10.05%	10.95%	4.2%	10.54%	11.46%	4.1%	11.03%	11.97%	4.0%	11.52%	12.48%
20.0	4.3%	9.09%	9.91%	4.2%	9.58%	10.42%	4.0%	10.08%	10.92%	3.9%	10.57%	11.43%	3.8%	11.06%	11.94%	3.8%	11.55%	12.45%
25.0	3.8%	9.14%	9.86%	3.7%	9.63%	10.37%	3.6%	10.12%	10.88%	3.5%	10.61%	11.39%	3.4%	11.10%	11.90%	3.4%	11.60%	12.40%
30.0	3.5%	9.17%	9.83%	3.4%	9.66%	10.34%	3.3%	10.15%	10.85%	3.2%	10.65%	11.35%	3.1%	11.14%	11.86%	3.1%	11.63%	12.37%
35.0	3.2%	9.19%	9.81%	3.1%	9.69%	10.31%	3.1%	10.18%	10.82%	3.0%	10.67%	11.33%	2.9%	11.17%	11.83%	2.8%	11.66%	12.34%
40.0	3.0%	9.21%	9.79%	2.9%	9.71%	10.29%	2.9%	10.20%	10.80%	2.8%	10.69%	11.31%	2.7%	11.19%	11.81%	2.7%	11.68%	12.32%
45.0	2.9%	9.23%	9.77%	2.8%	9.72%	10.28%	2.7%	10.22%	10.78%	2.6%	10.71%	11.29%	2.6%	11.21%	11.79%	2.5%	11.70%	12.30%
50.0	2.7%	9.24%	9.76%	2.6%	9.74%	10.26%	2.6%	10.23%	10.77%	2.5%	10.73%	11.27%	2.4%	11.22%	11.78%	2.4%	11.72%	12.28%
60.0	2.5%	9.27%	9.73%	2.4%	9.76%	10.24%	2.3%	10.25%	10.75%	2.3%	10.75%	11.25%	2.2%	11.24%	11.76%	2.2%	11.74%	12.26%
70.0	2.3%	9.28%	9.72%	2.2%	9.78%	10.22%	2.2%	10.27%	10.73%	2.1%	10.77%	11.23%	2.1%	11.26%	11.74%	2.0%	11.76%	12.24%
80.0	2.1%	9.30%	9.70%	2.1%	9.79%	10.21%	2.0%	10.29%	10.71%	2.0%	10.78%	11.22%	1.9%	11.28%	11.72%	1.9%	11.77%	12.23%
90.0	2.0%	9.31%	9.69%	2.0%	9.80%	10.20%	1.9%	10.30%	10.70%	1.9%	10.80%	11.20%	1.8%	11.29%	11.71%	1.8%	11.79%	12.21%
100.0	1.9%	9.32%	9.68%	1.9%	9.81%	10.19%	1.8%	10.31%	10.69%	1.8%	10.81%	11.19%	1.7%	11.30%	11.70%	1.7%	11.80%	12.20%

Direct Mail Projection Tables

95% Confidence Level - Standard Deviation: 1.960

ANTICIPATED PERCENT RESPONSE

Sample Size (000)	13.0% ±%	Variance Low	High	14.0% ±%	Variance Low	High	15.0% ±%	Variance Low	High	16.0% ±%	Variance Low	High	17.0% ±%	Variance Low	High	18.0% ±%	Variance Low	High
1.0	16.0%	10.92%	15.08%	15.4%	11.85%	16.15%	14.8%	12.79%	17.21%	14.2%	13.73%	18.27%	13.7%	14.67%	19.33%	13.2%	15.62%	20.38%
2.5	10.1%	11.68%	14.32%	9.7%	12.64%	15.36%	9.3%	13.60%	16.40%	9.0%	14.56%	17.44%	8.7%	15.53%	18.47%	8.4%	16.49%	19.51%
5.0	7.2%	12.07%	13.93%	6.9%	13.04%	14.96%	6.6%	14.01%	15.99%	6.4%	14.98%	17.02%	6.1%	15.96%	18.04%	5.9%	16.94%	19.06%
7.5	5.9%	12.24%	13.76%	5.6%	13.21%	14.79%	5.4%	14.19%	15.81%	5.2%	15.17%	16.83%	5.0%	16.15%	17.85%	4.8%	17.13%	18.87%
10.0	5.1%	12.34%	13.66%	4.9%	13.32%	14.68%	4.7%	14.30%	15.70%	4.5%	15.28%	16.72%	4.3%	16.26%	17.74%	4.2%	17.25%	18.75%
12.5	4.5%	12.41%	13.59%	4.3%	13.39%	14.61%	4.2%	14.37%	15.63%	4.0%	15.36%	16.64%	3.9%	16.34%	17.66%	3.7%	17.33%	18.67%
15.0	4.1%	12.46%	13.54%	4.0%	13.44%	14.56%	3.8%	14.43%	15.57%	3.7%	15.41%	16.59%	3.5%	16.40%	17.60%	3.4%	17.39%	18.61%
17.5	3.8%	12.50%	13.50%	3.7%	13.49%	14.51%	3.5%	14.47%	15.53%	3.4%	15.46%	16.54%	3.3%	16.44%	17.56%	3.2%	17.43%	18.57%
20.0	3.6%	12.53%	13.47%	3.4%	13.52%	14.48%	3.3%	14.51%	15.49%	3.2%	15.49%	16.51%	3.1%	16.48%	17.52%	3.0%	17.47%	18.53%
25.0	3.2%	12.58%	13.42%	3.1%	13.57%	14.43%	3.0%	14.56%	15.44%	2.8%	15.55%	16.45%	2.7%	16.53%	17.47%	2.6%	17.52%	18.48%
30.0	2.9%	12.62%	13.38%	2.8%	13.61%	14.39%	2.7%	14.60%	15.40%	2.6%	15.59%	16.41%	2.5%	16.57%	17.43%	2.4%	17.57%	18.43%
35.0	2.7%	12.65%	13.35%	2.6%	13.64%	14.36%	2.5%	14.63%	15.37%	2.4%	15.62%	16.38%	2.3%	16.61%	17.39%	2.2%	17.60%	18.40%
40.0	2.5%	12.67%	13.33%	2.4%	13.66%	14.34%	2.3%	14.65%	15.35%	2.2%	15.64%	16.36%	2.2%	16.63%	17.37%	2.1%	17.62%	18.38%
45.0	2.4%	12.69%	13.31%	2.3%	13.68%	14.32%	2.2%	14.67%	15.33%	2.1%	15.66%	16.34%	2.0%	16.65%	17.35%	2.0%	17.65%	18.35%
50.0	2.3%	12.71%	13.29%	2.2%	13.70%	14.30%	2.1%	14.69%	15.31%	2.0%	15.68%	16.32%	1.9%	16.67%	17.33%	1.9%	17.66%	18.34%
60.0	2.1%	12.73%	13.27%	2.0%	13.72%	14.28%	1.9%	14.71%	15.29%	1.8%	15.71%	16.29%	1.8%	16.70%	17.30%	1.7%	17.69%	18.31%
70.0	1.9%	12.75%	13.25%	1.8%	13.74%	14.26%	1.8%	14.74%	15.26%	1.7%	15.73%	16.27%	1.6%	16.72%	17.28%	1.6%	17.72%	18.28%
80.0	1.8%	12.77%	13.23%	1.7%	13.76%	14.24%	1.6%	14.75%	15.25%	1.6%	15.75%	16.25%	1.5%	16.74%	17.26%	1.5%	17.73%	18.27%
90.0	1.7%	12.78%	13.22%	1.6%	13.77%	14.23%	1.6%	14.77%	15.23%	1.5%	15.76%	16.24%	1.4%	16.75%	17.25%	1.4%	17.75%	18.25%
100.0	1.6%	12.79%	13.21%	1.5%	13.78%	14.22%	1.5%	14.78%	15.22%	1.4%	15.77%	16.23%	1.4%	16.77%	17.23%	1.3%	17.76%	18.24%

Direct Mail Projection Tables

95% Confidence Level - Standard Deviation: 1.960

ANTICIPATED PERCENT RESPONSE

Sample Size (000)	19.0% ±%	Variance Low	High	20.0% ±%	Variance Low	High	21.0% ±%	Variance Low	High	22.0% ±%	Variance Low	High	23.0% ±%	Variance Low	High	24.0% ±%	Variance Low	High
1.0	12.8%	16.57%	21.43%	12.4%	17.52%	22.48%	12.0%	18.48%	23.52%	11.7%	19.43%	24.57%	11.3%	20.39%	25.61%	11.0%	21.35%	26.65%
2.5	8.1%	17.46%	20.54%	7.8%	18.43%	21.57%	7.6%	19.40%	22.60%	7.4%	20.38%	23.62%	7.2%	21.35%	24.65%	7.0%	22.33%	25.67%
5.0	5.7%	17.91%	20.09%	5.5%	18.89%	21.11%	5.4%	19.87%	22.13%	5.2%	20.85%	23.15%	5.1%	21.83%	24.17%	4.9%	22.82%	25.18%
7.5	4.7%	18.11%	19.89%	4.5%	19.09%	20.91%	4.4%	20.08%	21.92%	4.3%	21.06%	22.94%	4.1%	22.05%	23.95%	4.0%	23.03%	24.97%
10.0	4.0%	18.23%	19.77%	3.9%	19.22%	20.78%	3.8%	20.20%	21.80%	3.7%	21.19%	22.81%	3.6%	22.18%	23.82%	3.5%	23.16%	24.84%
12.5	3.6%	18.31%	19.69%	3.5%	19.30%	20.70%	3.4%	20.29%	21.71%	3.3%	21.27%	22.73%	3.2%	22.26%	23.74%	3.1%	23.25%	24.75%
15.0	3.3%	18.37%	19.63%	3.2%	19.36%	20.64%	3.1%	20.35%	21.65%	3.0%	21.34%	22.66%	2.9%	22.33%	23.67%	2.8%	23.32%	24.68%
17.5	3.1%	18.42%	19.58%	3.0%	19.41%	20.59%	2.9%	20.40%	21.60%	2.8%	21.39%	22.61%	2.7%	22.38%	23.62%	2.6%	23.37%	24.63%
20.0	2.9%	18.46%	19.54%	2.8%	19.45%	20.55%	2.7%	20.44%	21.56%	2.6%	21.43%	22.57%	2.5%	22.42%	23.58%	2.5%	23.41%	24.59%
25.0	2.6%	18.51%	19.49%	2.5%	19.50%	20.50%	2.4%	20.50%	21.50%	2.3%	21.49%	22.51%	2.3%	22.48%	23.52%	2.2%	23.47%	24.53%
30.0	2.3%	18.56%	19.44%	2.3%	19.55%	20.45%	2.2%	20.54%	21.46%	2.1%	21.53%	22.47%	2.1%	22.52%	23.48%	2.0%	23.52%	24.48%
35.0	2.2%	18.59%	19.41%	2.1%	19.58%	20.42%	2.0%	20.57%	21.43%	2.0%	21.57%	22.43%	1.9%	22.56%	23.44%	1.9%	23.55%	24.45%
40.0	2.0%	18.62%	19.38%	2.0%	19.61%	20.39%	1.9%	20.60%	21.40%	1.8%	21.59%	22.41%	1.8%	22.59%	23.41%	1.7%	23.58%	24.42%
45.0	1.9%	18.64%	19.36%	1.8%	19.63%	20.37%	1.8%	20.62%	21.38%	1.7%	21.62%	22.38%	1.7%	22.61%	23.39%	1.6%	23.61%	24.39%
50.0	1.8%	18.65%	19.34%	1.8%	19.65%	20.35%	1.7%	20.64%	21.36%	1.7%	21.64%	22.36%	1.6%	22.63%	23.37%	1.6%	23.63%	24.37%
60.0	1.7%	18.69%	19.31%	1.6%	19.68%	20.32%	1.6%	20.67%	21.33%	1.5%	21.67%	22.33%	1.5%	22.66%	23.34%	1.4%	23.66%	24.34%
70.0	1.5%	18.71%	19.29%	1.5%	19.70%	20.30%	1.4%	20.70%	21.30%	1.4%	21.69%	22.31%	1.4%	22.69%	23.31%	1.3%	23.68%	24.32%
80.0	1.4%	18.73%	19.27%	1.4%	19.72%	20.28%	1.3%	20.72%	21.28%	1.3%	21.71%	22.29%	1.3%	22.71%	23.29%	1.2%	23.70%	24.30%
90.0	1.3%	18.74%	19.26%	1.3%	19.74%	20.26%	1.3%	20.73%	21.27%	1.2%	21.73%	22.27%	1.2%	22.73%	23.27%	1.2%	23.72%	24.28%
100.0	1.3%	18.76%	19.24%	1.2%	19.75%	20.25%	1.2%	20.75%	21.25%	1.2%	21.74%	22.26%	1.1%	22.74%	23.26%	1.1%	23.74%	24.26%

Direct Mail Projection Tables

95% Confidence Level - Standard Deviation: 1.960

Sample Size (000)	25.0% ±%	Variance Low	High	26.0% ±%	Variance Low	High	27.0% ±%	Variance Low	High	28.0% ±%	Variance Low	High	29.0% ±%	Variance Low	High	30.0% ±%	Variance Low	High
1.0	10.7%	22.32%	27.68%	10.5%	23.28%	28.72%	10.2%	24.25%	29.75%	9.9%	25.22%	30.78%	9.7%	26.19%	31.81%	9.5%	27.16%	32.84%
2.5	6.8%	23.30%	26.70%	6.6%	24.28%	27.72%	6.4%	25.26%	28.74%	6.3%	26.24%	29.76%	6.1%	27.22%	30.78%	6.0%	28.20%	31.80%
5.0	4.8%	23.80%	26.20%	4.7%	24.78%	27.22%	4.6%	25.77%	28.23%	4.4%	26.76%	29.24%	4.3%	27.74%	30.26%	4.2%	28.73%	31.27%
7.5	3.9%	24.02%	25.98%	3.8%	25.01%	26.99%	3.7%	26.00%	28.00%	3.6%	26.98%	29.02%	3.5%	27.97%	30.03%	3.5%	28.96%	31.04%
10.0	3.4%	24.15%	25.85%	3.3%	25.14%	26.86%	3.2%	26.13%	27.87%	3.1%	27.12%	28.88%	3.1%	28.11%	29.89%	3.0%	29.10%	30.90%
12.5	3.0%	24.24%	25.76%	3.0%	25.23%	26.77%	2.9%	26.22%	27.78%	2.8%	27.21%	28.79%	2.7%	28.20%	29.80%	2.7%	29.20%	30.80%
15.0	2.8%	24.31%	25.69%	2.7%	25.30%	26.70%	2.6%	26.29%	27.71%	2.6%	27.28%	28.72%	2.5%	28.27%	29.73%	2.4%	29.27%	30.73%
17.5	2.6%	24.36%	25.64%	2.5%	25.35%	26.65%	2.4%	26.34%	27.66%	2.4%	27.33%	28.67%	2.3%	28.33%	29.67%	2.3%	29.32%	30.68%
20.0	2.4%	24.40%	25.60%	2.3%	25.39%	26.61%	2.3%	26.38%	27.62%	2.2%	27.38%	28.62%	2.2%	28.37%	29.63%	2.1%	29.36%	30.64%
25.0	2.1%	24.46%	25.54%	2.1%	25.46%	26.54%	2.0%	26.45%	27.55%	2.0%	27.44%	28.56%	1.9%	28.44%	29.56%	1.9%	29.43%	30.57%
30.0	2.0%	24.51%	25.49%	1.9%	25.50%	26.50%	1.9%	26.50%	27.50%	1.8%	27.49%	28.51%	1.8%	28.49%	29.51%	1.7%	29.48%	30.52%
35.0	1.8%	24.55%	25.45%	1.8%	25.54%	26.46%	1.7%	26.53%	27.47%	1.7%	27.53%	28.47%	1.6%	28.52%	29.48%	1.6%	29.52%	30.48%
40.0	1.7%	24.58%	25.42%	1.7%	25.57%	26.43%	1.6%	26.56%	27.44%	1.6%	27.56%	28.44%	1.5%	28.56%	29.44%	1.5%	29.55%	30.45%
45.0	1.6%	24.60%	25.40%	1.6%	25.59%	26.41%	1.5%	26.59%	27.41%	1.5%	27.59%	28.41%	1.4%	28.58%	29.42%	1.4%	29.58%	30.42%
50.0	1.5%	24.62%	25.38%	1.5%	25.62%	26.38%	1.4%	26.61%	27.39%	1.4%	27.61%	28.39%	1.4%	28.60%	29.40%	1.3%	29.60%	30.40%
60.0	1.4%	24.65%	25.35%	1.3%	25.65%	26.35%	1.3%	26.64%	27.36%	1.3%	27.64%	28.36%	1.3%	28.64%	29.36%	1.2%	29.63%	30.37%
70.0	1.3%	24.68%	25.32%	1.2%	25.68%	26.32%	1.2%	26.67%	27.33%	1.2%	27.67%	28.33%	1.2%	28.66%	29.34%	1.1%	29.66%	30.34%
80.0	1.2%	24.70%	25.30%	1.2%	25.70%	26.30%	1.1%	26.69%	27.31%	1.1%	27.69%	28.31%	1.1%	28.69%	29.31%	1.1%	29.68%	30.32%
90.0	1.1%	24.72%	25.28%	1.1%	25.71%	26.29%	1.1%	26.71%	27.29%	1.0%	27.71%	28.29%	1.0%	28.70%	29.30%	1.0%	29.70%	30.30%
100.0	1.1%	24.73%	25.27%	1.0%	25.73%	26.27%	1.0%	26.72%	27.28%	1.0%	27.72%	28.28%	1.0%	28.72%	29.28%	.9%	29.72%	30.28%

Direct Mail Projection Tables

99% Confidence Level - Standard Deviation: 2.236

ANTICIPATED PERCENT RESPONSE

Sample Size (000)	.5% ±%	Variance Low	High	1.0% ±%	Variance Low	High	1.5% ±%	Variance Low	High	2.0% ±%	Variance Low	High	2.5% ±%	Variance Low	High	3.0% ±%	Variance Low	High
1.0	99.7%	.00%	1.00%	70.4%	.30%	1.70%	57.3%	.64%	2.36%	49.5%	1.01%	2.99%	44.2%	1.40%	3.60%	40.2%	1.79%	4.21%
2.5	63.1%	.18%	.82%	44.5%	.56%	1.44%	36.2%	.96%	2.04%	31.3%	1.37%	2.63%	27.9%	1.80%	3.20%	25.4%	2.24%	3.76%
5.0	44.6%	.28%	.72%	31.5%	.69%	1.31%	25.6%	1.12%	1.88%	22.1%	1.56%	2.44%	19.7%	2.01%	2.99%	18.0%	2.46%	3.54%
7.5	36.4%	.32%	.68%	25.7%	.74%	1.26%	20.9%	1.19%	1.81%	18.1%	1.64%	2.36%	16.1%	2.10%	2.90%	14.7%	2.56%	3.44%
10.0	31.5%	.34%	.66%	22.2%	.78%	1.22%	18.1%	1.23%	1.77%	15.7%	1.69%	2.31%	14.0%	2.15%	2.85%	12.7%	2.62%	3.38%
12.5	28.2%	.36%	.64%	19.9%	.80%	1.20%	16.2%	1.26%	1.74%	14.0%	1.72%	2.28%	12.5%	2.19%	2.81%	11.4%	2.66%	3.34%
15.0	25.8%	.37%	.63%	18.2%	.82%	1.18%	14.8%	1.28%	1.72%	12.8%	1.74%	2.26%	11.4%	2.21%	2.79%	10.4%	2.69%	3.31%
17.5	23.8%	.38%	.62%	16.8%	.83%	1.17%	13.7%	1.29%	1.71%	11.8%	1.76%	2.24%	10.6%	2.24%	2.76%	9.6%	2.71%	3.29%
20.0	22.3%	.39%	.61%	15.7%	.84%	1.16%	12.8%	1.31%	1.69%	11.1%	1.78%	2.22%	9.9%	2.25%	2.75%	9.0%	2.73%	3.27%
25.0	19.9%	.40%	.60%	14.1%	.86%	1.14%	11.5%	1.33%	1.67%	9.9%	1.80%	2.20%	8.8%	2.28%	2.72%	8.0%	2.76%	3.24%
30.0	18.2%	.41%	.59%	12.8%	.87%	1.13%	10.5%	1.34%	1.66%	9.0%	1.82%	2.18%	8.1%	2.30%	2.70%	7.3%	2.78%	3.22%
35.0	16.9%	.42%	.58%	11.9%	.88%	1.12%	9.7%	1.35%	1.65%	8.4%	1.83%	2.17%	7.5%	2.31%	2.69%	6.8%	2.80%	3.20%
40.0	15.8%	.42%	.58%	11.1%	.89%	1.11%	9.1%	1.36%	1.64%	7.8%	1.84%	2.16%	7.0%	2.33%	2.67%	6.4%	2.81%	3.19%
45.0	14.9%	.43%	.57%	10.5%	.90%	1.10%	8.5%	1.37%	1.63%	7.4%	1.85%	2.15%	6.6%	2.34%	2.66%	6.0%	2.82%	3.18%
50.0	14.1%	.43%	.57%	9.9%	.90%	1.10%	8.1%	1.38%	1.62%	7.0%	1.86%	2.14%	6.2%	2.34%	2.66%	5.7%	2.83%	3.17%
60.0	12.9%	.44%	.56%	9.1%	.91%	1.09%	7.4%	1.39%	1.61%	6.4%	1.87%	2.13%	5.7%	2.36%	2.64%	5.2%	2.84%	3.16%
70.0	11.9%	.44%	.56%	8.4%	.92%	1.08%	6.8%	1.40%	1.60%	5.9%	1.88%	2.12%	5.3%	2.37%	2.63%	4.8%	2.86%	3.14%
80.0	11.2%	.44%	.56%	7.9%	.92%	1.08%	6.4%	1.40%	1.60%	5.5%	1.89%	2.11%	4.9%	2.38%	2.62%	4.5%	2.87%	3.13%
90.0	10.5%	.45%	.55%	7.4%	.93%	1.07%	6.0%	1.41%	1.59%	5.2%	1.90%	2.10%	4.7%	2.38%	2.62%	4.2%	2.87%	3.13%
100.0	10.0%	.45%	.55%	7.0%	.93%	1.07%	5.7%	1.41%	1.59%	4.9%	1.90%	2.10%	4.4%	2.39%	2.61%	4.0%	2.88%	3.12%

Direct Mail Projection Tables

99% Confidence Level - Standard Deviation: 2.236

ANTICIPATED PERCENT RESPONSE

Sample Size (000)	3.5% ±%	Variance Low	High	4.0% ±%	Variance Low	High	4.5% ±%	Variance Low	High	5.0% ±%	Variance Low	High	5.5% ±%	Variance Low	High	6.0% ±%	Variance Low	High
1.0	37.1%	2.20%	4.80%	34.6%	2.61%	5.39%	32.6%	3.03%	5.97%	30.8%	3.46%	6.54%	29.3%	3.89%	7.11%	28.0%	4.32%	7.68%
2.5	23.5%	2.68%	4.32%	21.9%	3.12%	4.88%	20.6%	3.57%	5.43%	19.5%	4.03%	5.97%	18.5%	4.48%	6.52%	17.7%	4.94%	7.06%
5.0	16.6%	2.92%	4.08%	15.5%	3.38%	4.62%	14.6%	3.84%	5.16%	13.8%	4.31%	5.69%	13.1%	4.78%	6.22%	12.5%	5.25%	6.75%
7.5	13.6%	3.03%	3.97%	12.6%	3.49%	4.51%	11.9%	3.96%	5.04%	11.3%	4.44%	5.56%	10.7%	4.91%	6.09%	10.2%	5.39%	6.61%
10.0	11.7%	3.09%	3.91%	11.0%	3.56%	4.44%	10.3%	4.04%	4.96%	9.7%	4.51%	5.49%	9.3%	4.99%	6.01%	8.9%	5.47%	6.53%
12.5	10.5%	3.13%	3.87%	9.8%	3.61%	4.39%	9.2%	4.09%	4.91%	8.7%	4.56%	5.44%	8.3%	5.04%	5.96%	7.9%	5.53%	6.47%
15.0	9.6%	3.16%	3.84%	8.9%	3.64%	4.36%	8.4%	4.12%	4.88%	8.0%	4.60%	5.40%	7.6%	5.08%	5.92%	7.2%	5.57%	6.43%
17.5	8.9%	3.19%	3.81%	8.3%	3.67%	4.33%	7.8%	4.15%	4.85%	7.4%	4.63%	5.37%	7.0%	5.11%	5.89%	6.7%	5.60%	6.40%
20.0	8.3%	3.21%	3.79%	7.7%	3.69%	4.31%	7.3%	4.17%	4.83%	6.9%	4.66%	5.34%	6.6%	5.14%	5.86%	6.3%	5.62%	6.38%
25.0	7.4%	3.24%	3.76%	6.9%	3.72%	4.28%	6.5%	4.21%	4.79%	6.2%	4.69%	5.31%	5.9%	5.18%	5.82%	5.6%	5.66%	6.34%
30.0	6.8%	3.26%	3.74%	6.3%	3.75%	4.25%	5.9%	4.23%	4.77%	5.6%	4.72%	5.28%	5.4%	5.21%	5.79%	5.1%	5.69%	6.31%
35.0	6.3%	3.28%	3.72%	5.9%	3.77%	4.23%	5.5%	4.25%	4.75%	5.2%	4.74%	5.26%	5.0%	5.23%	5.77%	4.7%	5.72%	6.28%
40.0	5.9%	3.29%	3.71%	5.5%	3.78%	4.22%	5.2%	4.27%	4.73%	4.9%	4.76%	5.24%	4.6%	5.25%	5.75%	4.4%	5.73%	6.27%
45.0	5.5%	3.31%	3.69%	5.2%	3.79%	4.21%	4.9%	4.28%	4.72%	4.6%	4.77%	5.23%	4.4%	5.26%	5.74%	4.2%	5.75%	6.25%
50.0	5.3%	3.32%	3.68%	4.9%	3.80%	4.20%	4.6%	4.29%	4.71%	4.4%	4.78%	5.22%	4.1%	5.27%	5.73%	4.0%	5.76%	6.24%
60.0	4.8%	3.33%	3.67%	4.5%	3.82%	4.18%	4.2%	4.31%	4.69%	4.0%	4.80%	5.20%	3.8%	5.29%	5.71%	3.6%	5.78%	6.22%
70.0	4.4%	3.34%	3.66%	4.1%	3.83%	4.17%	3.9%	4.32%	4.68%	3.7%	4.82%	5.18%	3.5%	5.31%	5.69%	3.3%	5.80%	6.20%
80.0	4.2%	3.35%	3.65%	3.9%	3.85%	4.15%	3.6%	4.34%	4.66%	3.4%	4.83%	5.17%	3.3%	5.32%	5.68%	3.1%	5.81%	6.19%
90.0	3.9%	3.36%	3.64%	3.7%	3.85%	4.15%	3.4%	4.35%	4.65%	3.2%	4.84%	5.16%	3.1%	5.33%	5.67%	3.0%	5.82%	6.18%
100.0	3.7%	3.37%	3.63%	3.5%	3.86%	4.14%	3.3%	4.35%	4.65%	3.1%	4.85%	5.15%	2.9%	5.34%	5.66%	2.8%	5.83%	6.17%

Direct Mail Projection Tables

99% Confidence Level - Standard Deviation: 2.236

ANTICIPATED PERCENT RESPONSE

Sample Size (000)	6.5% ±%	Variance Low	High	7.0% ±%	Variance Low	High	7.5% ±%	Variance Low	High	8.0% ±%	Variance Low	High	8.5% ±%	Variance Low	High	9.0% ±%	Variance Low	High
1.0	26.8%	4.76%	8.24%	25.8%	5.20%	8.80%	24.8%	5.64%	9.36%	24.0%	6.08%	9.92%	23.2%	6.53%	10.47%	22.5%	6.98%	11.02%
2.5	17.0%	5.40%	7.60%	16.3%	5.86%	8.14%	15.7%	6.32%	8.68%	15.2%	6.79%	9.21%	14.7%	7.25%	9.75%	14.2%	7.72%	10.28%
5.0	12.0%	5.72%	7.28%	11.5%	6.19%	7.81%	11.1%	6.67%	8.33%	10.7%	7.14%	8.86%	10.4%	7.62%	9.38%	10.1%	8.10%	9.90%
7.5	9.8%	5.85%	7.14%	9.4%	6.34%	7.66%	9.1%	6.82%	8.18%	8.8%	7.30%	8.70%	8.5%	7.78%	9.22%	8.2%	8.26%	9.74%
10.0	8.5%	5.95%	7.05%	8.2%	6.43%	7.57%	7.9%	6.91%	8.09%	7.6%	7.39%	8.61%	7.3%	7.88%	9.12%	7.1%	8.36%	9.64%
12.5	7.6%	6.01%	6.99%	7.3%	6.49%	7.51%	7.0%	6.97%	8.03%	6.8%	7.46%	8.54%	6.6%	7.94%	9.06%	6.4%	8.43%	9.57%
15.0	6.9%	6.05%	6.95%	6.7%	6.53%	7.47%	6.4%	7.02%	7.98%	6.2%	7.50%	8.50%	6.0%	7.99%	9.01%	5.8%	8.48%	9.52%
17.5	6.4%	6.08%	6.92%	6.2%	6.57%	7.43%	5.9%	7.05%	7.95%	5.7%	7.54%	8.46%	5.5%	8.03%	8.97%	5.4%	8.52%	9.48%
20.0	6.0%	6.11%	6.89%	5.8%	6.60%	7.40%	5.6%	7.08%	7.92%	5.4%	7.57%	8.43%	5.2%	8.06%	8.94%	5.0%	8.55%	9.45%
25.0	5.4%	6.15%	6.85%	5.2%	6.64%	7.36%	5.0%	7.13%	7.87%	4.8%	7.62%	8.38%	4.6%	8.11%	8.89%	4.5%	8.60%	9.40%
30.0	4.9%	6.18%	6.82%	4.7%	6.67%	7.33%	4.5%	7.16%	7.84%	4.4%	7.65%	8.35%	4.2%	8.14%	8.86%	4.1%	8.63%	9.37%
35.0	4.5%	6.21%	6.79%	4.4%	6.70%	7.30%	4.2%	7.19%	7.81%	4.1%	7.68%	8.32%	3.9%	8.17%	8.83%	3.8%	8.66%	9.34%
40.0	4.2%	6.22%	6.78%	4.1%	6.71%	7.29%	3.9%	7.21%	7.79%	3.8%	7.70%	8.30%	3.7%	8.19%	8.81%	3.6%	8.68%	9.32%
45.0	4.0%	6.24%	6.76%	3.8%	6.73%	7.27%	3.7%	7.22%	7.78%	3.6%	7.71%	8.29%	3.5%	8.21%	8.79%	3.4%	8.70%	9.30%
50.0	3.8%	6.25%	6.75%	3.6%	6.74%	7.26%	3.5%	7.24%	7.76%	3.4%	7.73%	8.27%	3.3%	8.22%	8.78%	3.2%	8.71%	9.29%
60.0	3.5%	6.27%	6.73%	3.3%	6.77%	7.23%	3.2%	7.26%	7.74%	3.1%	7.75%	8.25%	3.0%	8.25%	8.75%	2.9%	8.74%	9.26%
70.0	3.2%	6.29%	6.71%	3.1%	6.78%	7.22%	3.0%	7.28%	7.72%	2.9%	7.77%	8.23%	2.8%	8.26%	8.74%	2.7%	8.76%	9.24%
80.0	3.0%	6.31%	6.69%	2.9%	6.80%	7.20%	2.8%	7.29%	7.71%	2.7%	7.79%	8.21%	2.6%	8.28%	8.72%	2.5%	8.77%	9.23%
90.0	2.8%	6.32%	6.68%	2.7%	6.81%	7.19%	2.6%	7.30%	7.70%	2.5%	7.80%	8.20%	2.4%	8.29%	8.71%	2.4%	8.79%	9.21%
100.0	2.7%	6.33%	6.67%	2.6%	6.82%	7.18%	2.5%	7.31%	7.69%	2.4%	7.81%	8.19%	2.3%	8.30%	8.70%	2.2%	8.80%	9.20%

Direct Mail Projection Tables

99% Confidence Level - Standard Deviation: 2.236

ANTICIPATED PERCENT RESPONSE

Sample Size (000)	9.5% ±%	Variance Low	High	10.0% ±%	Variance Low	High	10.5% ±%	Variance Low	High	11.0% ±%	Variance Low	High	11.5% ±%	Variance Low	High	12.0% ±%	Variance Low	High
1.0	21.8%	7.43%	11.57%	21.2%	7.88%	12.12%	20.6%	8.33%	12.67%	20.1%	8.79%	13.21%	19.6%	9.24%	13.76%	19.1%	9.70%	14.30%
2.5	13.8%	8.19%	10.81%	13.4%	8.66%	11.34%	13.1%	9.13%	11.87%	12.7%	9.60%	12.40%	12.4%	10.07%	12.93%	12.1%	10.55%	13.45%
5.0	9.8%	8.57%	10.43%	9.5%	9.05%	10.95%	9.2%	9.53%	11.47%	9.0%	10.01%	11.99%	8.8%	10.49%	12.51%	8.6%	10.97%	13.03%
7.5	8.0%	8.74%	10.26%	7.7%	9.23%	10.77%	7.5%	9.71%	11.29%	7.3%	10.19%	11.81%	7.2%	10.68%	12.32%	7.0%	11.16%	12.84%
10.0	6.9%	8.84%	10.16%	6.7%	9.33%	10.67%	6.5%	9.81%	11.19%	6.4%	10.30%	11.70%	6.2%	10.79%	12.21%	6.1%	11.27%	12.73%
12.5	6.2%	8.91%	10.09%	6.0%	9.40%	10.60%	5.8%	9.89%	11.11%	5.7%	10.37%	11.63%	5.5%	10.86%	12.14%	5.4%	11.35%	12.65%
15.0	5.6%	8.96%	10.04%	5.5%	9.45%	10.55%	5.3%	9.94%	11.06%	5.2%	10.43%	11.57%	5.1%	10.92%	12.08%	4.9%	11.41%	12.59%
17.5	5.2%	9.00%	10.00%	5.1%	9.49%	10.51%	4.9%	9.98%	11.02%	4.8%	10.47%	11.53%	4.7%	10.96%	12.04%	4.6%	11.45%	12.55%
20.0	4.9%	9.04%	9.96%	4.7%	9.53%	10.47%	4.6%	10.02%	10.98%	4.5%	10.51%	11.49%	4.4%	11.00%	12.00%	4.3%	11.49%	12.51%
25.0	4.4%	9.09%	9.91%	4.2%	9.58%	10.42%	4.1%	10.07%	10.93%	4.0%	10.56%	11.44%	3.9%	11.05%	11.95%	3.8%	11.54%	12.46%
30.0	4.0%	9.12%	9.88%	3.9%	9.61%	10.39%	3.8%	10.10%	10.90%	3.7%	10.60%	11.40%	3.6%	11.09%	11.91%	3.5%	11.58%	12.42%
35.0	3.7%	9.15%	9.85%	3.6%	9.64%	10.36%	3.5%	10.13%	10.87%	3.4%	10.63%	11.37%	3.3%	11.12%	11.88%	3.2%	11.61%	12.39%
40.0	3.5%	9.17%	9.83%	3.4%	9.66%	10.34%	3.3%	10.16%	10.84%	3.2%	10.65%	11.35%	3.1%	11.14%	11.86%	3.0%	11.64%	12.36%
45.0	3.3%	9.19%	9.81%	3.2%	9.68%	10.32%	3.1%	10.18%	10.82%	3.0%	10.67%	11.33%	2.9%	11.16%	11.84%	2.9%	11.66%	12.34%
50.0	3.1%	9.21%	9.79%	3.0%	9.70%	10.30%	2.9%	10.19%	10.81%	2.8%	10.69%	11.31%	2.8%	11.18%	11.82%	2.7%	11.68%	12.32%
60.0	2.8%	9.23%	9.77%	2.7%	9.73%	10.27%	2.7%	10.22%	10.78%	2.6%	10.71%	11.29%	2.5%	11.21%	11.79%	2.5%	11.70%	12.30%
70.0	2.6%	9.25%	9.75%	2.5%	9.75%	10.25%	2.5%	10.24%	10.76%	2.4%	10.74%	11.26%	2.3%	11.23%	11.77%	2.3%	11.73%	12.27%
80.0	2.4%	9.27%	9.73%	2.4%	9.76%	10.24%	2.3%	10.26%	10.74%	2.2%	10.75%	11.25%	2.2%	11.25%	11.75%	2.1%	11.74%	12.26%
90.0	2.3%	9.28%	9.72%	2.2%	9.78%	10.22%	2.2%	10.27%	10.73%	2.1%	10.77%	11.23%	2.1%	11.26%	11.74%	2.0%	11.76%	12.24%
100.0	2.2%	9.29%	9.71%	2.1%	9.79%	10.21%	2.1%	10.28%	10.72%	2.0%	10.78%	11.22%	2.0%	11.27%	11.73%	1.9%	11.77%	12.23%

Direct Mail Projection Tables

99% Confidence Level - Standard Deviation: 2.236

Sample Size (000)	13.0% ±%	Variance Low	High	14.0% ±%	Variance Low	High	15.0% ±%	Variance Low	High	16.0% ±%	Variance Low	High	17.0% ±%	Variance Low	High	18.0% ±%	Variance Low	High
1.0	18.3%	10.62%	15.38%	17.5%	11.55%	16.45%	16.8%	12.48%	17.52%	16.2%	13.41%	18.59%	15.6%	14.34%	19.66%	15.1%	15.28%	20.72%
2.5	11.6%	11.50%	14.50%	11.1%	12.45%	15.55%	10.6%	13.40%	16.60%	10.2%	14.36%	17.64%	9.9%	15.32%	18.68%	9.5%	16.28%	19.72%
5.0	8.2%	11.94%	14.06%	7.8%	12.90%	15.10%	7.5%	13.87%	16.13%	7.2%	14.84%	17.16%	7.0%	15.81%	18.19%	6.7%	16.79%	19.21%
7.5	6.7%	12.13%	13.87%	6.4%	13.10%	14.90%	6.1%	14.08%	15.92%	5.9%	15.05%	16.95%	5.7%	16.03%	17.97%	5.5%	17.01%	18.99%
10.0	5.8%	12.25%	13.75%	5.5%	13.22%	14.78%	5.3%	14.20%	15.80%	5.1%	15.18%	16.82%	4.9%	16.16%	17.84%	4.8%	17.14%	18.86%
12.5	5.2%	12.33%	13.67%	5.0%	13.31%	14.69%	4.8%	14.29%	15.71%	4.6%	15.27%	16.73%	4.4%	16.25%	17.75%	4.3%	17.23%	18.77%
15.0	4.7%	12.39%	13.61%	4.5%	13.37%	14.63%	4.3%	14.35%	15.65%	4.2%	15.33%	16.67%	4.0%	16.31%	17.69%	3.9%	17.30%	18.70%
17.5	4.4%	12.43%	13.57%	4.2%	13.41%	14.59%	4.0%	14.40%	15.60%	3.9%	15.38%	16.62%	3.7%	16.37%	17.63%	3.6%	17.35%	18.65%
20.0	4.1%	12.47%	13.53%	3.9%	13.45%	14.55%	3.8%	14.44%	15.56%	3.6%	15.42%	16.58%	3.5%	16.41%	17.59%	3.4%	17.39%	18.61%
25.0	3.7%	12.52%	13.48%	3.5%	13.51%	14.49%	3.4%	14.50%	15.50%	3.2%	15.48%	16.52%	3.1%	16.47%	17.53%	3.0%	17.46%	18.54%
30.0	3.3%	12.57%	13.43%	3.2%	13.55%	14.45%	3.1%	14.54%	15.46%	3.0%	15.53%	16.47%	2.9%	16.52%	17.48%	2.8%	17.50%	18.50%
35.0	3.1%	12.60%	13.40%	3.0%	13.59%	14.41%	2.8%	14.57%	15.43%	2.7%	15.56%	16.44%	2.6%	16.55%	17.45%	2.6%	17.54%	18.46%
40.0	2.9%	12.62%	13.38%	2.8%	13.61%	14.39%	2.7%	14.60%	15.40%	2.6%	15.59%	16.41%	2.5%	16.58%	17.42%	2.4%	17.57%	18.43%
45.0	2.7%	12.65%	13.35%	2.6%	13.63%	14.37%	2.5%	14.62%	15.38%	2.4%	15.61%	16.39%	2.3%	16.60%	17.40%	2.2%	17.60%	18.40%
50.0	2.6%	12.66%	13.34%	2.5%	13.65%	14.35%	2.4%	14.64%	15.36%	2.3%	15.63%	16.37%	2.2%	16.62%	17.38%	2.1%	17.62%	18.38%
60.0	2.4%	12.69%	13.31%	2.3%	13.68%	14.32%	2.2%	14.67%	15.33%	2.1%	15.67%	16.33%	2.0%	16.66%	17.34%	1.9%	17.65%	18.35%
70.0	2.2%	12.72%	13.28%	2.1%	13.71%	14.29%	2.0%	14.70%	15.30%	1.9%	15.69%	16.31%	1.9%	16.68%	17.32%	1.8%	17.68%	18.32%
80.0	2.0%	12.73%	13.27%	2.0%	13.73%	14.27%	1.9%	14.72%	15.28%	1.8%	15.71%	16.29%	1.7%	16.70%	17.30%	1.7%	17.70%	18.30%
90.0	1.9%	12.75%	13.25%	1.8%	13.74%	14.26%	1.8%	14.73%	15.27%	1.7%	15.73%	16.27%	1.6%	16.72%	17.28%	1.6%	17.71%	18.29%
100.0	1.8%	12.76%	13.24%	1.8%	13.75%	14.25%	1.7%	14.75%	15.25%	1.6%	15.74%	16.26%	1.6%	16.73%	17.27%	1.5%	17.73%	18.27%

Direct Mail Projection Tables

99% Confidence Level - Standard Deviation: 2.236

ANTICIPATED PERCENT RESPONSE

Sample Size (000)	19.0% ±%	Variance Low	High	20.0% ±%	Variance Low	High	21.0% ±%	Variance Low	High	22.0% ±%	Variance Low	High	23.0% ±%	Variance Low	High	24.0% ±%	Variance Low	High
1.0	14.6%	16.23%	21.77%	14.1%	17.17%	22.83%	13.7%	18.12%	23.88%	13.3%	19.07%	24.93%	12.9%	20.02%	25.98%	12.6%	20.98%	27.02%
2.5	9.2%	17.25%	20.75%	8.9%	18.21%	21.79%	8.7%	19.18%	22.82%	8.4%	20.15%	23.85%	8.2%	21.12%	24.88%	8.0%	22.09%	25.91%
5.0	6.5%	17.76%	20.24%	6.3%	18.74%	21.26%	6.1%	19.71%	22.29%	6.0%	20.69%	23.31%	5.8%	21.67%	24.33%	5.6%	22.65%	25.35%
7.5	5.3%	17.99%	20.01%	5.2%	18.97%	21.03%	5.0%	19.95%	22.05%	4.9%	20.93%	23.07%	4.7%	21.91%	24.09%	4.6%	22.90%	25.10%
10.0	4.6%	18.12%	19.88%	4.5%	19.11%	20.89%	4.3%	20.09%	21.91%	4.2%	21.07%	22.93%	4.1%	22.06%	23.94%	4.0%	23.05%	24.95%
12.5	4.1%	18.22%	19.78%	4.0%	19.20%	20.80%	3.9%	20.19%	21.81%	3.8%	21.17%	22.83%	3.7%	22.16%	23.84%	3.6%	23.15%	24.85%
15.0	3.8%	18.28%	19.72%	3.7%	19.27%	20.73%	3.5%	20.26%	21.74%	3.4%	21.24%	22.76%	3.3%	22.23%	23.77%	3.2%	23.22%	24.78%
17.5	3.5%	18.34%	19.66%	3.4%	19.32%	20.68%	3.3%	20.31%	21.69%	3.2%	21.30%	22.70%	3.1%	22.29%	23.71%	3.0%	23.28%	24.72%
20.0	3.3%	18.38%	19.62%	3.2%	19.37%	20.63%	3.1%	20.36%	21.64%	3.0%	21.35%	22.65%	2.9%	22.33%	23.67%	2.8%	23.32%	24.68%
25.0	2.9%	18.45%	19.55%	2.8%	19.43%	20.57%	2.7%	20.42%	21.58%	2.7%	21.41%	22.59%	2.6%	22.40%	23.60%	2.5%	23.40%	24.60%
30.0	2.7%	18.49%	19.51%	2.6%	19.48%	20.52%	2.5%	20.47%	21.53%	2.4%	21.47%	22.53%	2.4%	22.46%	23.54%	2.3%	23.45%	24.55%
35.0	2.5%	18.53%	19.47%	2.4%	19.52%	20.48%	2.3%	20.51%	21.49%	2.3%	21.50%	22.50%	2.2%	22.50%	23.50%	2.1%	23.49%	24.51%
40.0	2.3%	18.56%	19.44%	2.2%	19.55%	20.45%	2.2%	20.54%	21.46%	2.1%	21.54%	22.46%	2.0%	22.53%	23.47%	2.0%	23.52%	24.48%
45.0	2.2%	18.59%	19.41%	2.1%	19.58%	20.42%	2.0%	20.57%	21.43%	2.0%	21.56%	22.44%	1.9%	22.56%	23.44%	1.9%	23.55%	24.45%
50.0	2.1%	18.61%	19.39%	2.0%	19.60%	20.40%	1.9%	20.59%	21.41%	1.9%	21.59%	22.41%	1.8%	22.58%	23.42%	1.8%	23.57%	24.43%
60.0	1.9%	18.64%	19.36%	1.8%	19.63%	20.37%	1.8%	20.63%	21.37%	1.7%	21.62%	22.38%	1.7%	22.62%	23.38%	1.6%	23.61%	24.39%
70.0	1.7%	18.67%	19.33%	1.7%	19.66%	20.34%	1.6%	20.66%	21.34%	1.6%	21.65%	22.35%	1.5%	22.64%	23.36%	1.5%	23.64%	24.36%
80.0	1.6%	18.69%	19.31%	1.6%	19.68%	20.32%	1.5%	20.68%	21.32%	1.5%	21.67%	22.33%	1.4%	22.67%	23.33%	1.4%	23.66%	24.34%
90.0	1.5%	18.71%	19.29%	1.5%	19.70%	20.30%	1.4%	20.70%	21.30%	1.4%	21.69%	22.31%	1.4%	22.69%	23.31%	1.3%	23.68%	24.32%
100.0	1.5%	18.72%	19.28%	1.4%	19.72%	20.28%	1.4%	20.71%	21.29%	1.3%	21.71%	22.29%	1.3%	22.70%	23.30%	1.3%	23.70%	24.30%

Direct Mail Projection Tables

99% Confidence Level - Standard Deviation: 2.236

ANTICIPATED PERCENT RESPONSE

Sample Size (000)	25.0% ±%	Variance Low	High	26.0% ±%	Variance Low	High	27.0% ±%	Variance Low	High	28.0% ±%	Variance Low	High	29.0% ±%	Variance Low	High	30.0% ±%	Variance Low	High
1.0	12.2%	21.94%	28.06%	11.9%	22.90%	29.10%	11.6%	23.86%	30.14%	11.3%	24.83%	31.17%	11.1%	25.79%	32.21%	10.8%	26.76%	33.24%
2.5	7.7%	23.06%	26.94%	7.5%	24.04%	27.96%	7.4%	25.01%	28.99%	7.2%	25.99%	30.01%	7.0%	26.97%	31.03%	6.8%	27.95%	32.05%
5.0	5.5%	23.63%	26.37%	5.3%	24.61%	27.39%	5.2%	25.60%	28.40%	5.1%	26.58%	29.42%	4.9%	27.57%	30.43%	4.8%	28.55%	31.45%
7.5	4.5%	23.88%	26.12%	4.4%	24.87%	27.13%	4.2%	25.85%	28.15%	4.1%	26.84%	29.16%	4.0%	27.83%	30.17%	3.9%	28.82%	31.18%
10.0	3.9%	24.03%	25.97%	3.8%	25.02%	26.98%	3.7%	26.01%	27.99%	3.6%	27.00%	29.00%	3.5%	27.99%	30.01%	3.4%	28.98%	31.02%
12.5	3.5%	24.13%	25.87%	3.4%	25.12%	26.88%	3.3%	26.11%	27.89%	3.2%	27.10%	28.90%	3.1%	28.09%	29.91%	3.1%	29.08%	30.92%
15.0	3.2%	24.21%	25.79%	3.1%	25.20%	26.80%	3.0%	26.19%	27.81%	2.9%	27.18%	28.82%	2.9%	28.17%	29.83%	2.8%	29.16%	30.84%
17.5	2.9%	24.27%	25.73%	2.9%	25.26%	26.74%	2.8%	26.25%	27.75%	2.7%	27.24%	28.76%	2.6%	28.23%	29.77%	2.6%	29.23%	30.77%
20.0	2.7%	24.32%	25.68%	2.7%	25.31%	26.69%	2.6%	26.30%	27.70%	2.5%	27.29%	28.71%	2.5%	28.28%	29.72%	2.4%	29.28%	30.72%
25.0	2.4%	24.39%	25.61%	2.4%	25.38%	26.62%	2.3%	26.37%	27.63%	2.3%	27.37%	28.63%	2.2%	28.36%	29.64%	2.2%	29.35%	30.65%
30.0	2.2%	24.44%	25.56%	2.2%	25.43%	26.57%	2.1%	26.43%	27.57%	2.1%	27.42%	28.58%	2.0%	28.41%	29.59%	2.0%	29.41%	30.59%
35.0	2.1%	24.48%	25.52%	2.0%	25.48%	26.52%	2.0%	26.47%	27.53%	1.9%	27.46%	28.54%	1.9%	28.46%	29.54%	1.8%	29.45%	30.55%
40.0	1.9%	24.52%	25.48%	1.9%	25.51%	26.49%	1.8%	26.50%	27.50%	1.8%	27.50%	28.50%	1.7%	28.49%	29.51%	1.7%	29.49%	30.51%
45.0	1.8%	24.54%	25.46%	1.8%	25.54%	26.46%	1.7%	26.53%	27.47%	1.7%	27.53%	28.47%	1.6%	28.52%	29.48%	1.6%	29.52%	30.48%
50.0	1.7%	24.57%	25.43%	1.7%	25.56%	26.44%	1.6%	26.56%	27.44%	1.6%	27.55%	28.45%	1.6%	28.55%	29.45%	1.5%	29.54%	30.46%
60.0	1.6%	24.60%	25.40%	1.5%	25.60%	26.40%	1.5%	26.59%	27.41%	1.5%	27.59%	28.41%	1.4%	28.59%	29.41%	1.4%	29.58%	30.42%
70.0	1.5%	24.63%	25.37%	1.4%	25.63%	26.37%	1.4%	26.62%	27.38%	1.4%	27.62%	28.38%	1.3%	28.62%	29.38%	1.3%	29.61%	30.39%
80.0	1.4%	24.66%	25.34%	1.3%	25.65%	26.35%	1.3%	26.65%	27.35%	1.3%	27.65%	28.35%	1.2%	28.64%	29.36%	1.2%	29.64%	30.36%
90.0	1.3%	24.68%	25.32%	1.3%	25.67%	26.33%	1.2%	26.67%	27.33%	1.2%	27.67%	28.33%	1.2%	28.66%	29.34%	1.1%	29.66%	30.34%
100.0	1.2%	24.69%	25.31%	1.2%	25.69%	26.31%	1.2%	26.69%	27.31%	1.1%	27.68%	28.32%	1.1%	28.68%	29.32%	1.1%	29.68%	30.32%

Direct Mail Projection Tables

90% Confidence Level - Standard Deviation: 1.645

| | ANTICIPATED PERCENT RESPONSE | | | | | | | | | | | | | | | | | |
| Sample Size (000) | .5% | | | 1.0% | | | 1.5% | | | 2.0% | | | 2.5% | | | 3.0% | | |
	±%	Variance Low	High	±%	Variance Low	High	±%	Variance Low	High	±%	Variance Low	High	±%	Variance Low	High	±%	Variance Low	High
1.0	73.4%	.13%	.87%	51.8%	.48%	1.52%	42.2%	.87%	2.13%	36.4%	1.27%	2.73%	32.5%	1.69%	3.31%	29.6%	2.11%	3.89%
2.5	46.4%	.27%	.73%	32.7%	.67%	1.33%	26.7%	1.10%	1.90%	23.0%	1.54%	2.46%	20.5%	1.99%	3.01%	18.7%	2.44%	3.56%
5.0	32.8%	.34%	.66%	23.1%	.77%	1.23%	18.9%	1.22%	1.78%	16.3%	1.67%	2.33%	14.5%	2.14%	2.86%	13.2%	2.60%	3.40%
7.5	26.8%	.37%	.63%	18.9%	.81%	1.19%	15.4%	1.27%	1.73%	13.3%	1.73%	2.27%	11.9%	2.20%	2.80%	10.8%	2.68%	3.32%
10.0	23.2%	.38%	.62%	16.4%	.84%	1.16%	13.3%	1.30%	1.70%	11.5%	1.77%	2.23%	10.3%	2.24%	2.76%	9.4%	2.72%	3.28%
12.5	20.8%	.40%	.60%	14.6%	.85%	1.15%	11.9%	1.32%	1.68%	10.3%	1.79%	2.21%	9.2%	2.27%	2.73%	8.4%	2.75%	3.25%
15.0	18.9%	.41%	.59%	13.4%	.87%	1.13%	10.9%	1.34%	1.66%	9.4%	1.81%	2.19%	8.4%	2.29%	2.71%	7.6%	2.77%	3.23%
17.5	17.5%	.41%	.59%	12.4%	.88%	1.12%	10.1%	1.35%	1.65%	8.7%	1.83%	2.17%	7.8%	2.31%	2.69%	7.1%	2.79%	3.21%
20.0	16.4%	.42%	.58%	11.6%	.88%	1.12%	9.4%	1.36%	1.64%	8.1%	1.84%	2.16%	7.3%	2.32%	2.68%	6.6%	2.80%	3.20%
25.0	14.7%	.43%	.57%	10.4%	.90%	1.10%	8.4%	1.37%	1.63%	7.3%	1.85%	2.15%	6.5%	2.34%	2.66%	5.9%	2.82%	3.18%
30.0	13.4%	.43%	.57%	9.4%	.91%	1.09%	7.7%	1.38%	1.62%	6.6%	1.87%	2.13%	5.9%	2.35%	2.65%	5.4%	2.84%	3.16%
35.0	12.4%	.44%	.56%	8.7%	.91%	1.09%	7.1%	1.39%	1.61%	6.2%	1.88%	2.12%	5.5%	2.36%	2.64%	5.0%	2.85%	3.15%
40.0	11.6%	.44%	.56%	8.2%	.92%	1.08%	6.7%	1.40%	1.60%	5.8%	1.88%	2.12%	5.1%	2.37%	2.63%	4.7%	2.86%	3.14%
45.0	10.9%	.45%	.55%	7.7%	.92%	1.08%	6.3%	1.41%	1.59%	5.4%	1.89%	2.11%	4.8%	2.38%	2.62%	4.4%	2.87%	3.13%
50.0	10.4%	.45%	.55%	7.3%	.93%	1.07%	6.0%	1.41%	1.59%	5.1%	1.90%	2.10%	4.6%	2.39%	2.61%	4.2%	2.87%	3.13%
60.0	9.5%	.45%	.55%	6.7%	.93%	1.07%	5.4%	1.42%	1.58%	4.7%	1.91%	2.09%	4.2%	2.40%	2.60%	3.8%	2.89%	3.11%
70.0	8.8%	.46%	.54%	6.2%	.94%	1.06%	5.0%	1.42%	1.58%	4.4%	1.91%	2.09%	3.9%	2.40%	2.60%	3.5%	2.89%	3.11%
80.0	8.2%	.46%	.54%	5.8%	.94%	1.06%	4.7%	1.43%	1.57%	4.1%	1.92%	2.08%	3.6%	2.41%	2.59%	3.3%	2.90%	3.10%
90.0	7.7%	.46%	.54%	5.5%	.95%	1.05%	4.4%	1.43%	1.57%	3.8%	1.92%	2.08%	3.4%	2.41%	2.59%	3.1%	2.91%	3.09%
100.0	7.3%	.46%	.54%	5.2%	.95%	1.05%	4.2%	1.44%	1.56%	3.6%	1.93%	2.07%	3.2%	2.42%	2.58%	3.0%	2.91%	3.09%

Direct Mail Projection Tables

90% Confidence Level - Standard Deviation: 1.645

ANTICIPATED PERCENT RESPONSE

Sample Size (000)	3.5%			4.0%			4.5%			5.0%			5.5%			6.0%		
	±%	Variance Low	High	±%	Variance Low	High	±%	Variance Low	High	±%	Variance Low	High	±%	Variance Low	High	±%	Variance Low	High
1.0	27.3%	2.54%	4.46%	25.5%	2.98%	5.02%	24.0%	3.42%	5.58%	22.7%	3.87%	6.13%	21.6%	4.31%	6.69%	20.6%	4.76%	7.24%
2.5	17.3%	2.90%	4.10%	16.1%	3.36%	4.64%	15.2%	3.82%	5.18%	14.3%	4.28%	5.72%	13.6%	4.75%	6.25%	13.0%	5.22%	6.78%
5.0	12.2%	3.07%	3.93%	11.4%	3.54%	4.46%	10.7%	4.02%	4.98%	10.1%	4.49%	5.51%	9.6%	4.97%	6.03%	9.2%	5.45%	6.55%
7.5	10.0%	3.15%	3.85%	9.3%	3.63%	4.37%	8.8%	4.11%	4.89%	8.3%	4.59%	5.41%	7.9%	5.07%	5.93%	7.5%	5.55%	6.45%
10.0	8.6%	3.20%	3.80%	8.1%	3.68%	4.32%	7.6%	4.16%	4.84%	7.2%	4.64%	5.36%	6.8%	5.12%	5.88%	6.5%	5.61%	6.39%
12.5	7.7%	3.23%	3.77%	7.2%	3.71%	4.29%	6.8%	4.19%	4.81%	6.4%	4.68%	5.32%	6.1%	5.16%	5.84%	5.8%	5.65%	6.35%
15.0	7.1%	3.25%	3.75%	6.6%	3.74%	4.26%	6.2%	4.22%	4.78%	5.9%	4.71%	5.29%	5.6%	5.19%	5.81%	5.3%	5.68%	6.32%
17.5	6.5%	3.27%	3.73%	6.1%	3.76%	4.24%	5.7%	4.24%	4.76%	5.4%	4.73%	5.27%	5.2%	5.22%	5.78%	4.9%	5.70%	6.30%
20.0	6.1%	3.29%	3.71%	5.7%	3.77%	4.23%	5.4%	4.26%	4.74%	5.1%	4.75%	5.25%	4.8%	5.23%	5.77%	4.6%	5.72%	6.28%
25.0	5.5%	3.31%	3.69%	5.1%	3.80%	4.20%	4.8%	4.28%	4.72%	4.5%	4.77%	5.23%	4.3%	5.26%	5.74%	4.1%	5.75%	6.25%
30.0	5.0%	3.33%	3.67%	4.7%	3.81%	4.19%	4.4%	4.30%	4.70%	4.1%	4.79%	5.21%	3.9%	5.28%	5.72%	3.8%	5.77%	6.23%
35.0	4.6%	3.34%	3.66%	4.3%	3.83%	4.17%	4.1%	4.32%	4.68%	3.8%	4.81%	5.19%	3.6%	5.30%	5.70%	3.5%	5.79%	6.21%
40.0	4.3%	3.35%	3.65%	4.0%	3.84%	4.16%	3.8%	4.33%	4.67%	3.6%	4.82%	5.18%	3.4%	5.31%	5.69%	3.3%	5.80%	6.20%
45.0	4.1%	3.36%	3.64%	3.8%	3.85%	4.15%	3.6%	4.34%	4.66%	3.4%	4.83%	5.17%	3.2%	5.32%	5.68%	3.1%	5.82%	6.18%
50.0	3.9%	3.36%	3.64%	3.6%	3.86%	4.14%	3.4%	4.35%	4.65%	3.2%	4.84%	5.16%	3.0%	5.33%	5.67%	2.9%	5.83%	6.17%
60.0	3.5%	3.38%	3.62%	3.3%	3.87%	4.13%	3.1%	4.36%	4.64%	2.9%	4.85%	5.15%	2.8%	5.35%	5.65%	2.7%	5.84%	6.16%
70.0	3.3%	3.39%	3.61%	3.0%	3.88%	4.12%	2.9%	4.37%	4.63%	2.7%	4.86%	5.14%	2.6%	5.36%	5.64%	2.5%	5.85%	6.15%
80.0	3.1%	3.39%	3.61%	2.8%	3.89%	4.11%	2.7%	4.38%	4.62%	2.5%	4.87%	5.13%	2.4%	5.37%	5.63%	2.3%	5.86%	6.14%
90.0	2.9%	3.40%	3.60%	2.7%	3.89%	4.11%	2.5%	4.39%	4.61%	2.4%	4.88%	5.12%	2.3%	5.37%	5.63%	2.2%	5.87%	6.13%
100.0	2.7%	3.40%	3.60%	2.5%	3.90%	4.10%	2.4%	4.39%	4.61%	2.3%	4.89%	5.11%	2.2%	5.38%	5.62%	2.1%	5.88%	6.12%

257

Direct Mail Projection Tables

90% Confidence Level - Standard Deviation: 1.645

ANTICIPATED PERCENT RESPONSE

Sample Size (000)	6.5% ±%	Variance Low	High	7.0% ±%	Variance Low	High	7.5% ±%	Variance Low	High	8.0% ±%	Variance Low	High	8.5% ±%	Variance Low	High	9.0% ±%	Variance Low	High
1.0	19.7%	5.22%	7.78%	19.0%	5.67%	8.33%	18.3%	6.13%	8.87%	17.6%	6.59%	9.41%	17.1%	7.05%	9.95%	16.5%	7.51%	10.49%
2.5	12.5%	5.69%	7.31%	12.0%	6.16%	7.84%	11.6%	6.63%	8.37%	11.2%	7.11%	8.89%	10.8%	7.58%	9.42%	10.5%	8.06%	9.94%
5.0	8.8%	5.93%	7.07%	8.5%	6.41%	7.59%	8.2%	6.89%	8.11%	7.9%	7.37%	8.63%	7.6%	7.85%	9.15%	7.4%	8.33%	9.67%
7.5	7.2%	6.03%	6.97%	6.9%	6.52%	7.48%	6.7%	7.00%	8.00%	6.4%	7.48%	8.52%	6.2%	7.97%	9.03%	6.0%	8.46%	9.54%
10.0	6.2%	6.09%	6.91%	6.0%	6.58%	7.42%	5.8%	7.07%	7.93%	5.6%	7.55%	8.45%	5.4%	8.04%	8.96%	5.2%	8.53%	9.47%
12.5	5.6%	6.14%	6.86%	5.4%	6.62%	7.38%	5.2%	7.11%	7.89%	5.0%	7.60%	8.40%	4.8%	8.09%	8.91%	4.7%	8.58%	9.42%
15.0	5.1%	6.17%	6.83%	4.9%	6.66%	7.34%	4.7%	7.15%	7.85%	4.6%	7.64%	8.36%	4.4%	8.13%	8.87%	4.3%	8.62%	9.38%
17.5	4.7%	6.19%	6.81%	4.5%	6.68%	7.32%	4.4%	7.17%	7.83%	4.2%	7.66%	8.34%	4.1%	8.15%	8.85%	4.0%	8.64%	9.36%
20.0	4.4%	6.21%	6.79%	4.2%	6.70%	7.30%	4.1%	7.19%	7.81%	3.9%	7.68%	8.32%	3.8%	8.18%	8.82%	3.7%	8.67%	9.33%
25.0	3.9%	6.24%	6.76%	3.8%	6.73%	7.27%	3.7%	7.23%	7.77%	3.5%	7.72%	8.28%	3.4%	8.21%	8.79%	3.3%	8.70%	9.30%
30.0	3.6%	6.27%	6.73%	3.5%	6.76%	7.24%	3.3%	7.25%	7.75%	3.2%	7.74%	8.26%	3.1%	8.24%	8.76%	3.0%	8.73%	9.27%
35.0	3.3%	6.28%	6.72%	3.2%	6.78%	7.22%	3.1%	7.27%	7.73%	3.0%	7.76%	8.24%	2.9%	8.25%	8.75%	2.8%	8.75%	9.25%
40.0	3.1%	6.30%	6.70%	3.0%	6.79%	7.21%	2.9%	7.28%	7.72%	2.8%	7.78%	8.22%	2.7%	8.27%	8.73%	2.6%	8.76%	9.24%
45.0	2.9%	6.31%	6.69%	2.8%	6.80%	7.20%	2.7%	7.30%	7.70%	2.6%	7.79%	8.21%	2.5%	8.28%	8.72%	2.5%	8.78%	9.22%
50.0	2.8%	6.32%	6.68%	2.7%	6.81%	7.19%	2.6%	7.31%	7.69%	2.5%	7.80%	8.20%	2.4%	8.29%	8.71%	2.3%	8.79%	9.21%
60.0	2.5%	6.33%	6.67%	2.4%	6.83%	7.17%	2.4%	7.32%	7.68%	2.3%	7.82%	8.18%	2.2%	8.31%	8.69%	2.1%	8.81%	9.19%
70.0	2.4%	6.35%	6.65%	2.3%	6.84%	7.16%	2.2%	7.34%	7.66%	2.1%	7.83%	8.17%	2.0%	8.33%	8.67%	2.0%	8.82%	9.18%
80.0	2.2%	6.36%	6.64%	2.1%	6.85%	7.15%	2.0%	7.35%	7.65%	2.0%	7.84%	8.16%	1.9%	8.34%	8.66%	1.8%	8.83%	9.17%
90.0	2.1%	6.36%	6.64%	2.0%	6.86%	7.14%	1.9%	7.36%	7.64%	1.9%	7.85%	8.15%	1.8%	8.35%	8.65%	1.7%	8.84%	9.16%
100.0	2.0%	6.37%	6.63%	1.9%	6.87%	7.13%	1.8%	7.36%	7.64%	1.8%	7.86%	8.14%	1.7%	8.35%	8.65%	1.7%	8.85%	9.15%

Direct Mail Projection Tables

90% Confidence Level - Standard Deviation: 1.645

ANTICIPATED PERCENT RESPONSE

Sample Size (000)	9.5% ±%	Variance Low	High	10.0% ±%	Variance Low	High	10.5% ±%	Variance Low	High	11.0% ±%	Variance Low	High	11.5% ±%	Variance Low	High	12.0% ±%	Variance Low	High
1.0	16.1%	7.97%	11.03%	15.6%	8.44%	11.56%	15.2%	8.91%	12.09%	14.8%	9.37%	12.63%	14.4%	9.84%	13.16%	14.1%	10.31%	13.69%
2.5	10.2%	8.54%	10.46%	9.9%	9.01%	10.99%	9.6%	9.49%	11.51%	9.4%	9.97%	12.03%	9.1%	10.45%	12.55%	8.9%	10.93%	13.07%
5.0	7.2%	8.82%	10.18%	7.0%	9.30%	10.70%	6.8%	9.79%	11.21%	6.6%	10.27%	11.73%	6.5%	10.76%	12.24%	6.3%	11.24%	12.76%
7.5	5.9%	8.94%	10.06%	5.7%	9.43%	10.57%	5.5%	9.92%	11.08%	5.4%	10.41%	11.59%	5.3%	10.89%	12.11%	5.1%	11.38%	12.62%
10.0	5.1%	9.02%	9.98%	4.9%	9.51%	10.49%	4.8%	10.00%	11.00%	4.7%	10.49%	11.51%	4.6%	10.98%	12.02%	4.5%	11.47%	12.53%
12.5	4.5%	9.07%	9.93%	4.4%	9.56%	10.44%	4.3%	10.05%	10.95%	4.2%	10.54%	11.46%	4.1%	11.03%	11.97%	4.0%	11.52%	12.48%
15.0	4.1%	9.11%	9.89%	4.0%	9.60%	10.40%	3.9%	10.09%	10.91%	3.8%	10.58%	11.42%	3.7%	11.07%	11.93%	3.6%	11.56%	12.44%
17.5	3.8%	9.14%	9.86%	3.7%	9.63%	10.37%	3.6%	10.12%	10.88%	3.5%	10.61%	11.39%	3.4%	11.10%	11.90%	3.4%	11.60%	12.40%
20.0	3.6%	9.16%	9.84%	3.5%	9.65%	10.35%	3.4%	10.14%	10.86%	3.3%	10.64%	11.36%	3.2%	11.13%	11.87%	3.1%	11.62%	12.38%
25.0	3.2%	9.19%	9.81%	3.1%	9.69%	10.31%	3.0%	10.18%	10.82%	3.0%	10.67%	11.33%	2.9%	11.17%	11.83%	2.8%	11.66%	12.34%
30.0	2.9%	9.22%	9.78%	2.8%	9.72%	10.28%	2.8%	10.21%	10.79%	2.7%	10.70%	11.30%	2.6%	11.20%	11.80%	2.6%	11.69%	12.31%
35.0	2.7%	9.24%	9.76%	2.6%	9.74%	10.26%	2.6%	10.23%	10.77%	2.5%	10.72%	11.28%	2.4%	11.22%	11.78%	2.4%	11.71%	12.29%
40.0	2.5%	9.26%	9.74%	2.5%	9.75%	10.25%	2.4%	10.25%	10.75%	2.3%	10.74%	11.26%	2.3%	11.24%	11.76%	2.2%	11.73%	12.27%
45.0	2.4%	9.27%	9.73%	2.3%	9.77%	10.23%	2.3%	10.26%	10.74%	2.2%	10.76%	11.24%	2.2%	11.25%	11.75%	2.1%	11.75%	12.25%
50.0	2.3%	9.28%	9.72%	2.2%	9.78%	10.22%	2.1%	10.27%	10.73%	2.1%	10.77%	11.23%	2.0%	11.27%	11.73%	2.0%	11.76%	12.24%
60.0	2.1%	9.30%	9.70%	2.0%	9.80%	10.20%	2.0%	10.29%	10.71%	1.9%	10.79%	11.21%	1.9%	11.29%	11.71%	1.8%	11.78%	12.22%
70.0	1.9%	9.32%	9.68%	1.9%	9.81%	10.19%	1.8%	10.31%	10.69%	1.8%	10.81%	11.19%	1.7%	11.30%	11.70%	1.7%	11.80%	12.20%
80.0	1.8%	9.33%	9.67%	1.7%	9.83%	10.17%	1.7%	10.32%	10.68%	1.7%	10.82%	11.18%	1.6%	11.31%	11.69%	1.6%	11.81%	12.19%
90.0	1.7%	9.34%	9.66%	1.6%	9.84%	10.16%	1.6%	10.33%	10.67%	1.6%	10.83%	11.17%	1.5%	11.33%	11.67%	1.5%	11.82%	12.18%
100.0	1.6%	9.35%	9.65%	1.6%	9.84%	10.16%	1.5%	10.34%	10.66%	1.5%	10.84%	11.16%	1.4%	11.33%	11.67%	1.4%	11.83%	12.17%

Direct Mail Projection Tables

90% Confidence Level - Standard Deviation: 1.645

ANTICIPATED PERCENT RESPONSE

Sample Size (000)	13.0% ±%	Variance Low	High	14.0% ±%	Variance Low	High	15.0% ±%	Variance Low	High	16.0% ±%	Variance Low	High	17.0% ±%	Variance Low	High	18.0% ±%	Variance Low	High
1.0	13.5%	11.25%	14.75%	12.9%	12.19%	15.81%	12.4%	13.14%	16.86%	11.9%	14.09%	17.91%	11.5%	15.05%	18.95%	11.1%	16.00%	20.00%
2.5	8.5%	11.89%	14.11%	8.2%	12.86%	15.14%	7.8%	13.83%	16.17%	7.5%	14.79%	17.21%	7.3%	15.76%	18.24%	7.0%	16.74%	19.26%
5.0	6.0%	12.22%	13.78%	5.8%	13.19%	14.81%	5.5%	14.17%	15.83%	5.3%	15.15%	16.85%	5.1%	16.13%	17.87%	5.0%	17.11%	18.89%
7.5	4.9%	12.36%	13.64%	4.7%	13.34%	14.66%	4.5%	14.32%	15.68%	4.4%	15.30%	16.70%	4.2%	16.29%	17.71%	4.1%	17.27%	18.73%
10.0	4.3%	12.45%	13.55%	4.1%	13.43%	14.57%	3.9%	14.41%	15.59%	3.8%	15.40%	16.60%	3.6%	16.38%	17.62%	3.5%	17.37%	18.63%
12.5	3.8%	12.51%	13.49%	3.6%	13.49%	14.51%	3.5%	14.47%	15.53%	3.4%	15.46%	16.54%	3.3%	16.45%	17.55%	3.1%	17.43%	18.57%
15.0	3.5%	12.55%	13.45%	3.3%	13.53%	14.47%	3.2%	14.52%	15.48%	3.1%	15.51%	16.49%	3.0%	16.50%	17.50%	2.9%	17.48%	18.52%
17.5	3.2%	12.58%	13.42%	3.1%	13.57%	14.43%	3.0%	14.56%	15.44%	2.8%	15.54%	16.46%	2.7%	16.53%	17.47%	2.7%	17.52%	18.48%
20.0	3.0%	12.61%	13.39%	2.9%	13.60%	14.40%	2.8%	14.58%	15.42%	2.7%	15.57%	16.43%	2.6%	16.56%	17.44%	2.5%	17.55%	18.45%
25.0	2.7%	12.65%	13.35%	2.6%	13.64%	14.36%	2.5%	14.63%	15.37%	2.4%	15.62%	16.38%	2.3%	16.61%	17.39%	2.2%	17.60%	18.40%
30.0	2.5%	12.68%	13.32%	2.4%	13.67%	14.33%	2.3%	14.66%	15.34%	2.2%	15.65%	16.35%	2.1%	16.64%	17.36%	2.0%	17.64%	18.36%
35.0	2.3%	12.70%	13.30%	2.2%	13.69%	14.31%	2.1%	14.69%	15.31%	2.0%	15.68%	16.32%	1.9%	16.67%	17.33%	1.9%	17.66%	18.34%
40.0	2.1%	12.72%	13.28%	2.0%	13.71%	14.29%	2.0%	14.71%	15.29%	1.9%	15.70%	16.30%	1.8%	16.69%	17.31%	1.8%	17.68%	18.32%
45.0	2.0%	12.74%	13.26%	1.9%	13.73%	14.27%	1.8%	14.72%	15.28%	1.8%	15.72%	16.28%	1.7%	16.71%	17.29%	1.7%	17.70%	18.30%
50.0	1.9%	12.75%	13.25%	1.8%	13.74%	14.26%	1.8%	14.74%	15.26%	1.7%	15.73%	16.27%	1.6%	16.72%	17.28%	1.6%	17.72%	18.28%
60.0	1.7%	12.77%	13.23%	1.7%	13.77%	14.23%	1.6%	14.76%	15.24%	1.5%	15.75%	16.25%	1.5%	16.75%	17.25%	1.4%	17.74%	18.26%
70.0	1.6%	12.79%	13.21%	1.5%	13.78%	14.22%	1.5%	14.78%	15.22%	1.4%	15.77%	16.23%	1.4%	16.77%	17.23%	1.3%	17.76%	18.24%
80.0	1.5%	12.80%	13.20%	1.4%	13.80%	14.20%	1.4%	14.79%	15.21%	1.3%	15.79%	16.21%	1.3%	16.78%	17.22%	1.2%	17.78%	18.22%
90.0	1.4%	12.82%	13.18%	1.4%	13.81%	14.19%	1.3%	14.80%	15.20%	1.3%	15.80%	16.20%	1.2%	16.79%	17.21%	1.2%	17.79%	18.21%
100.0	1.3%	12.83%	13.17%	1.3%	13.82%	14.18%	1.2%	14.81%	15.19%	1.2%	15.81%	16.19%	1.1%	16.80%	17.20%	1.1%	17.80%	18.20%

Direct Mail Projection Tables

90% Confidence Level - Standard Deviation: 1.645

ANTICIPATED PERCENT RESPONSE

Sample Size (000)	19.0%			20.0%			21.0%			22.0%			23.0%			24.0%		
	±%	Variance Low	High	±%	Variance Low	High	±%	Variance Low	High	±%	Variance Low	High	±%	Variance Low	High	±%	Variance Low	High
1.0	10.7%	16.96%	21.04%	10.4%	17.92%	22.08%	10.1%	18.88%	23.12%	9.8%	19.85%	24.15%	9.5%	20.81%	25.19%	9.3%	21.78%	26.22%
2.5	6.8%	17.71%	20.29%	6.6%	18.68%	21.32%	6.4%	19.66%	22.34%	6.2%	20.64%	23.36%	6.0%	21.62%	24.38%	5.9%	22.59%	25.41%
5.0	4.8%	18.09%	19.91%	4.7%	19.07%	20.93%	4.5%	20.05%	21.95%	4.4%	21.04%	22.96%	4.3%	22.02%	23.98%	4.1%	23.01%	24.99%
7.5	3.9%	18.25%	19.75%	3.8%	19.24%	20.76%	3.7%	20.23%	21.77%	3.6%	21.21%	22.79%	3.5%	22.20%	23.80%	3.4%	23.19%	24.81%
10.0	3.4%	18.35%	19.65%	3.3%	19.34%	20.66%	3.2%	20.33%	21.67%	3.1%	21.32%	22.68%	3.0%	22.31%	23.69%	2.9%	23.30%	24.70%
12.5	3.0%	18.42%	19.58%	2.9%	19.41%	20.59%	2.9%	20.40%	21.60%	2.8%	21.39%	22.61%	2.7%	22.38%	23.62%	2.6%	23.37%	24.63%
15.0	2.8%	18.47%	19.53%	2.7%	19.46%	20.54%	2.6%	20.45%	21.55%	2.5%	21.44%	22.56%	2.5%	22.43%	23.57%	2.4%	23.43%	24.57%
17.5	2.6%	18.51%	19.49%	2.5%	19.50%	20.50%	2.4%	20.49%	21.51%	2.3%	21.48%	22.52%	2.3%	22.48%	23.52%	2.2%	23.47%	24.53%
20.0	2.4%	18.54%	19.46%	2.3%	19.53%	20.47%	2.3%	20.53%	21.47%	2.2%	21.52%	22.48%	2.1%	22.51%	23.49%	2.1%	23.50%	24.50%
25.0	2.1%	18.59%	19.41%	2.1%	19.58%	20.42%	2.0%	20.58%	21.42%	2.0%	21.57%	22.43%	1.9%	22.56%	23.44%	1.9%	23.56%	24.44%
30.0	2.0%	18.63%	19.37%	1.9%	19.62%	20.38%	1.8%	20.61%	21.39%	1.8%	21.61%	22.39%	1.7%	22.60%	23.40%	1.7%	23.59%	24.41%
35.0	1.8%	18.66%	19.34%	1.8%	19.65%	20.35%	1.7%	20.64%	21.36%	1.7%	21.64%	22.36%	1.6%	22.63%	23.37%	1.6%	23.62%	24.38%
40.0	1.7%	18.68%	19.32%	1.6%	19.67%	20.33%	1.6%	20.66%	21.34%	1.5%	21.66%	22.34%	1.5%	22.65%	23.35%	1.5%	23.65%	24.35%
45.0	1.6%	18.70%	19.30%	1.6%	19.69%	20.31%	1.5%	20.68%	21.32%	1.5%	21.68%	22.32%	1.4%	22.67%	23.33%	1.4%	23.67%	24.33%
50.0	1.5%	18.71%	19.29%	1.5%	19.71%	20.29%	1.4%	20.70%	21.30%	1.4%	21.70%	22.30%	1.3%	22.69%	23.31%	1.3%	23.69%	24.31%
60.0	1.4%	18.74%	19.26%	1.3%	19.73%	20.27%	1.3%	20.73%	21.27%	1.3%	21.72%	22.28%	1.2%	22.72%	23.28%	1.2%	23.71%	24.29%
70.0	1.3%	18.76%	19.24%	1.2%	19.75%	20.25%	1.2%	20.75%	21.25%	1.2%	21.74%	22.26%	1.1%	22.74%	23.26%	1.1%	23.73%	24.27%
80.0	1.2%	18.77%	19.23%	1.2%	19.77%	20.23%	1.1%	20.76%	21.24%	1.1%	21.76%	22.24%	1.1%	22.76%	23.24%	1.0%	23.75%	24.25%
90.0	1.1%	18.78%	19.22%	1.1%	19.78%	20.22%	1.1%	20.78%	21.22%	1.0%	21.77%	22.23%	1.0%	22.77%	23.23%	1.0%	23.77%	24.23%
100.0	1.1%	18.80%	19.20%	1.0%	19.79%	20.21%	1.0%	20.79%	21.21%	1.0%	21.78%	22.22%	1.0%	22.78%	23.22%	.9%	23.78%	24.22%

Direct Mail Projection Tables

90% Confidence Level - Standard Deviation: 1.645

ANTICIPATED PERCENT RESPONSE

Sample Size (000)	25.0% ±%	Variance Low	High	26.0% ±%	Variance Low	High	27.0% ±%	Variance Low	High	28.0% ±%	Variance Low	High	29.0% ±%	Variance Low	High	30.0% ±%	Variance Low	High
1.0	9.0%	22.75%	27.25%	8.8%	23.72%	28.28%	8.6%	24.69%	29.31%	8.3%	25.66%	30.34%	8.1%	26.64%	31.36%	7.9%	27.62%	32.38%
2.5	5.7%	23.58%	26.42%	5.6%	24.56%	27.44%	5.4%	25.54%	28.46%	5.3%	26.52%	29.48%	5.1%	27.51%	30.49%	5.0%	28.49%	31.51%
5.0	4.0%	23.99%	26.01%	3.9%	24.98%	27.02%	3.8%	25.97%	28.03%	3.7%	26.96%	29.04%	3.6%	27.94%	30.06%	3.6%	28.93%	31.07%
7.5	3.3%	24.18%	25.82%	3.2%	25.17%	26.83%	3.1%	26.16%	27.84%	3.0%	27.15%	28.85%	3.0%	28.14%	29.86%	2.9%	29.13%	30.87%
10.0	2.8%	24.29%	25.71%	2.8%	25.28%	26.72%	2.7%	26.27%	27.73%	2.6%	27.26%	28.74%	2.6%	28.25%	29.75%	2.5%	29.25%	30.75%
12.5	2.5%	24.36%	25.64%	2.5%	25.35%	26.65%	2.4%	26.35%	27.65%	2.4%	27.34%	28.66%	2.3%	28.33%	29.67%	2.2%	29.33%	30.67%
15.0	2.3%	24.42%	25.58%	2.3%	25.41%	26.59%	2.2%	26.40%	27.60%	2.2%	27.40%	28.60%	2.1%	28.39%	29.61%	2.1%	29.38%	30.62%
17.5	2.2%	24.46%	25.54%	2.1%	25.45%	26.55%	2.0%	26.45%	27.55%	2.0%	27.44%	28.56%	1.9%	28.44%	29.56%	1.9%	29.43%	30.57%
20.0	2.0%	24.50%	25.50%	2.0%	25.49%	26.51%	1.9%	26.48%	27.52%	1.9%	27.48%	28.52%	1.8%	28.47%	29.53%	1.8%	29.47%	30.53%
25.0	1.8%	24.55%	25.45%	1.8%	25.54%	26.46%	1.7%	26.54%	27.46%	1.7%	27.53%	28.47%	1.6%	28.53%	29.47%	1.6%	29.52%	30.48%
30.0	1.6%	24.59%	25.41%	1.6%	25.58%	26.42%	1.6%	26.58%	27.42%	1.5%	27.57%	28.43%	1.5%	28.57%	29.43%	1.5%	29.56%	30.44%
35.0	1.5%	24.62%	25.38%	1.5%	25.61%	26.39%	1.4%	26.61%	27.39%	1.4%	27.61%	28.39%	1.4%	28.60%	29.40%	1.3%	29.60%	30.40%
40.0	1.4%	24.64%	25.36%	1.4%	25.64%	26.36%	1.4%	26.63%	27.37%	1.3%	27.63%	28.37%	1.3%	28.63%	29.37%	1.3%	29.62%	30.38%
45.0	1.3%	24.66%	25.34%	1.3%	25.66%	26.34%	1.3%	26.66%	27.34%	1.2%	27.65%	28.35%	1.2%	28.65%	29.35%	1.2%	29.64%	30.36%
50.0	1.3%	24.68%	25.32%	1.2%	25.68%	26.32%	1.2%	26.67%	27.33%	1.2%	27.67%	28.33%	1.2%	28.67%	29.33%	1.1%	29.66%	30.34%
60.0	1.2%	24.71%	25.29%	1.1%	25.71%	26.29%	1.1%	26.70%	27.30%	1.1%	27.70%	28.30%	1.1%	28.70%	29.30%	1.0%	29.69%	30.31%
70.0	1.1%	24.73%	25.27%	1.0%	25.73%	26.27%	1.0%	26.72%	27.28%	1.0%	27.72%	28.28%	1.0%	28.72%	29.28%	.9%	29.72%	30.28%
80.0	1.0%	24.75%	25.25%	1.0%	25.74%	26.26%	1.0%	26.74%	27.26%	.9%	27.74%	28.26%	.9%	28.74%	29.26%	.9%	29.73%	30.27%
90.0	.9%	24.76%	25.24%	.9%	25.76%	26.24%	.9%	26.76%	27.24%	.9%	27.75%	28.25%	.9%	28.75%	29.25%	.8%	29.75%	30.25%
100.0	.9%	24.77%	25.23%	.9%	25.77%	26.23%	.9%	26.77%	27.23%	.8%	27.77%	28.23%	.8%	28.76%	29.24%	.8%	29.76%	30.24%

Appendix C

A Typical Questionnaire

Figure C.1 is a reproduction of a recent database questionnaire distributed by Donnelly Marketing and reprinted with their permission.

These usually combine speculative questions asked so that the distributor can offer the names to interested advertisers, and custom questions where arrangements have been made in advance by a company seeking to gather data on a specific field. Such custom questions generally vary in cost depending on the space required and the number of names expected to be produced.

Every such survey usually has an exclusive arrangement with a tobacco manufacturer. It is likely that this questionnaire is the product of arrangements with a home permanent packaged goods manufacturer as well as at least one beverage and home remedy manufacturer.

Note the permission lines agreeing to accept samples of cigarettes and nonprescription medicines, and the notice that the list will be shared with other businesses, and the option to prohibit this.

Carol Wright® Wants To Know.

"Help me tell major manufacturers what's right for you. They'll be able to send free samples, money saving coupons and special offers that meet your particular needs. Please complete and mail this survey today."

I am 18 years of age or older and agree to accept a free, non-prescription medicine sample. A1

First Name |___|___|___|___|___|___|___|___|___|___|___|___|___|___|___|
Last Name |___|___|___|___|___|___|___|___|___|___|___|___|___|___|___| M___ F___ Age___
Address |___|___|___|___|___|___|___|___|___|___|___|___|___|___| Apt # |___|___|___|___|
City |___|___|___|___|___|___|___|___|___|___| State |___|___| Zip |___|___|___|___|___|
Spouse's First Name |___|___|___|___|___|___|___|___|___|___|___| M___ F___ Age___
Married 1.☐   Single 2.☐   Rent Home or Apartment 3.☐   Own Home 4.☐
Please send me your completed survey no later than March 31, 1993.

1. How many glasses of carbonated soft drinks are consumed in your home each week?

0-5	5-10	10+
1.☐	2.☐	3.☐

1a. Which brand(s) are consumed? (check all that apply)

	Regular	Diet	Caffeine Free
Coca-Cola	01.☐	11.☐	21.☐
Pepsi	02.☐	12.☐	22.☐
Dr. Pepper	03.☐	13.☐	23.☐
Cherry Coke	04.☐	14.☐	24.☐
Cherry 7-Up	05.☐	15.☐	25.☐
7-Up	06.☐	16.☐	26.☐
Slice	07.☐	17.☐	27.☐
Sprite	08.☐	18.☐	28.☐
Gatorade	09.☐	19.☐	29.☐
Other	10.☐	20.☐	30.☐

2. Which brand(s) of beer have you purchased in the last month?

Number of Six Packs

	1-3	4-7	8 or more
Bud Light	01.☐	11.☐	21.☐
Coors Light	02.☐	12.☐	22.☐
Miller Light	03.☐	13.☐	23.☐
Budweiser	04.☐	14.☐	24.☐
Coors	05.☐	15.☐	25.☐
Miller High Life	06.☐	16.☐	26.☐
Miller Genuine Draft	07.☐	17.☐	27.☐
Busch	08.☐	18.☐	28.☐
Imported	09.☐	19.☐	29.☐
Other	10.☐	20.☐	30.☐

3. Which brand(s) of pain/fever relievers have been used in your household by adults in the past three months?

	Have Used (Check all that apply)	Use Most Often (Check only one)
Advil	01.☐	11.☐
Anacin	02.☐	12.☐
Bayer	03.☐	13.☐
Bufferin	04.☐	14.☐
Excedrin	05.☐	15.☐
Motrin IB	06.☐	16.☐
Nuprin	07.☐	17.☐
Tylenol	08.☐	18.☐
Store Brand	09.☐	19.☐
	10.☐	20.☐

3a. How often are pain/fever relievers used?

Daily	1.☐	Monthly	4.☐
3-5 Times a Week	2.☐	Occasionally	5.☐
1-2 Times a Week	3.☐		

4. Which brand(s) of cold and allergy/sinus remedies are used most often in your household?

Actifed	01.☐	Nyquil	12.☐
Alka Seltzer Plus	02.☐	Sine Aid	13.☐
Benadryl	03.☐	Sine-Off	14.☐
Comtrex	04.☐	Sinus Excedrin	15.☐
Contac	05.☐	Sinutab	16.☐
Co-Tylenol	06.☐	Sudafed	17.☐
Dimetapp	07.☐	Sudafed Plus	18.☐
Dimetapp Plus	08.☐	Triaminic	19.☐
Dristan	09.☐	Tylenol Sinus	20.☐
Drixoral	10.☐	Store Brand	21.☐
Drixoral Plus	11.☐	Other	22.☐

4a. How often are cold and allergy/sinus remedies used?

Daily	1.☐	Monthly	4.☐
3-5 Times a Week	2.☐	Occasionally	5.☐
1-2 Times a Week	3.☐		

5. Please write the ages of all persons in your household. Please circle your age.

Female Ages _____ _____ _____ _____
Male Ages _____ _____ _____ _____

6. Check all interests or hobbies pursued in your household.

Fishing	01.☐	Gourmet Cooking	13.☐
Camping	02.☐	Physical Fitness/Exer.	14.☐
Hunting	03.☐	Diet Conscious	15.☐
Tennis	04.☐	Photography	16.☐
Golf	05.☐	Stamps/Coins	17.☐
Snow Skiing	06.☐	Gardening	18.☐
Cycling	07.☐	Foreign Travel	19.☐
Casino Gambling	08.☐	Woodworking	20.☐
Sewing	09.☐	Needlecraft	21.☐
Books	10.☐	Quilting	22.☐
Do-it-Yourself	11.☐	Scuba Diving	23.☐
Sweepstakes/Lottery	12.☐	Symphony/Ballet/Opera	24.☐

7. Please check all that apply to your household:

Have a Cellular Phone	01.☐
Support Health Charities	02.☐
Have a Compact Disc Player	03.☐
Have a VCR	04.☐
Have a Personal Computer	05.☐
Have American Express	06.☐
Have MasterCard/Visa	07.☐
Have a Dog	08.☐
Have a Cat	09.☐
Military Veteran in the Household	10.☐
Recently Donated by Mail	11.☐

8. What types of magazines/books do you or your family members read?

Best Seller	01.☐	Fashion	09.☐
Business/News	02.☐	Mystery	10.☐
Classics	03.☐	Romance	11.☐
Cooking/Wine	04.☐	Science Fiction	12.☐
Crafts/Needlework	05.☐	Sports	13.☐
Devotional/Bible	06.☐	Travel/Entertain.	14.☐
Home/Gardening	07.☐	Young Children	15.☐
Health/Beauty	08.☐		

9. Does anyone in your household suffer from: (check all those that apply)

Allergies	01.☐	Gastritis	14.☐
Alzheimer's Disease	02.☐	Heart Disease	15.☐
Angina	03.☐	Hearing Difficulty	16.☐
Arthritis/Rheumatism	04.☐	High Blood Pressure	17.☐
Asthma	05.☐	High Cholesterol	18.☐
Bladder Control/ Incontinence	06.☐	Migraines	19.☐
		Osteoporosis	20.☐
Bleeding Gums/ Gingivitis	07.☐	Parkinson's Disease	21.☐
		Physical Handicap	22.☐
Blindness/Visual Impairment	08.☐	Sensitive Skin	23.☐
		Sinusitis	24.☐
Diabetes	09.☐	Thinning Hair/ Balding	25.☐
Emphysema	10.☐		
Epilepsy	11.☐	Ulcer	26.☐
Frequent Headaches	12.☐	Yeast Infection	27.☐
Frequent Heartburn	13.☐		

10. If you or anyone in your household colors their hair, which brand(s) is used most often?

Nice & Easy	1.☐	Ultress	4.☐
Loving Care	2.☐	Color at a Salon	5.☐
Miss Clairol	3.☐	Other	6.☐

10a. If you or anyone in your household perms their hair, do you?

Perm at a Salon   1.☐   Perm at Home   2.☐

11. How many times have you shopped by mail in the last six months?

Once or Twice   1.☐   Three or More Times   2.☐

11a. In total, how much did you spend?

Under $50   1.☐   Over $50   2.☐

FOR SMOKERS ONLY
"By completing the following questions you are certifying that all smokers listed are 21 years of age or older, and want to receive free samples of cigarettes and incentive items in the mail, subject to applicable state and federal law."

12. You

First Name |___|___|___|___|___|___|___|___|___|___|___|___|
Last Name |___|___|___|___|___|___|___|___|___|___|___|___|___|
Birth Date (required) |___|___| |___|___| |___|___|
                        Month   Day   Year
Gender   Male   1.☐   Female   2.☐
What is your regular brand of cigarettes?
|___|___|___|___|___|___|___|___|___|___|___|___|___|
What other brand, if any, do you smoke?
|___|___|___|___|___|___|___|___|___|___|___|___|___|
Is your regular brand? (check one in each column)
Filter   3.☐ | Menthol   5.☐ | Reg./King   7.☐
Non-Filter   4.☐ | Non-Menthol   6.☐ | Long/100s   8.☐
                                      Extra Long/120s   9.☐
How many packs of cigarettes have you smoked in the last month?
Regular _____   Other _____

X _____
Signature (required)

13. Other Smoker

First Name |___|___|___|___|___|___|___|___|___|___|___|___|
Last Name |___|___|___|___|___|___|___|___|___|___|___|___|___|
Birth Date (required) |___|___| |___|___| |___|___|
                        Month   Day   Year
Gender   Male   1.☐   Female   2.☐
What is your regular brand of cigarettes?
|___|___|___|___|___|___|___|___|___|___|___|___|___|
What other brand, if any, do you smoke?
|___|___|___|___|___|___|___|___|___|___|___|___|___|
Is your regular brand? (check one in each column)
Filter   3.☐ | Menthol   5.☐ | Reg./King   7.☐
Non-Filter   4.☐ | Non-Menthol   6.☐ | Long/100s   8.☐
                                      Extra Long/120s   9.☐
How many packs of cigarettes have you smoked in the last month?
Regular _____   Other _____

X _____
Signature (required)

Thank you for completing this questionnaire. Your responses benefit manufacturers and marketers of goods and services who are interested in satisfying your wants and needs. The information collected (unless you choose otherwise by checking this box ☐) may later be shared with other reputable businesses.

Mailing is as easy as 1-2-3!

1. Fold top of survey down.
2. Fold in half once more.
3. Moisten or tape edge, affix postage and mail. Thank you!

264

Appendix D
Database Marketing General Terms

The following list was compiled by Amy Zipkin, a researcher and writer living in Westport, Connecticut. Note that any phrases not found may be defined in the next section, a separate glossary of technical terms.

Activey buyer: A customer who has made a purchase during the last twelve months. Also known as an active customer.

Additions: New names added to a mailing list.

Advertising allowance: Financial assistance for all or part of a direct marketing effort in return for featuring a manufacturer's products or brand name.

Advocate: A product's best and most loyal customers who receive incentives and information to help build business.

Aspiration imagery: A concept which illustrates that people don't want to identify with individuals exactly like themselves, but with those who represent a reasonably achievable improvement.

Back-end: Activities or promotions directed at previous buyers or respondents.

Benefits: The features of a product or service which enhance its appeal and/or marketability.

Booklet: A multi-page brochure, usually bound.

Bounce-back: An offer enclosed with the mailing which is sent to the customer when his order is filled. May be included in bills, premium deliveries or other communications.

Brochure: A high quality pamphlet, usually 6 or more sides with specially designed layout and illustrations. May include a BRC (business replay card).

Bulk mail: A third-class mail category where identical pieces of mail, addressed to different names, are processed for mailing before being sent to the post office.

Business list: A compilation of names of individuals and/or companies. May be based on business associated interest, inquiry, subscription, purchase, or membership.

Buyer: Anyone who purchases a product or service including merchandise, books, records or information at least once. (*See also* First time buyer.)

Cash buyer: A purchaser who encloses payment with order.

Cash on delivery (COD): A customer who pays for the balance of an order when it is received.

Catalog: A book or booklet describing merchandise available for purchase. May include prices, sizes, warranties where applicable.

Circulars: Any simple form of printed advertising, including direct mail.

Conquest marketing: A concentration of advertising spending on a competitor's customers.

Consultative selling: Personalized sales method which offers advice on a customer's needs and then sells a product or service to meet those needs.

Conversion: The process of turning a first time buyer into a repeat purchaser.

Consumer list: A list of names which results from an inquiry or buying activity indicating a general purchasing interest.

Customer: A buyer with the need and the finances to purchase your product.

Database: A collection of related data organized for efficient retrieval and manipulation.

Database marketing: An evolving group of direct marketing techniques emanating from the use of data collection on customer and/or prospect information.

Demographics: Statistical population data including age, occupation, income, education.

Envelope stuffer: Any advertising or promotional material included with letters, statements, or invoices.

Expire: A former customer, no longer an active buyer.

Field: A category of data.

File: A collection of like records.

First time buyer: A customer who buys a product or service for the first time. Also known as respondents, triers, starters.

Former buyer: A purchaser who has bought from a company one or more times from the past, with no purchases recorded in the previous year.

Free-ride: See Envelope stuffer.

Friend of a friend: Name of an individual who may be interested in an advertiser's product or service. Provided by a third party who is already a user of the product.

Front end: The necessary direct marketing activities to obtain an order which include package, offer and reply card.

Genderization: A program run to add gender to mailing lists, based on first names.

Gift buyer: An individual who buys a product or a service for another.

Giftees: Lists of individuals who are sent gifts by mail by friends, donors or businesses. Also known as beneficiaries.

Guarantee: A pledge of satisfaction made by the seller to the buyer indicating the terms by which the seller insures his merchandise against defects, etc.

Half life: A formula for estimating the total response expected from a direct-response effort shortly after the first responses are received.

High ticket buyers: Buyers who have purchased expensive items by mail.

House list: Any list of names owned by a company compiled through purchases or buyer inquiries that is used to promote the company's products or services.

In-house: Products or services which can be produced by the advertiser.

Individual: Mailing to a person by name rather than to a box, apartment number, residential address, or occupant.

Influentials: Those individuals in business who have the decision-making power about what to buy. In consumer mailings, those individuals whose opinion is valued in their community, church, local school district.

Installment buyer: A customer who orders goods or services and pays for them in two or more periodic payments after delivery.

Lead generation: Mailing used to solicit inquiries for sales follow-up.

Lead qualification: Determining by telemarketing a customer's level of interest, willingness and ability to buy a product or service.

Lifestyle selectivity: Substantiation of lifestyle habits through lists of what people need, what people own, what people join and what people support. Also movers, marriages, births.

Lifetime value: The total profit or loss estimated or realized from a customer over the active life of a customer record.

List criteria: The factors on a mailing list that differentiate one segment from another. The criteria can be demographic, psychographic, or physical in nature.

List segmentation: Use of subgroups within a list.

Magalog: A mail order catalog similar to a magazine format.

Mail order: Promoting merchandise and/or services directly to the customer. Orders are received by mail, telephone and/or fax and the merchandise is shipped by mail.

Mail order buyer: A customer who orders a product or service for delivery by mail or other means.

Market: The total of all individuals or organizations that represent potential buyers.

Marketing mix: The various marketing elements and strategies that must be used together to achieve maximum effectiveness.

Media: Plural of medium. The means of transmitting information or an advertising message.

Member: A customer enrolled in a promotional program.

Member-get-member: A promotion where existing members are offered a gift for enrolling new members.

Multiple buyer: A customer who has bought two or more times.

New households: Data on new connects by local phone companies that are coming to the marketplace.

Offer: The terms promoting a specific product or service.

One-time buyer: A purchaser who has not ordered a second time or made a second purchase of a product.

Package: All of the elements of a mailing piece.

Package insert: Any promotional piece included in merchandise packages that advertise goods or services available from the same or different sellers.

Past buyer: See Former buyer, sometimes called an "Expire".

Penetration: Percentage of the numbers of individuals and/or families on a particular list compared to the total number possible.

Personalization: The means of adding an individual name to a mailing piece.

Premium: An item offered to a buyer, either free or at nominal cost, as an incentive to purchase, or receive for trial, a product or service offered by direct marketing.

Premium buyer: A customer who buys a product or service to get another product or service, or who responds to an offer of a special premium on the package or label of another product.

Promotional add on: A name added to a customer list as a by-product of promotional response.

Prospect: A consumer who might reasonably be expected to purchase your product in the near future.

Psychographics: Characteristics or qualities used to denote the lifestyles or attitudes of potential or actual customers.

Questionnaire: A list of questions designed for a specific audience which solicits answers to specific questions.

Record: A collection of fields.

Referral name: See friend of a friend.

Refined RFM models: The ability to target customers when product category differences are important.

Regression analysis: A statistical means to improve the predictability of response based on an analysis of relationships within a file.

Relationship marketing: Establishment of connection between the company and the consumer. Also known as loyalty marketing.

Sale: A formal agreement to buy.

Segment: A portion of a list or file selected on the basis of a special set of characteristics.

Selective binding: Method which allows different advertisements to be inserted into different individual issues of several participating magazines.

Sequential files: Files in sequence by field such as last name, social security number, etc.

Simple RFM models: The ability to target in simple situations where neither product category differences nor lifestyles are important.

Single: One person or a single-person household.

Stuffer: Advertising enclosures placed in other media.

Suspect: Someone on a mailing list who for some reason is more likely to become a customer than the general public.

Take-one: Leaflet display at the point of sale or where consumers congregate.

Targeting model: A method of selecting better customers for a given promotion using a scoring algorithm or a popular regression technique.

Telemarketing: Using the telephone as an interactive medium for promotion.

Telephone marketing: Any activity in direct mail using the telephone.

Test market: Trial market for a new product, service, or offer.

Till forbid: An order which is scheduled to continue until specifically cancelled by the buyer.

Trial buyer: A customer who buys a product with the understanding that it may be examined, used or tested for a specific time before deciding whether to pay for it or return it.

Trial subscriber: Person who orders a service or publication conditionally.

Universe: A group of lists, publications, or stations with common characteristics.

User: A consumer who is known to have purchased your product at least once.

Zip code selection models: The means of targeting customers and select names in areas of high incidence.

Database Marketing Technical Terms

This glossary has been compiled by and is reprinted by permission of the Direct Marketing Association. It is reprinted from "Managing Database Marketing Technology for Success," a study conducted by Deloitte & Touche.

AID (automatic interaction detection): A technique developed in the 1960s that continuously splits the mailing sample into two groups based on the value of significant predictor variables. See also: CHAID.

CD-ROM (compact disk read-only memory): High-capacity, moderate-cost optical storage medium used for nontransactional databases. Current CD-ROM capacity is 660 megabytes or up to 1.2 gigabytes using data compression. CD-ROMs have slower access times than hard disks.

CHAID (chi-squared automatic interaction detection): A technique developed in the 1970s that continuously splits the mailing sample based on variables that appear to be predictors of response rates. Unlike AID, CHAID can split a variable into two or more groups. *See also* AID.

Client: *See* Client/server architecture.

Client/server architecture: A method for distributing the workload among an interconnected group of computers. To obtain data or perform specialized functions, the "client" (often, but not exclusively, a PC or workstation) usually handles interactions with users and initiates requests to one or more *servers*. An individual computer is often assigned exclusively to the *client* or *server* role, but may perform both functions in some situations.

Count: The number of records that meet a set of selection conditions.

Cross-tabs: A tabular report with one set of criteria arranged horizontally and another set arranged vertically to form cells. The number in each cell shows the count of names or households that meet the criteria corresponding to the row and criteria of that cell.

Data compression: A means of compacting the amount of storage space required by digital data, using various mathematical formulas. Used when disk space or transmission capacity is scarce and numerical processing power is relatively abundant.

Data dictionary: A central file in which the data items contained in database tables are cataloged and defined to maintain consistency. A *data repository*, a more ambitious version of data dictionary, is designed to catalog all of the data in an enterprise, where that data is used, and the business functions it supports.

Database administrator (DBA): The person responsible for maintaining the accuracy, consistency and security of a database.

Database: A collection of related data organized for efficient retrieval and manipulation.

Database hygiene: General term to describe data maintenance tasks such as "de-duping" (*See* De-dupe), correcting addresses and errors, adding missing data and reorganizing the data for efficiency.

Database machine: A special-purpose computer designed to efficiently manipulate large databases. Usually attaches to a conventional computer via a high-speed data link.

Database management system (DBMS): Proprietary software used to create and maintain a database. Provides a layer of transparency between the physical data and application programs.

Database marketing: Broad term for an evolving group of direct marketing techniques that are driven by a database of customer and prospect information. The systematic use of analytical tools and customer data to build customer relationships.

De-dupe: The process of identifying and removing duplicate names from a file, usually as part of a merge/purge operation.

Direct access storage device (DASD): Mainframe-era jargon for magnetic disk storage. Acronym pronounced "daz-dee."

Distributed database: A database consisting of segments located on interconnected computers disbursed throughout an organization.

Enhancement: The process of adding demographic or other predictive data to a customer or prospect database, usually by contracting with a service bureau.

Expert system: Software that attempts to replicate the decision-making or pattern recognition skills of a human expert in a narrowly defined field.

Extract file: A subset of a large database used for analysis, often formatted as a flat file for downloading to a personal computer or workstation.

Field: The basic data element that forms a record in a file or relational database (for example, name, zip code, source code).

Flat file: A data file containing related records with no internal indexes or pointers. Usually refers to a file that was not created with a DBMS. May be accessed directly by application programs or through a file management system that uses external indexes.

Fourth generation language (4GL): A powerful, high-productivity programming language that is suitable for professional programmers and end users. Most 4GLs run on more than one type of computer. Programs written in 4GLs often require more computing resources than a similar program written in a 3GL.

Gains chart: A graph or table that shows the incremental and cumulative orders (and, in some versions, profitability) for a mailing, after the data have been sorted according to the best to worst responding groups. As a graph, the X-axis is usually the cumulative percentage of the population receiving the offer and the Y-axis is the percentage of the population responding to the offer.

Geocoding: Using the mailing address that enhances a list with potential segmentation data (such as income or age range, household size, family statistics) based on U.S. Census Bureau block groups and enumeration districts.

Gigabyte (Gbyte): One billion bytes (characters).

Graphical user interface (GUI): Software that allows users to interact with programs by manipulating graphical images on a screen using a mouse or other pointing device.

Hierarchical database: Organized as a tree structure, with predefined access paths from parent records to child records.

House file: Active and inactive purchasers or responders.

Index: Used to reduce the time needed to locate a specific record in a database.

Indexed sequential access method (ISAM): A standard file management subsystem that is usually derived from application programs.

Inverted file database: A data storage method that provides very fast access to most complex queries, but requires a fairly wide number of computer resources to build and update. Generally not recommended in high-volume transaction environments or where the data is often processed sequentially.

JOIN: In relational databases, the operation used to combine two or more tables that have a common key. For example, JOIN could be used to combine a customer master record from one table with a customer's transactions stored in another table where the customer number is the common key.

Key: A field within a data record that is used to uniquely identify that record.

Knowledge-based system: *See* Expert system.

Lift: A measure of segmentation effectiveness, calculated as the percentage increase in (actual or predicted) response rate for a segment, over the response rate for the entire group. For example, if the overall response rate to a mailing is 3 percent and the response rate of a second decile is 3.6 percent, the lift is 20 percent. Lift is often expressed as an index number (120 in the previous example) rather than a percentage.

Local area network (LAN): A method of linking computers within a department or building to allow the sharing of files or printers and the exchange of electronic mail.

Logistic regression: A statistical technique used for model development when there is reason to believe that the predictor variables are not normally distributed.

Logit analysis: A type of log-linear modeling that allows for the exploration of interaction among variables—well-suited to direct marketing data.

Megabyte (Mbyte): One million bytes (characters).

Merge/purge: The process of combining two or more mailing lists into a single list based on specified criteria.

Micromarketing: Marketing programs tailored to small geographic areas or individual stores based on demographic data and a database of store-level information.

Multivariate regression: A set of statistical techniques used in advanced segmentation models, with a dependent variable and multiple independent variables.

NCOA (National Change of Address): File maintained by the U.S. Postal Service and used by licensed service bureaus to update addresses in a mailing list that are incorrect because the addressee has moved.

Network model database: A data storage method that supports multiple-parent relationships and several navigation paths through the data.

Neural network: An arrangement of interconnected processing elements that can be used to model nonlinear relationships in databases. *Backpropagation* is currently the most widely used neural network topology of the dozens that have been developed.

Object-oriented database management system (ODBMS): An emerging database management technique that is especially suited to storing complex data structures such as those used in computer-aided engineering.

Open systems: Hardware and system-level software that adhere to formal or *de facto* industry standards to facilitate interconnection of components, design flexibility and portability.

Optical disk: High-capacity storage medium frequently used in document imaging systems and as an archival medium for large databases.

Outsourcing: Turning over an existing data processing function to be managed for profit by an external vendor. Often involves the transfer of employees and sale of existing equipment and facilities to the outsourcing contractor.

Overlay: Addition of new database fields such as demographics or psychographics to allow for more sophisticated modeling and better targeting of promotions.

Parallel processor: A computer using several processors working simultaneously to achieve significant speed improvements. A massively parallel processor uses hundreds or thousands of interconnected processors.

Proprietary systems: Systems unique to a particular vendor, usually based on unpublished specifications with limited or no compliance to international standards (the opposite of open systems).

QBE (query by example): *See* Query.

Query: A question designed to retrieve information from a database. The result can be a count of the number of records meeting a set of criteria or a report containing the data. Depending on the software available, the query may be expressed in (1) natural language, (2) structured query language (SQL), (3) a proprietary format, or (4) by selecting items from a menu or by providing an example.

Query optimizer: Software that analyzes and rearranges a query in order to minimize the amount of computer resources needed to produce the answer.

Record: A row of data about an entity in a relational table or a flat file.

Redundant array of inexpensive disks (RAID): A mass storage device built from dozens of hard disks of the type used in PCs, designed to provide reliable but inexpensive storage for very large databases.

Re-engineering: Redesigning business processes from the ground up, and often with the help of new information technologies, to achieve dramatic cost reduction and time compression.

Relational database: A database built using the relational model, based on tables linked by a common key. Relational databases do not have any predefined access paths, and the order of records within each table is arbitrary.

Relationship marketing: Blanket term for a marketing philosophy and various practices designed to identify the customer, treat customers as individuals, build loyalty, and measure programs on the basis of contribution to long-term value.

Selects: The names meeting selection criteria.

Sequential file: A file that is read or written one record, or record group, at a time, from beginning to end.

Server: *See* Client/server architecture.

Software re-engineering: Rewriting aging but critical computer applications to take advantage of advances in hardware, database management systems and development tools. Often accomplished with the assistance of specialized software tools that analyze and help convert old programs and files.

Structured query language (SQL): A nonprocedural industry-standard language used to perform queries and manipulate data in relational databases. SQL can be entered by a user or embedded in programs, and SQL interfaces are available for some nonrelational databases. Example of a simple SQL statement that finds all females with a net worth over $250,000:

```
SELECT*
FROM CUSTOMER_FILE
WHERE SEX = F
AND NETWORTH>250000;
```

Table: The basic data structure in a relational database, made up of rows (records) and columns (data items or fields).

Terabyte (Tbyte): One trillion bytes (characters).

Third generation language (3GL): Programming languages such as COBOL, FORTRAN, and C, which are generally considered inappropriate for end-user development.

View: Virtually, a table. In relational databases, a method of storing the commands needed to recreate a particular combination of frequently used data.

Virtual storage access method (VSAM): A set of file access methods that uses indexes to help locate data quickly. Although VSAM does not provide many of the functions or benefits found in a DBMS, it is a very efficient means of handling large files. Associated with IBM mainframe computers.

Workstation: A powerful desktop or deskside computer, often using a reduced instruction set computer (RISC) processor and connected to other computers in a local area network. Occasionally used to refer to high-end PCs.

Appendix F

Bibliography

Burnett, Ed. *The Complete Direct Mail List Handbook: Everything You Need to Know About Lists and How to Use Them for Greater Profit.* Englewood Cliffs, NJ: Prentice-Hall, 1988. 736 pp.

Clancy, Kevin J. and Shulman, Robin S. *The Marketing Revolution. A Radical Manifesto for Dominating the Marketplace.* New York: Harper, 1992. 314 pp.

Deloitte & Touche. "Managing Database Marketing Technology for Success. A Study of Experiences and 'Best Practices' in Leading Marketing Organizations." Commissioned and published by Direct Marketing Association, 1992. 120 pp.

Eicoff, Al. *Eicoff on Broadcast Direct Marketing.* Chicago: National Textbook Company, 1988. 191 pp.

Harper, Rose. *Mailing List Stragegies: A guide to Direct Mail Success.* New York: McGraw-Hill, 1986. 214 pp.

Holtmann, Arthur F., & Mann, Donald C. *New Age of Financial Services Marketing.* Sourcebooks 1991, 322 pp.

Nash, Edward L. *Direct Marketing Handbook,* 2nd ed. New York: McGraw-Hill, 1991. 832 pp.

Nash, Edward L. *Direct Marketing: Strategy/Planning/Execution,* 2nd ed. New York: McGraw-Hill, 1992. 472 pp.

Posch, Robert J. *The Direct Marketer's Legal Adviser.* New York: McGraw-Hill, 1983. 242. pp.

Rapp, Stan and Collins, Tom. *Maximarketing: The New Direction in Advertising, Promotion and Strategy.* (hardcover) New York: McGraw-Hill, 1989. (softcover) New York: NAL-Dutton, 1990. 265 pp.

Shepard, David and Associates. *New Direct Marketing: How to Implement a Profit Driven Database Marketing Strategy,* 2nd ed. New York: Business One Irwin, 1993. 535 pp.

Index

About the Author

Edward L. Nash, executive vice president of Bozell, Jacobs, Kenyon & Eckhardt, is responsible for strategic development of direct marketing programs in Bozell's offices throughout the United States and worldwide. In 1990, his agency won the prestigious Henry Hoke Award for excellence in direct marketing. Mr. Nash has also been marketing vice president for Lasalle Extension University, president of Capitol Record Club, executive vice president of Rapp & Collins, and CEO of BBDO Direct, which he founded and ran for five years.

Renowned in the industry as its "master strategist," Mr. Nash is a frequent keynote speaker at direct marketing conferences worldwide. He is the author of *Direct Marketing: Strategy/Planning/Execution* and editor-in-chief of *The Direct Marketing Handbook,* both published by McGraw-Hill.